AI and Machine Learning for Network and Security Management

AI and Machine Learning for Network and Security Management

Yulei Wu
University of Exeter
UK

Jingguo Ge
IIE Chinese Academy of Sciences
China

Tong Li
IIE Chinese Academy of Sciences
China

**IEEE Press
Series on
Networks and
Services Management**

**Dr. Veli Sahin and
Dr. Mehmet Ulema,** *Series Editors*

IEEE PRESS
WILEY

Published by John Wiley & Sons, Inc., Hoboken, New Jersey.
Published simultaneously in Canada.

For general information on our other products and services or for technical support, please contact our Customer Care Department within the United States at (800) 762-2974, outside the United States at (317) 572-3993 or fax (317) 572-4002.

Wiley also publishes its books in a variety of electronic formats. Some content that appears in print may not be available in electronic formats. For more information about Wiley products, visit our web site at www.wiley.com.

Library of Congress Cataloging-in-Publication Data applied for:
Hardback ISBN: 9781119835875

Cover Design: Wiley
Cover Image: © Bill Donnelley

Set in 9.5/12.5pt STIXTwoText by Straive, Chennai, India

Contents

Author Biographies

Yulei Wu, is a Senior Lecturer with the Department of Computer Science, Faculty of Environment, Science and Economy, University of Exeter, UK. His research focuses on networking, Internet of Things, edge intelligence, information security, and ethical AI. He serves as an Associate Editor for IEEE Transactions on Network and Service Management, and IEEE Transactions on Network Science and Engineering, as well as an Editorial Board Member of Computer Networks, Future Generation Computer Systems, and Nature Scientific Reports at Nature Portfolio. He is a Senior Member of the IEEE and the ACM, and a Fellow of the HEA (Higher Education Academy).

Jingguo Ge, is currently a Professor of the Institute of Information Engineering, Chinese Academy of Sciences (CAS), and also a Professor of School of Cyber Security, University of Chinese Academy of Sciences. His research focuses on Future Network Architecture, 5G/6G, Software-defined networking (SDN), Cloud Native networking, Zero Trust Architecture. He has published more than 60 research papers and is the holder of 28 patents. He participated in the formulation of 3 ITU standards on IMT2020.

Tong Li, is currently a Senior Engineer of Institute of Information Engineering at the Chinese Academy of Sciences (CAS). His research and engineering focus on Computer Networks, Cloud Computing, Software-Defined Networking (SDN), and Distributed Network and Security Management. He participated 2 ITU standards on IMT2020 and developed many large-scale software systems on SDN, network management and orchestration.

Preface

With the fast development of networking technologies, the communication network has gone through four generations and is in the process of deploying the fifth-generation system (5G) worldwide. 5G has its unique feature of accommodating diversified services on top of a shared infrastructure. These services not only include the telecommunication service that we use every day for our daily lives, but also encompass a wide variety of services in support of many important vertical industries including energy, health, water, manufacturing, environment, to name a few. These services are mainly classified into three broad categories: enhanced Mobile Broadband (eMBB), Ultra Reliable Low Latency Communications (URLLC), and massive Machine Type Communications (mMTC). The deployment of 5G to support eMBB services has already started in the globe, and that of supporting URLLC and mMTC will start in the foreseeable future. Meanwhile, research of next-generation communication systems, i.e. beyond 5G (B5G) or 6G, has already started with many research centers and groups established globally.

To meet requirements of diverse services running on top of 5G/B5G/6G infrastructure, many networking and computing techniques have been incorporated into the communication system, including reconfigurable intelligent surface, Millimeter-wave/THz links, high-capacity backhaul connectivity, cloud nativeness, machine-type communications, edge intelligence, blockchain, and quantum computing. This immediately results in the increasing complexity of modern networking and communication systems which will be at a scale and scope we have never seen before. This also remarkably raises the bar for network and service management. Since network security is an integral part of network management, the broad understanding of network management shall cover both network management and security management. The closed-form models created for individual protocols, applications, and systems have been successful for network and security management in the past 20 years. However, the networking systems of today are too complicated for closed-form analysis.

Network automation is being pursued by the community to facilitate network and security management. Artificial intelligence (AI) and machine learning (especially deep learning) have been widely used in a number of fields, e.g. image recognition and computer vision as well as natural language processing, to enhance the automation of relevant tasks. The networking community started to adopt AI and machine learning techniques to achieve the goal of network automation in recent years. Due to the complexity of today's networking systems, it is essentially hard to make a fully autonomous system. The current start-of-the-art shows a promising progress of developing AI and machine learning models to automate certain tasks for network and security management, including network planning and routing, resource allocation and scheduling, encrypted traffic classification, anomaly detection, zero trust networks, and security operations.

This book covers the key tasks of network and security management, and elaborates how advanced AI and machine learning techniques can improve the network automation. It will not only address the problems from the computing point of view, but also explore how the cognitive means, e.g. knowledge transfer, can help with the network and security management. Network automation has become a burning issue for network and security management. This book will be useful and helpful for network engineers to tackle network automation issues, and it will also be a good textbook for education in universities. The book can also help policy-makers understand how network automation works in the field of network and security management.

Yulei Wu
Exeter, UK

Jingguo Ge
Beijing, China

Tong Li
Beijing, China

Acknowledgments

Many thanks to all the contributors of this book, including Guozhi Lin, Lei Zhang, Zhaoxue Jiang, Peijie Sun, Jin Cheng, Zhenguo Zhang, and Zhibin Xu.

Acronyms

1D-CNN	one-dimension convolutional network
2D-CNN	two-dimension convolutional network
5G	fifth-generation mobile communication system
ABAC	attribute-based access control
ACL	access control list
ACU	adaptive context unit
ADASYN	oversample using adaptive synthetic
AE	AutoEncoder
AH	accepting host
AI	artificial intelligence
AIOps	artificial intelligence for it operations
ANN	artificial neural network
AP	access proxy
ART	adversarial robustness tool
Bi-GRU	bidirectional gate recurrent unit
Bi-LSTM	bidirectional long-short term memory
CAPEX	capital expenditure
CART	classification and regression tree
CNN	convolutional neural network
CPU	central processing unit
CSTNET	China Science and Technology Network
CVAE	conditional variational autoencoder
DAE	denoising AutoEncoder
DBSCAN	density-based spatial clustering of applications with noise
DDM	drift detection method
DDQN	double deep Q network
DNS	domain name system

E2E	end-to-end
EDR	endpoint detection and response
EM	expectation maximum
EPG	end point group
FAR	false alarm rate
FN	false negative
FP	false positive
GAN	generative adversarial network
GBP	group-based police
GCN	graph convolutional network
GDPR	general data protection regulation
GFE	Google front end
GPU	graphics processing unit
HEA	high-level VNE agent
HMM	hidden Markov model
HRL	hierarchical reinforcement learning
HTTP	hypertext transfer protocol
HTTPS	hypertext transfer protocol over secure socket layer
ICT	information and communication technology
IDS	intrusion detection system
IH	initiating host
IIoT	Industrial Internet of Things
ILP	integer linear programming
InP	infrastructure provider
IoT	Internet of Things
ISE	identity services engine
ISP	internet service provider
KNN	K-nearest neighbor
KPI	key performance indicator
LEA	low-level VNE agent
LSTM	long short-term memory
MCTS	Monte Carlo tree search
MDP	Markov decision process
MEC	mobile edge computing
MILP	mixed-integer linear programming
ML	machine learning
MRE	machine reasoning engine
MSE	mean square error
NFV	network functions virtualization
NGMN	next generation mobile network

O&M	operation and maintenance
ONF	open networking foundation
OPEX	operating expenditure
PA	policy administrator
PCA	principal component analysis
PE	policy engine
PEP	policy enforcement point
PKI	public key infrastructure
PSO	particle swarm optimization
QoS	quality of service
QUIC	quick UDP Internet connection
RBM	restricted Boltzmann machine
ResNet	residual network
RL	reinforcement learning
RNN	recurrent neural network
SAE	sparse AutoEncoder
SDN	software-defined networking
SDP	software-defined perimeter
SD-RAN	software-defined radio access network
SD-WAN	software-defined wide area network
seq2seq	sequence to sequence
SIEM	security information and event management
SLA	service-level agreement
SMDP	semi-Markov decision process
SMOTE	synthetic minority over-sampling technique
SMTP	simple mail transfer protocol
SN	substrate network
SN	substrate network
SNI	service name indication
SP	service provider
SSI	symbolic structure inferring
SSL	symbolic semantic learning
SSO	single sign-on
SVM	support vector machine
TA	trust algorithm
TCP	transmission control protocol
TDG	traffic dispersion graph
TDR	true detection rate
TP	true positive

VAE	variational autoencoder
VLAN	virtual local area network
VN	virtual network
VNE	virtual network embedding
VNR	virtual network request
VoIP	voice over internet protocol
VPN	virtual private network
VR	virtual reality
VXLAN	virtual extensible local area network
ZTN	zero trust network

1

Introduction

1.1 Introduction

Networking systems have been experiencing rapid advancement in recent years, due to the fast development of 5G (Cheng et al., 2018, 2020b, Wu et al., 2021b), Internet of Things (IoT) (Wu et al., 2021c, Wu, 2021), Cloud/Edge Computing (Zhang et al., 2020, Wu, 2020), and Industry 4.0 (Wu et al., 2021a, Turner et al., 2021). On the one hand, many advanced networking techniques have been developed, such as software-defined networking (SDN) (Miao et al., 2016, Wang et al., 2018, Yang et al., 2020), network functions virtualization (NFV) (Miao et al., 2019, Cheng et al., 2020b), and network slicing (Wang et al., 2019, 2020) to facilitate network and service deployment and management. On the other hand, cybersecurity is a major concern for networking systems due to the increase in system exposure to the Internet (Wu et al., 2021a, Garg et al., 2020, Culot et al., 2019). Many security mechanisms, e.g. intrusion detection, traffic classification, and anomaly detection, have been developed to facilitate the security management of networking systems (Huang et al., 2017, 2018, Zuo et al., 2020, Sun et al., 2020).

Telecommunication networks such as 5G have received significant attention in the past few years because of their capabilities of accommodating diverse vertical industry applications (Wang et al., 2019, 2020). Along with the diversified services as well as their changing and/or stringent service requirements, 5G networks have become a complex system that requires advanced artificial intelligence (AI) and machine-learning (ML) techniques to manage and maintain high-standard services to users (Yan et al., 2020). From the perspective of network operators, it is important to maximize the resource utilization of 5G infrastructure, while minimizing the violation of service-level agreement (SLA) (Wang et al., 2019). The research of next-generation telecommunication networks, the so-called 6G (Wu et al., 2021d), has been initiated by many countries, such as United Kingdom, USA, China, Finland, just to name a few. "AI Everywhere" is an important component for 6G to ensure an automatic, healthy, and secure networking system.

AI and Machine Learning for Network and Security Management, First Edition.
Yulei Wu, Jingguo Ge, and Tong Li.
© 2023 The Institute of Electrical and Electronics Engineers, Inc. Published 2023 by John Wiley & Sons, Inc.

The fast advancement of IoT and Industrial Internet of Things (IIoT) is transforming many traditional industries (many of them are critical infrastructures), such as energy, healthcare, factory, and transportation, toward the goal of Industry 4.0 (Wu et al., 2021a). Such a complex networking system, connecting tens of billions of devices to the Internet, is collecting a huge amount of data every day. AI and ML techniques can leverage the knowledge learned from the data to automate many tasks for these industries (Lin et al., 2021), resulting in the so-called "smart energy, smart factory, smart transportation," to name a few. Such an automation remarkably increases the efficiency of system operation of industries. However, since traditional form of these industries is much more isolated, the exposure of these industries to the Internet as a result of the transformation, calls for significant security management to ensure the safety of these critical infrastructures (Culot et al., 2019, Wu et al., 2021a).

In order to properly apply AI and ML technologies into the field of network and security management, many real-world conditions and challenges need to be considered. For example, network intent is a key piece of information to enable autonomous network management (Lin et al., 2021). How to gain accurate network intent from network big data and how to ensure that the learned network intent can be readily used across different network environments is nontrivial. Reinforcement learning (RL) is a useful tool for autonomous network management (Yan et al., 2020). Successfully applying RL in various network management tasks is challenging. In many real-world conditions, such as IoT/IIoT, lightweight learning models are required (Cheng et al., 2020a). How to devise such models while maintaining the model performance is still worth to investigate for the field of network and security management. In addition, learning from encrypted data, e.g. encrypted traffic, is crucial, due to the increase in the volume of such traffic enforced by data regulations like the general data protection regulation (GDPR) (Liu et al., 2020). Further, because of the changing condition of real-world networking systems, network data are not ideal in many cases. They are usually evolving, changing, and imbalanced, and new data that have not been seen before may present from time to time. Besides, network data are usually hard to label, resulting in few-shot issues. How to effectively learn useful information from such "noisy" data is of paramount importance to ensure the success of AI-enabled network and security management (Sun et al., 2020).

In this book, we provide our insights and potential solutions to the above issues and challenges and consider various applications to network and security management including autonomous networks, resource allocation, traffic processing, traffic classification, anomaly detection, anomaly classification, and zero trust networks (ZTNs). In Section 1.2, we will explain the rationale under which the chapters in this book are organized.

1.2   Organization of the Book

There are two strands in this book. The first strand is in Chapter 2, where we provide a comprehensive review of potential AI and ML techniques for network and security management, the existing industry products, standards, projects, and proof-of-concepts. The second strand is across Chapters 3–9, where we elaborate the application of AI and ML techniques in various network and security management tasks. In Chapter 10, we elaborate an intelligent network management and operation system and discuss the deployment of the proposed solutions in this book. In Chapter 11, we conclude this book and provide potential research challenges and open issues that will be useful for future research in this area. Figure 1.1 shows the chapter organization of this book. In what follows, we briefly introduce each chapter to facilitate readers understand the content of this book.

Chapter 2. This chapter discusses the status and limitations of current network and security management and proposes an architecture for ML-empowered network and security management. Well-known AI and ML techniques that are useful for network and security management are reviewed and discussed. We also investigate existing industry products, standards, and proof-of-concepts for network and security management.

Chapter 3. The realization of network autonomy requires network knowledge to manage the network. The abstract intent of network management tasks

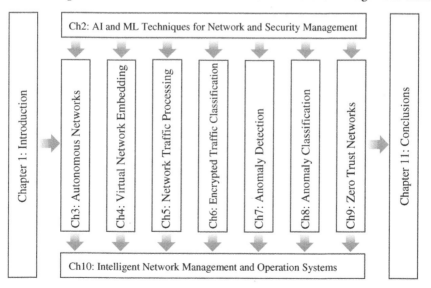

Figure 1.1   The chapter organization of this book.

can be considered as part of network knowledge. In this chapter, we treat abstract intents of network management tasks as a composite structure of symbols. Each symbol expresses the intention of the network management task in a certain aspect. The combinations of symbols, representing a network management task, should be able to be transferred and implemented across different networks. In this regard, we design a reference mechanism for learning intention symbols and their structures from network data. Taking path selection as an example, we describe in detail how to implement this mechanism to obtain the intent structure of the path selection task. It has been proved by experiments that the knowledge learnt by the proposed solution can be transferred and effectively leveraged in different network environments.

Chapter 4. Due to the outstanding performance of automatic exploration and quick development, RL methods have been applied to the virtual network embedding (VNE) problem. In this chapter, we find that a proactive VNE algorithm can benefit from hierarchical reinforcement learning (HRL). In this algorithm, a two-level agent is responsible for executing the VNE task, considering both the long-term impact and short-term impact. At the high level, the agent selects a feasible request from a batch, which aims to maximize the long-term revenue. At the low level, the agent manages to embed the selected request with the minimum cost.

Chapter 5. Although network traffic classification algorithms based on machine learning can alleviate the limitations imposed by traditional techniques, most of them are carried out by learning an underlying concept (i.e. data distribution) from a static dataset. Due to the exponential increase in the available network data, considerable attention has been received on processing network data as a stream. In this scenario, due to unforeseen circumstances in the network, the phenomenon of concept drift will degrade the performance of the classifier. In this chapter, after measuring the impact of concept drift on network traffic classifiers, we present a concept drift detector based on conditional variational autoencoders (CVAEs) under the semisupervised learning. In addition, we deploy the detector in a real-world environment, and experimental results show that this algorithm plays a great role in stabilizing the performance of a classifier.

Chapter 6. The surge in the volume of encrypted traffic and the nontransparency of encrypted traffic leads to high computational overheads in efficient network management. In this chapter, we introduce a lightweight and online approach for traffic classification, which adopts the multihead attention mechanism and the convolutional networks. Due to the one-step interaction of all packets and the parallel computing, the multihead attention mechanism can significantly reduce the number of model parameters and the running time. In addition, the effectiveness and efficiency of convolutional networks are proved in traffic classification.

Chapter 7. As the scale of networking systems expands, a fast-growing number of logs are produced. This chapter proposes a robust context-aware method for log anomaly detection. It combines word embedding with region embedding to conduct log vectorization. Such rich semantic information enables the proposed method to deal with unseen log data and understand imbalanced log data better and deeper. The proposed method combines semisupervised learning to make full use of labeled data and unlabeled data.

Chapter 8. ML-based log anomaly classification methods have been widely studied to ensure the stability and reliability of large-scale systems. This chapter briefly introduces the feature extraction in log analysis and the few-shot problem by examples. Then, we propose OpenLog, an anomaly classification method based on meta-learning. OpenLog uses a two-layer semantic encoder to simplify the complex feature engineering. It adopts the meta-learning strategy to train the models using sufficient auxiliary datasets to enhance its performance. OpenLog transforms the multiclassification task into a binary-classification task, and it can classify unseen anomalies without retraining.

Chapter 9. In recent years, many advanced persistent attacks (APTs) have occurred on corporate internal networks. Traditional perimeter-based security defense techniques such as firewalls, which assume that users and devices inside a network are safe and trustworthy, can no longer provide sufficient security protection. The concept of ZTN was therefore proposed. In ZTN, every request, whether it comes from an internal network or an external network, must be authenticated and authorized before accessing resources. In this chapter, we provide a brief introduction of ZTN, including its concept, its architecture, and its current implementation schemes such as access proxy-based, software-defined perimeter (SDP)-based, microsegmentation-based solutions, to name a few. Since ZTN needs to authenticate and authorize requests, it is necessary to consider as many devices, users, and environmental information as possible to make decisions. As there are a large number of services, traffic, and equipment logs in the corporate intranet, ML-based information fusion and decision-making methods may improve authentication and authorization performance. Therefore, in this chapter, we evaluate the possibility of using ML in ZTN.

Chapter 10. Although various intelligent operation and management technologies based on deep learning are being developed, how to efficiently apply them to real-world products is one of the core challenges faced by deep learning. In this chapter, we introduce various open source tools, frameworks, and characteristics in the field of operations management and security. Furthermore, we analyze existing security operations and management systems based on deep learning. Finally, we propose a security framework for intelligent operation and management based on network big data and describe the core functions and interfaces in the framework.

Chapter 11. This chapter provides a brief summary of this book, followed by a list of important research challenges and open issues that can be used for further research on AI and ML for network and security management.

1.3 Conclusion

This chapter provided a brief introduction of this book, emphasizing the motivation of writing this book and the chapter organization of the book. In addition, a brief review of each chapter is also provided, facilitating readers understand the content of this book.

References

Xiangle Cheng, Yulei Wu, Geyong Min, and Albert Y. Zomaya. Network function virtualization in dynamic networks: A stochastic perspective. *IEEE Journal on Selected Areas in Communications*, 36(10):2218–2232, 2018. doi: 10.1109/JSAC.2018.2869958.

Jin Cheng, Runkang He, E Yuepeng, Yulei Wu, Junling You, and Tong Li. Real-time encrypted traffic classification via lightweight neural networks. In *GLOBECOM 2020 - 2020 IEEE Global Communications Conference*, pages 1–6, 2020a. doi: 10.1109/GLOBECOM42002.2020.9322309.

Xiangle Cheng, Yulei Wu, Geyong Min, Albert Y. Zomaya, and Xuming Fang. Safeguard network slicing in 5G: A learning augmented optimization approach. *IEEE Journal on Selected Areas in Communications*, 38(7):1600–1613, 2020b. doi: 10.1109/JSAC.2020.2999696.

Giovanna Culot, Fabio Fattori, Matteo Podrecca, and Marco Sartor. Addressing industry 4.0 cybersecurity challenges. *IEEE Engineering Management Review*, 47(3):79–86, 2019. doi: 10.1109/EMR.2019.2927559.

Sahil Garg, Kuljeet Kaur, Georges Kaddoum, and Kim-Kwang Raymond Choo. Toward secure and provable authentication for internet of things: Realizing industry 4.0. *IEEE Internet of Things Journal*, 7(5):4598–4606, 2020. doi: 10.1109/JIOT.2019.2942271.

Chengqiang Huang, Geyong Min, Yulei Wu, Yiming Ying, Ke Pei, and Zuochang Xiang. Time series anomaly detection for trustworthy services in cloud computing systems. *IEEE Transactions on Big Data*, 1, 2017. doi: 10.1109/TBDATA.2017.2711039.

Chengqiang Huang, Yulei Wu, Yuan Zuo, Ke Pei, and Geyong Min. Towards experienced anomaly detector through reinforcement learning. *Proceedings of the AAAI Conference on Artificial Intelligence*, 32(1), 2018. URL https://ojs.aaai.org/index.php/AAAI/article/view/12130.

Guozhi Lin, Jingguo Ge, Yulei Wu, Hui Li, Tong Li, Wei Mi, and E Yuepeng. Network automation for path selection: A new knowledge transfer approach. In *2021 IFIP Networking Conference*, 2021.

Xun Liu, Junling You, Yulei Wu, Tong Li, Liangxiong Li, Zheyuan Zhang, and Jingguo Ge. Attention-based bidirectional GRU networks for efficient https traffic classification. *Information Sciences*, 541:297–315, 2020. ISSN 0020-0255. doi: 10.1016/j.ins.2020.05.035. URL https://www.sciencedirect.com/science/article/pii/S002002552030445X.

Wang Miao, Geyong Min, Yulei Wu, Haozhe Wang, and Jia Hu. Performance modelling and analysis of software-defined networking under bursty multimedia traffic. *ACM Transactions on Multimedia Computing, Communications, and Applications*, 12(5s):2016. ISSN 1551-6857. doi: 10.1145/2983637. URL https://doi.org/10.1145/2983637.

Wang Miao, Geyong Min, Yulei Wu, Haojun Huang, Zhiwei Zhao, Haozhe Wang, and Chunbo Luo. Stochastic performance analysis of network function virtualization in future internet. *IEEE Journal on Selected Areas in Communications*, 37(3):613–626, 2019. doi: 10.1109/JSAC.2019.2894304.

Peijie Sun, E Yuepeng, Tong Li, Yulei Wu, Jingguo Ge, Junling You, and Bingzhen Wu. Context-aware learning for anomaly detection with imbalanced log data. In *2020 IEEE 22nd International Conference on High Performance Computing and Communications; IEEE 18th International Conference on Smart City; IEEE 6th International Conference on Data Science and Systems (HPCC/SmartCity/DSS)*, pages 449–456, 2020. doi: 10.1109/HPCC-SmartCity-DSS50907.2020.00055.

Christopher J. Turner, John Oyekan, Lampros Stergioulas, and David Griffin. Utilizing industry 4.0 on the construction site: Challenges and opportunities. *IEEE Transactions on Industrial Informatics*, 17(2):746–756, 2021. doi: 10.1109/TII.2020.3002197.

Guodong Wang, Yanxiao Zhao, Jun Huang, and Yulei Wu. An effective approach to controller placement in software defined wide area networks. *IEEE Transactions on Network and Service Management*, 15(1):344–355, 2018. doi: 10.1109/TNSM.2017.2785660.

Haozhe Wang, Yulei Wu, Geyong Min, Jie Xu, and Pengcheng Tang. Data-driven dynamic resource scheduling for network slicing: A deep reinforcement learning approach. *Information Sciences*, 498:106–116, 2019. ISSN 0020-0255. doi: 10.1016/j.ins.2019.05.012. https://www.sciencedirect.com/science/article/pii/S0020025519303986.

Haozhe Wang, Yulei Wu, Geyong Min, and Wang Miao. A graph neural network-based digital twin for network slicing management. *IEEE Transactions on Industrial Informatics*, 1, 2020. doi: 10.1109/TII.2020.3047843.

Yulei Wu. Cloud-edge orchestration for the internet-of-things: Architecture and AI-powered data processing. *IEEE Internet of Things Journal*, 1, 2020. doi: 10.1109/JIOT.2020.3014845.

Yulei Wu. Robust learning-enabled intelligence for the internet of things: A survey from the perspectives of noisy data and adversarial examples. *IEEE Internet of Things Journal*, 8(12):9568–9579, 2021. doi: 10.1109/JIOT.2020.3018691.

Yulei Wu, Hong-Ning Dai, and Hao Wang. Convergence of blockchain and edge computing for secure and scalable IIoT critical infrastructures in industry 4.0. *IEEE Internet of Things Journal*, 8(4):2300–2317, 2021a. doi: 10.1109/JIOT.2020.3025916.

Yulei Wu, Hong-Ning Dai, Hao Wang, and Kim-Kwang Raymond Choo. Blockchain-based privacy preservation for 5G-enabled drone communications. *IEEE Network*, 35(1):50–56, 2021b. doi: 10.1109/MNET.011.2000166.

Yulei Wu, Zehua Wang, Yuxiang Ma, and Victor C.M. Leung. Deep reinforcement learning for blockchain in industrial IoT: A survey. *Computer Networks*, 191:108004, 2021c. ISSN 1389-1286. doi: 10.1016/j.comnet.2021.108004. URL https://www.sciencedirect.com/science/article/pii/S1389128621001213.

Y. Wu, S. Singh, T. Taleb, A. Roy, H.S. Dhillon, M.R. Kanagarathinam, and A. De. *6G Mobile Wireless Networks*. Springer, 2021d).

Zhongxia Yan, Jingguo Ge, Yulei Wu, Liangxiong Li, and Tong Li. Automatic virtual network embedding: A deep reinforcement learning approach with graph convolutional networks. *IEEE Journal on Selected Areas in Communications*, 38(6):1040–1057, 2020. doi: 10.1109/JSAC.2020.2986662.

Shu Yang, Laizhong Cui, Xinhao Deng, Qi Li, Yulei Wu, Mingwei Xu, Dan Wang, and Jianping Wu. FISE: A forwarding table structure for enterprise networks. *IEEE Transactions on Network and Service Management*, 17(2):1181–1196, 2020. doi: 10.1109/TNSM.2019.2951426.

Juan Zhang, Yulei Wu, Geyong Min, Fei Hao, and Laizhong Cui. Balancing energy consumption and reputation gain of UAV scheduling in edge computing. *IEEE Transactions on Cognitive Communications and Networking*, 6(4):1204–1217, 2020. doi: 10.1109/TCCN.2020.3004592.

Yuan Zuo, Yulei Wu, Geyong Min, Chengqiang Huang, and Ke Pei. An intelligent anomaly detection scheme for micro-services architectures with temporal and spatial data analysis. *IEEE Transactions on Cognitive Communications and Networking*, 6(2):548–561, 2020. doi: 10.1109/TCCN.2020.2966615.

2

When Network and Security Management Meets AI and Machine Learning

2.1 Introduction

With the fast development of cloud computing, Internet of Things (IoT), and new-generation mobile communication technologies (Wu, 2021, Wu et al., 2022, Cheng et al., 2020b), network services and systems are growing exponentially. Such an advancement of network technologies has brought about social progress, business innovation, and convenience of life, and at the same time, it inevitably causes the increase in the complexity of network management and security management. In this context, network and security management that is carried out manually or that which relies on automation rules are overwhelming, and there is an urgent need for help from emerging AI technologies (Wu et al., 2021). In this chapter, we will discuss why, how, and where AI technologies can empower network and security management.

Adopting artificial intelligence (AI) and machine learning (ML) is to realize automated and intelligent network and security management. The architecture usually considers a closed-loop feedback iterative model of perception-analysis-control. The top-down management channel is intent description, strategy selection, and configuration generation. The bottom-up management channel is data fusion, behavior analysis, strategy selection, and configuration generation. The intelligence engine based on AI and ML is at the center of and is the core of the architecture.

In addition to the discussion around the architectural aspects, in this chapter, we also introduce several main types of ML techniques, including supervised learning, semisupervised/unsupervised learning, and RL, and provide examples of network and security management applications based on various ML techniques.

Further, we investigate and summarize the industrial applications and standards in the field of network and security management. The literature shows a significant growth of ML-empowered products, demonstrating the significance and potential impact of AI and ML in the field of networking. However, how to

AI and Machine Learning for Network and Security Management, First Edition.
Yulei Wu, Jingguo Ge, and Tong Li.

leverage ML technologies efficiently, accurately, and stably in realistic networks with uncertainties is still an area worthy of research.

The remainder of this chapter is organized as follows: Section 2.2 introduces the architecture of ML-empowered network and security management. Sections 2.3–2.5 introduce existing network and security management applications based on different types of ML techniques. Sections 2.6–2.9 summarize the industry products, standards, projects, and proof-of-concepts on network and security management. Finally, Section 2.10 concludes this chapter.

2.2 Architecture of Machine Learning-Empowered Network and Security Management

Nowadays, network and security management relies heavily on human experience and skills. Telecommunication network is becoming increasingly complex under the heavy historical burden. Especially with the advent of 5G and cloud/edge computing, the scale of the network has increased by 10 times, and the network traffic is showing great uncertainties, which has exceeded the reach of human professional knowledge and ability. Facing the future, a large number of real-time services are beyond the reach of human response speed. At the same time, the quality of network services is constantly improving. For example, services can be accessed quickly, network faults can be eliminated in a timely manner, and end-to-end (E2E) service quality can be guaranteed. Therefore, industry puts forward clear requirements for the intelligentization of the network. The current device-centric network operation and maintenance model has been difficult to effectively achieve the above aims. Only by building a truly user experience-centric network can it effectively meet the demands of end users and support the commercial success of network service providers. With the maturity of cloud computing, big data, and AI technologies, network solutions driven by user intents have emerged. It builds an intelligent network brain between the physical network and the business intent to achieve user experience-centric networks.

This section presents the overall architecture of the application of AI and ML in network and security management. The technical idea is to adopt a closed-loop feedback iterative model of perception-analysis-control. As shown in Figure 2.1, the architecture consists of a smart brain layer empowered by AI and ML techniques and a network infrastructure layer.

The smart brain layer aims to achieve the intelligent management and control of the network. It accepts the business intentions of operators and accurately transforms the intentions to network strategies. The smart brain automatically verifies and implements the strategies to physical networks. It perceives the states of the physical network in real time, detects anomalies, and issues early warnings in time

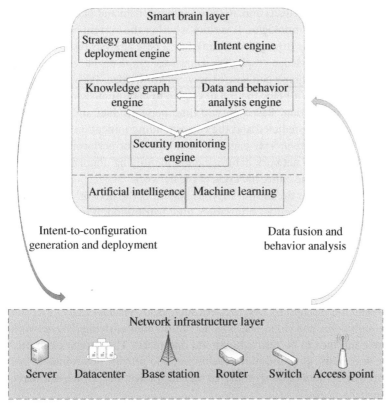

Figure 2.1 The overall architecture of AI- and ML-empowered network and security management.

to provide advice on how to handle anomalies and ensure that the network meets the business intents. It can quickly troubleshoot anomalies or optimize network performance based on the telemetry data and the experience knowledge graph database. Through continuous modeling and network behavioral learning, it can identify, e.g. short-term congestion points that are prone to occur in advance and migrate important services or improve scheduling strategies.

The smart brain layer has five functional modules, including an intent engine, a strategy automation deployment engine, a data and behavior analysis engine, a knowledge graph engine, and a security-monitoring engine. The *intent* engine is responsible for receiving and translating business intents into network strategies, simulating and verifying network strategies. The *strategy automation deployment engine* transforms network strategies into specific network commands and delivers it to network devices automatically through standard interfaces. The *data and behavior analysis engine* collects and analyzes network data and behaviors based on real-time telemetry technologies. It verifies whether the current network conforms to the user's intents through AI techniques. These analysis results are also used to construct a knowledge graph. The *knowledge graph engine* continuously improves the experience graph database of network knowledge. Taking advantage of the knowledge graph, it helps the intent engine to continuously optimize the ability of intents translation. Based on real-time network data and knowledge graphs, risky events are predicted and the corresponding mitigation suggestions are given. The *security monitoring engine* is responsible for performing security threat analysis based on network behavior data, identifying abnormal network traffic, and monitoring the entire life cycle of the network.

The smart brain layer is the central nervous system of the network. It achieves the data acquisition, verification, translation, and distribution of user intentions in a top-down manner, so as to build a user-centric automation and intelligent network. Its bottom-up channel is to use AI techniques to analyze various measurement data and service behaviors of the entire life cycle of networks to achieve the automated and intelligent network and security management.

The network infrastructure layer is the cornerstone. It needs to meet the high bandwidth demand brought by new services such as 4K/virtual reality (VR) and other ultra-high-definition video, 5G, as well as autonomous driving. The network architecture continues to be restructured and optimized. The network can provide elastic scalability, plug-and-play capabilities, and provide deterministic low latency for future 5G services and industrial special applications, which is to serve different business needs.

2.3 Supervised Learning

Supervised learning is the process of using a set of samples with known labels to learn appropriate parameters and construct a learner. Therefore, the learner can map the newly arrived unlabeled data to the category (label) to which it belongs. The core of supervised learning is to label data, that is, learning from historical experience. Typical examples of supervised ML applications are shown in Table 2.1.

2.3.1 Classification

Classification is a typical supervised learning process. Based on the known categories, what the classification needs to do is to classify each unlabeled data into the corresponding category. The information of each category must be known in advance, and all data items to be classified have the corresponding categories by

Table 2.1 Examples of supervised ML applications.

Applications	Works	Features
Traffic analysis	Peng et al. (2016) and Soysal and Schmidt (2010)	Compare multiple machine learning classifiers applied to traffic classification
	Goseva-Popstojanova et al. (2014)	Expose common threats in the Web to be identified
	Belavagi and Muniyal (2016)	Compare several supervised machine learning classifiers for intrusion detection
Anomaly detection	Liu et al. (2015)	Automatically select the appropriate detector-parameter combinations and the thresholds
Log analysis	Liang et al. (2007)	Train three classifiers for log prediction
	Zhang et al. (2019)	Automatically learn the importance of different log events for anomaly detection
	Li et al. (2018a)	Suggest the most appropriate level for newly-added logging statements
	Farshchi et al. (2015)	Find the correlation between the logs and the effect of operation activities on cloud resources
	He et al. (2018)	Detect the cause of system performance degradation

default. Thus, classification algorithms have limitations on whether they can meet the above conditions. Common classification algorithms include decision trees, support vector machine (SVM), K-nearest neighbor (KNN) and neural networks, to name a few.

The idea of decision trees is to use a tree structure to classify. Taking binary classification as an example, it is expected the model that learns from a given labeled dataset can classify new data. This task of classifying samples can be regarded as a "decision" for the question of "is the current sample normal?" Essentially, the decision-making process of decision trees is the process of "decision" for a certain attribute of a sample. Due to the visualized tree structure, the decision tree has strong interpretability and has low requirements on the scale of training data. However, decision tree algorithms may generate very complex tree models, and the decision tree is usually based on a heuristic algorithm, so it may be unstable. Commonly used decision tree algorithms include Iterative Dichotomiser three (ID3) (Quinlan, 1986), C4.5 (Quinlan, 1993), Classification and Regression Tree(CART) (Breiman et al., 1984), etc.

One of the ideas of classification is to find a partitioning hyperplane in the sample space based on the labeled training dataset to separate samples of different categories. The idea of SVM is to find the maximum margin hyperplane with the best tolerance. The classification idea of SVM is simple, and the performance is usually good. SVM using the kernel function, can solve nonlinear classification issue, and it is suitable for classification tasks with less-training data. However, when the data scale is large, the space and time overhead of SVM increases, and SVM is mainly suitable for binary classification problems.

KNN has a simple idea, that is, each sample can be represented by the KNN samples. If most of the KNN samples belong to a certain category, the sample also belongs to this category. KNN uses the Euclidean distance as a distance metric measuring two samples. KNN is simple and easy to use and implement, but it is easily affected by the configuration of k and the impression of noise.

Generally, neural networks refer to the artificial neural network, which is an algorithmic mathematical model that imitates the behavioral characteristics of animal neural networks and performs distributed parallel information processing. This kind of networks relies on the complexity of the system and achieves the purpose of processing information by adjusting the interconnection between a large number of internal nodes. Neural network algorithms are based on a set of interconnected input and output units, and each connection between the units is associated with a weight. In the learning phase, neural network algorithms adjust the weight to achieve the correspondence between the input sample and its category. The neural network classification algorithm is accurate and flexible and can be adapted to various types of data, but correspondingly, the time and space overhead of neural networks is much greater than other types of classification algorithms.

Classification has been widely used in various scenarios and tasks of network and security management, such as anomaly detection (Liu et al., 2015, Wu et al., 2022, Guo et al., 2021, Huang et al., 2022, 2018), traffic classification (Rezaei and Liu, 2019b, Soysal and Schmidt, 2010, Cheng et al., 2020a, 2021, Liu et al., 2020), log classification (Liang et al., 2007, Zhang et al., 2019, Sun et al., 2020, Zuo et al., 2020), etc.

The works in Peng et al. (2016) and Soysal and Schmidt (2010) compared multiple machine learning classifiers applied to traffic classification. For anomalous or malicious traffic detection, Goseva-Popstojanova et al. (2014) exposed common threats in the Web to be identified. Belavagi and Muniyal (2016) compared several supervised machine learning classifiers for intrusion detection. For KPI (key performance indicator) anomaly detection, Liu et al. (2015) proposed a novel supervised approach called Opprentice and trained a random forest classifier to automatically select the appropriate detector-parameter combinations and the thresholds. For log analysis, Liang et al. (2007) trained three classifiers of the Ripper, SVM, and KNN to predict whether the newly arrived log is at the FATAL or FAILURE level so as to achieve the purpose of anomaly detection. Zhang et al. (2019) proposed LogRobust, which used the neural network algorithm long short term memory(LSTM), to fully mine the context, semantics, syntax, and structural features of the log sequence, and automatically learn the importance of different log events to the detection target.

2.3.2 Regression

The most classic regression algorithm is linear regression. It assumes that a linear function can fit the target data and then uses some error analysis to determine a function that best fits the target data. Nonlinear problems can be solved by transforming variables into linear regression problems. Curve regression algorithm, also known as polynomial regression, refers to the use of continuous curves to approximately describe the functional relationship between the coordinates represented by a set of discrete points on a plane. It is a method of approximating discrete data with analytical expressions. The decision tree algorithm CART mentioned in Section 2.3.1 can also be used as a regression algorithm. Unlike the classification-enabled CART based on the Gini index, the regression-enabled CART is based on the square error minimization criterion for feature selection and generates a binary tree. Among the samples contained in the leaf nodes of the regression tree, the average value of the output variables is the predicted result.

In network and security management, regression analysis can be used for event mining that gathers a variety of data and performs event correlation analysis. For log analysis, Li et al. (2018a) leveraged ordinal regression models to suggest the most appropriate level for newly added logging statements automatically for anomaly detection and fault localization. Farshchi et al. (2015) presented a regression-based analysis method to find the correlation between the logs and the effect of operation activities on cloud resources. He et al. (2018) proposed Log3C to detect the cause of system performance degradation based on the cascading clustering algorithm and a multivariate linear regression model.

2.4 Semisupervised and Unsupervised Learning

Supervised learning has been able to guide and solve many problems in network and security management. However, in many real-world scenarios, we inevitably encounter such problems of the difficulty on obtaining the labels of samples for supervised learning, the high cost of manual labeling, and the insufficiency of prior knowledge and experience. Unsupervised and semisupervised learning can, to some extent, address these challenges. Unsupervised learning does not need labeled data and only relies on differences between samples or extracting some similar patterns of samples to achieve the purpose of learning. Common unsupervised learning methods include clustering, dimension reduction, etc. Semisupervised learning is different from supervised learning and unsupervised learning. It uses not only a large amount of unlabeled data but also uses labeled data to achieve the purpose of learning. Semisupervised learning has lower requirements for labeled data but also can bring high accuracy at the same time. Therefore, it is receiving more attention. Typical examples of semi- and un-supervised ML applications are shown in Table 2.2.

Table 2.2 Examples of semi- and unsupervised ML applications.

Application	Works	Function
Traffic analysis	Shaikh et al. (2013) and Namdev et al. (2015)	Network flow classification
	Mu et al. (2013)	Purity the traffic flow in deep packet inspection
	Botta et al. (2012)	Analyze traffic behavior to identify P2P traffic
	Fahad et al. (2013)	Traffic classification using PCA for features selection
	Rezaei and Liu (2019a)	Semisupervised traffic classification methods
Network prediction	Gwon and Kung (2014)	A semisupervised model to classify frame/packet patterns and infer the properties of flows in a Wi-Fi network
Log analysis	Fu et al. (2009), Hamooni et al. (2016), and Shima (2016)	Log parsers based on clustering
	Lin et al. (2016)	Problem identification based on a agglomerative hierarchical clustering algorithm
	Meng et al. (2018)	A data-driven system to detect and classify anomalies based on a semisupervised learning algorithm

2.4.1 Clustering

Clustering refers to the process of dividing a sample set into clusters composed of similar samples. A good clustering method can make the samples in a cluster as similar as possible, and the samples in different clusters are as different as possible.

K-means (Macqueen, 1966) is one of the simplest and popular clustering algorithms. It is based on distance, and it expects that the closer the distance between two targets, the greater the similarity. It starts with K random cluster centers and calculates the distances with the remaining samples in the sample set to the K cluster centers. It then assigns them to the clusters corresponding to the cluster centers with the smallest distance.

Density-based spatial clustering of applications with noise (DBSCAN) (Ester et al., 1996) is a density-based clustering algorithm. Unlike K-means, DBSCAN does not need to specify the number of clusters in advance, so the final number of clusters is also uncertain. It divides the sample points into core points, boundary points, and noise points based on the preset parameters, Eps (distance) and MinPts (minimum number of points). The core point refers to the point that contains more than MinPts in the radius Eps. The boundary point refers to the point whose number of points in the radius Eps is less than MinPts, but falls in the neighborhood of the core point. The noise point refers to a point that is neither a core point nor a boundary point. DBSCAN deletes noise points and then it assigns an edge between all core points within Eps. Each group of connected core points forms a cluster, and each boundary point is assigned to a cluster of core points associated with it.

In network and security management, clustering can be used in traffic classification, problem identification, and log classification, etc. Shaikh et al. (2013) and Namdev et al. (2015) classified network flows using K-means and DBSCAN algorithms. Mu et al. (2013) proposed a deep packet inspection (DPI) method based on K-means, to purity the traffic flow. Botta et al. (2012) analyzed traffic behaviors to identify P2P traffic, where the first step is to cluster similar flows using K-means, and then clusters are represented by a traffic dispersion graph (TDG). In the domain of log analysis, log key extraction (LKE) (Fu et al., 2009), LogMine (Hamooni et al., 2016), and LenMa (Shima, 2016) are the proposed log parsers that follow the idea of clustering. Lin et al. (2016) proposed LogCluster, which clusters the logs based on the agglomerative hierarchical clustering (AHC) for problem identification.

2.4.2 Dimension Reduction

Dimension reduction in the field of machine learning refers to the use of a certain mapping method to map data points in the original high-dimensional space to the low-dimensional space. In the original high-dimensional space, the data contain redundant and noise information, which may cause errors in practical applications and reduce accuracy. Through dimension reduction, we hope to reduce the errors caused by redundant information and improve the accuracy of the task, and find the intrinsic structural characteristics of the data through dimension reduction algorithms. In many algorithms, dimension reduction has become part of data preprocessing.

The most commonly used dimension reduction algorithm is principal component analysis (PCA). The goal of PCA is to map high-dimensional data to a low-dimensional space representation through a certain linear projection and expects that the variance of the data in the projected dimension is the largest, so as to use fewer data dimensions while retaining the larger characteristics of multiple original data points. In work Fahad et al. (2013) of traffic classification, PCA was used as a flow feature selection technique. Xu et al. (2009) proposed an anomaly detection method based on frequent pattern filtering and PCA.

2.4.3 Semisupervised Learning

Semisupervised learning can be divided into semisupervised classification, semisupervised regression, semisupervised clustering, semisupervised dimensionality reduction, and other related algorithms according to the application. Based on the theory, it can also be divided into transductive semisupervised learning and inductive semisupervised learning. As a broad concept, semisupervision can be applied to traditional machine learning algorithm (e.g. SVM, clustering) and deep learning models (e.g. CNN, LSTM).

In the domain of traffic classification, Rezaei and Liu (2019a) proposed a semisupervised encrypted traffic classification approach based on a one-dimensional CNN. The model was trained to predict the statistical features of the entire flow from a few sampled packets with a large unlabeled dataset. In network prediction, Gwon and Kung (2014) proposed a semisupervised model to classify received frame/packet patterns and infer the original properties of flows in a Wi-Fi network. Meng et al. (2018) proposed LogClass, a data-driven system to detect and classify anomalies based on a semisupervised learning algorithm Positive-Unlabeled learning and supervised classifier SVM, to tackle the challenges of device-agnostic vocabulary and partial labels.

2.5 Reinforcement Learning

RL is a subclass of ML, where an agent extracts knowledge from the surrounding environment and aims to maximize the long-term accumulative reward. Due to the automatic exploration, RL is adequate to complex and perplexing environments. Figure 2.2 shows the basic work procedure of RL. In RL, an agent starts

Figure 2.2 The framework of reinforcement learning.

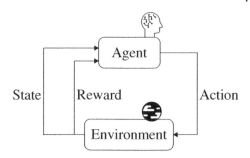

from scratch and gradually learns desirable behavior (e.g. strategy) by exploring the external environment automatically. After getting the environment state, the agent transforms the state to advanced features and generates actions. The environment performs the action and returns a reward to the agent. Based on the current reward, the agent can estimate the long-term accumulative reward and optimize its strategy to maximize the long-term accumulative reward. Different from the traditional ML method, the objective of RL is to optimize the strategy for better performance in the future. Using the optimized strategy, the agent generates another action according to the new environment. As the optimization iterative goes on, the agent eventually converges to a strategy that maximizes the long-term reward without any explicit objective functions and targets. When the agent finishes the training, it only needs to extract the environment state and generate actions. It is obvious that the procedure of optimizing the strategy of the agent can be completed automatically by predefined training routines without much human efforts.

RL has shown great potential in dealing with a set of complex tasks, such as the game of Go. Due to the excellent exploration ability, RL has been applied widely in the control tasks in the area of network management, such as virtual network embedding (VNE), software defined networks (SDNs), and Blockchain.

RL-based VNE. VNE is the major challenge of network virtualization, which aims to effectively allocate substrate network (SN) resources to virtual networks. As shown in Figure 2.3, the VNE problem includes two parts: node mapping and link mapping, and it has been proved to be NP-hard. A large number of heuristic algorithms have been proposed, but most of them rely on artificial rules to rank nodes and make mapping decisions, where the parameters are always fixed and cannot be optimized. Therefore, embedding algorithms of the heuristic method are always sub-optimal. In recent years, due to the excellent performance of automatic exploration and fast deployment, RL begins to surface in the VNE field. Aiming to maximize long-term reward, RL-based VNE can greatly alleviate the suboptimal problem. In VNE problems, the actions can be defined as node mapping (i.e. map a virtual network node to a substrate network node) and link mapping (i.e.

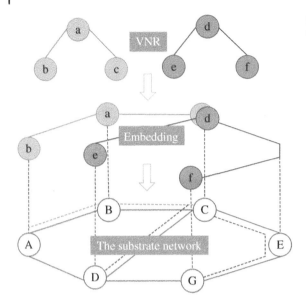

Figure 2.3 The description of the VNE process.

according to the node mapping, find substrate network paths to embed the virtual link). The environment state consists of the state of the substrate network and virtual networks. The rewards are defined on the consideration of request acceptance, long-term revenue, load balance, and so on. At present, many RL methods, such as Q-learning, Monte Carlo tree search (MCTS), and deep RL, have been successfully applied to the VNE task.

RL-based SDN. SDN facilitates organizations to deploy applications and enable flexible delivery. In the traditional network infrastructure, the control plane and data plane are closely coupled, where the variety and the complexity of network elements make their maintenance very expensive and underlying infrastructure less flexible when a new service is deployed. Therefore, SDN proposed a new approach to increase network flexibility and controllability. In SDN, the control operations are centralized in a controller that issues network policies, such as network slice, load balance, routing, and traffic engineering. However, most of the operations are NP-hard, which challenges the SDN technology greatly. Recently, RL-based SDN controllers significantly optimize the SDN functions due to the excellent performance of automatic exploration. In the SDN problem, the actions can be defined as the issued controlling strategy. The environment state consists of the state of the control plane and data plane. The rewards are defined on the consideration of load balance, congestion control, traffic engineering, and so on.

RL-based blockchain. As a revolutionary technology, Blockchain makes a great impact on modern society due to transparency, decentralization, and encryption. Blockchain gets lots of attention since the first appearance of Cryptocurrencies.

Blockchain is defined as the chain of digital blocks connected with each other as an open distributed ledger. Many applications can benefit from Blockchain to protect their information exchanges, which enables users to verify, preserve, and synchronize the contents of the ledger replicated by multiple users. By combining the benefits of Blockchain and RL, many RL-based Blockchain technologies have been applied in the network and security management area. On the one hand, the application of Blockchain can ensure the security and privacy of the management. On the other hand, the usage of RL can optimize management strategies without too much human efforts.

Generally, RL is classified into policy-based and value-based categories according to the optimization objective. Both of them have been widely applied in network and security management. Next, we will introduce the application of RL in network management and security in a more general way.

2.5.1 Policy-Based

Policy-based RL approaches directly optimize the accumulative long-term rewards while remaining relatively stable and improving with a small learning rate. In every epoch, the policy gradient is estimated from a single trajectory, of which the variance is tremendous due to the sample inefficiency. We will take the MCTS algorithm as an example to illustrate the procedure of policy-based RL. The idea of this algorithm is to create a trajectory tree, instead of exploring all the trajectories, wherein in each epoch, only the most promising trajectory will be selected. The algorithm contains four steps that repeat multiple episodes as shown in Figure 2.4. (i) *Selection*. The RL agent starts from the root node and then moves toward the children nodes with the highest possibility of winning. (ii) *Expansion*. After selecting the right node, expansion is applied to extend the actions further by

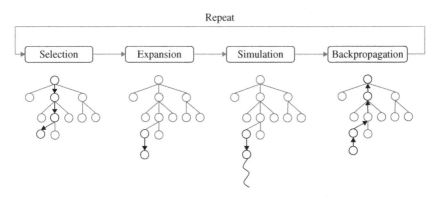

Figure 2.4 The framework of MCTS.

Table 2.3 Examples of policy-based RL applications.

Application	Works	Function
VNE	Haeri and Trajković (2017)	Solve virtual node mapping with MCTS
	Soualah et al. (2015)	Propose a batch-embedding strategy based on MCTS
	Xiao et al. (2019)	Adopt a policy gradient-based method to improve efficiency
	Zheng et al. (2020)	Propose a batch-embedding strategy based on MCTS
SDN	Zhang et al. (2020)	Balance link utilization with policy-based method
	Li et al. (2018b)	Attain the global optimal load balancing

expanding the selected nodes and creating many children nodes. (iii) *Simulation.* The agent rolls out one or multiple simulations with rewards accumulated for each simulation. (iv) *Backup.* Due to the rewards, the total rewards of their parent nodes should be updated by going back up the tree one by one. Finally, the state of the tree is changed and will influence the future node of the selection process.

Due to the excellent performance in convergence and high-dimensional action spaces, policy-based methods are widely used in network and security management. Some related works in network and security management are shown in Table 2.3. Haeri and Trajković (2017) formalized the virtual node mapping problem by using the Markov decision process (MDP) and devised action policies for the proposed MDP using the MCTS algorithm, which improved the embedding solutions by shortening the computation time. In work Zheng et al. (2020), the combination of MCTS with node importance sped up the extraction of domain-specific knowledge. Zhang et al. (2020) proposed a RL-based flow rerouting method which learned a policy to select critical flows automatically so as to balance link utilization.

2.5.2 Value-Based

Value-based RL approaches can learn from many trajectories sampled from the same environment. In the value-based approach, the value function is selected initially and then find new value function according to different trajectories. The process will repeat until it finds the optimal value function. According to the value function, the agent can always choose the action with the highest value. For example, *Q*-learning is a representative value-based RL algorithm that seeks

Table 2.4 Examples of value-based RL applications.

Application	Works	Function
VNE	Yan et al. (2020)	Combine GCN and Q-learning in the field of VNE
	Yao et al. (2018)	Decompose the VNE into three steps with RL
SDN	Sun et al. (2021)	Combine control theory with deep Q-learning methods
	Rischke et al. (2020)	Enable multiple routing paths by a RL-based approach
	Guo et al. (2019)	Propose a value-based QoS-aware secure routing protocol
	Chen et al. (2020)	Suggest better routing paths with a value-based RL method
	Jalodia et al. (2019)	Manage dynamic resources with a value-based RL method
Blockchain	He et al. (2020)	Design a smart contract within a private Blockchain network
	Yang et al. (2020)	Formulate the resource allocation as an MDP
	Feng et al. (2019)	Cooperate computation offloading and resource allocation

to find the best action to take, given the current state. The "Q" in Q-learning represents how useful a given action is in accumulating some future rewards. On the one hand, the Q-value can be learned by deep learning, which is called deep Q-learning. On the other hand, the Q-value can be defined in a table, which is named tabular Q-learning.

Due to the high-sample efficiency and low variance, value-based methods are widely used in network and security management. Some related works are shown in Table 2.4. Yan et al. (2020) first combined the Graph Convolutional Network with the Q-learning method to solve the VNE problem, which improved the acceptance ratio remarkably and achieved good robustness. To get convincing results, Yao et al. (2018) proposed a value-based dynamic attribute matrix representation algorithm for VNE, which decomposed the process of node mapping into three steps and reduced the algorithm complexity. To fix the scalability problem in SDN, Sun et al. (2021) proposed to combine the control theory and deep Q-learning technology to achieve an efficient network control scheme for traffic engineering. Guo et al. (2019) dynamically optimized the routing policy in SDN by a value-based quality of service (QoS)-aware secure routing method, which improved security and efficiency. Chen et al. (2020) considered comprehensive network information for state representation and used one-to-many network configuration for routing choice. Simulation results showed that the RL-routing could obtain higher rewards and enable a host to transfer a large file faster than the state-of-the-art method. He et al. (2020) first elaborated on the security and privacy issues of edge computing-enabled IoT and exploited a value-based RL method to allocate edge computing resources. Feng et al. (2019) jointly designed and optimized the performance of Blockchain and mobile edge computing (MEC) based on the deep Q-learning method.

2.6 Industry Products on Network and Security Management

2.6.1 Network Management

A summary of network management products is shown in Table 2.5.

2.6.1.1 Cisco DNA Center

Cisco DNA Center is an intent-based management and control platform for users' networks. Cisco DNA Center software resides on the Cisco DNA Center appliance and controls all of Cisco physical and virtual devices. The following are applications of AI in Cisco DNA Center.

- Cisco DNA Center translates business intents into network policies and applies those policies, such as access control, traffic routing, and QoS, consistently over the entire wired and wireless infrastructure. Policy-based access control and network segmentation is a critical function of the Cisco Software-Defined Access (SD-Access) solution built from Cisco DNA Center and Cisco Identity Services Engine (ISE). Cisco AI Network Analytics and Cisco Group-Based Policy Analytics running in the Cisco DNA Center identify endpoints, group

Table 2.5 Summary of network management products.

Company	Product	Type
Cisco	DNA center	Intent-based device
Loom systems	Sophie	Logs based monitoring software
Juniper	Ex4400 switch	Security switch
	Juniper SRX series services gateway	SD-WAN security router
H3C	SeerAnalyzer	Intelligent analysis software

similar endpoints, and determine group communication behaviors. Cisco DNA Center then facilitates creating policies that determine the form of communication allowed between and within members of each group. ISE then activates the underlying infrastructure and segments the network creating a virtual overlay to follow these policies consistently. Such segmenting implements zero-trust security in the workplace, reduces risk, contains threats, and helps verify regulatory compliance by giving endpoints just the right level of access they need.

- Cisco DNA Assurance, using AI/ML, enables every point on the network to become a sensor, sending continuous streaming telemetry on application performance and user connectivity in real time. The clean and simple dashboard shows detailed network health and flags issues. Then, guided remediation automates resolution to keep the network performing at its optimal with less mundane troubleshooting work. The outcome is a consistent experience and proactive optimization of the network, with less time spent on troubleshooting tasks.

- AI Analysis Security Announcement uses Machine Reasoning Engine (MRE) to identify potential vulnerabilities in the network. The MRE can be dynamically updated from the machine inference knowledge base to discover new security issues. The switches and routers supported by Cisco DNA Center can be scanned to identify software images with security announcements.

2.6.1.2 Sophie

Sophie is an AIOps-powered IT monitoring tool. It can prevent IT incidents before customers are affected and provide corresponding solutions. Sophie automatically parses and analyzes all of network devices' logs, learns the baseline of the environment, and alerts to both previously known and unknown issues. By enriching the alerts with the root-cause and insights, Sophie enables users to become proactive and improve the mean-time-to-resolution (MTTR) by 45%.

2.6.1.3 Juniper EX4400 Switch

EX4400 switch can provide Mist AI engine with the rich streaming data and metadata needed for true AIOps. By introducing Wired Assurance and Marvis VNA powered by Mist AI in EX4400 switch, operators can easily find "minor" problems, such as faulty cables and misconfigured VLANs, and use simple queries to gain insights into the wired switching domain.

2.6.1.4 Juniper SRX Series Services Gateway

Juniper SRX Series Services Gateway is the flagship product in the Software Defined Wide Area Network (SD-WAN) security router field, with an integrated advanced security firewall. Mist AI was extended to SRX Series Services Gateway in 2020. It allows customers to set and implement service levels, ensures a good user experience across the WAN, and customers can use Marvis VNA for simple troubleshooting and gain insights. By extracting telemetry data from the Session Smart router to the Mist AI engine, customers can now set, monitor, and implement service levels across the WAN, proactively monitor abnormal conditions and other edge events, and further enhance their understanding of WAN conditions to ensure excellent user experience. In addition, the Marvis virtual network assistant (powered by Mist AI) can troubleshoot the Session Smart SD-WAN environment by using natural language queries and take proactive measures to correct problems before users are affected.

2.6.1.5 H3C SeerAnalyzer

H3C SeerAnalyzer is a new generation of network intelligent analysis systems supported by big data and AI. SeerAnalyzer uses telemetry and other technologies to collect real-time and full-scale network operating status data, uses big data technology to efficiently preprocess and store these data, and uses a big data distributed computing engine to perform real-time and offline calculations on massive amounts of data. The algorithm intelligently analyzes complex data, gains insight into the health status and problems of the entire network, combines expert knowledge and associated algorithms to locate the root cause of the problem, and performs AI prediction on key faults. The result data collected and analyzed by SeerAnalyzer provide an open API interface to facilitate the integration of upper-level application systems. Below are applications of AI in H3C SeerAnalyzer.

- SeerAnalyzer uses distributed computing engines such as Spark and Flink to provide high reliability through cluster capabilities and uses AI algorithms to complete data online/offline analysis tasks to meet the needs of intelligent operation and maintenance analysis in various scenarios. It can support up to millions of levels per minute data flow analysis capabilities.
- It realizes network-wide state awareness by collecting network equipment status data, protocol message data, traffic forwarding data, user access process data, log data, etc., and uses ML algorithms and expert systems to realize real-time perception of network faults and intelligent fault root cause location. It also provides repair suggestions for operation and maintenance personnel.
- It uses AI analysis of massive data to evaluate the quality of the network, user experience, application, etc., and provides network optimization capabilities and key guarantee capabilities.
- It utilizes high-performance acquisition, real-time expert system, and AI algorithm calculation to complete the isolation of the fault environment verification, fault detection, impact verification, and isolated push.

- SeerAnalyzer uses intelligent algorithms to continuously analyze the historical data accumulated in the network, thereby predicting network failures and performance bottlenecks, and providing a basis for preintervention and planning of operation and maintenance personnel.

2.6.2 Security Management

A summary of security management products is shown in Table 2.6.

2.6.2.1 SIEM, IBM QRadar Advisor with Watson

IBM QRadar Advisor with Watson is a SIEM (Security Information and Event Management) tool, which is a built-in AI solution that integrates log analysis, network traffic analysis, and automatic Security Operations Center (SOC) task generation functions. Cognitive computing is an advanced AI that uses various forms of AI, including machine learning algorithms and deep learning networks, to constantly enhance and improve the level of intelligence over time. Watson is IBM's cognitive AI technology that can learn through every interaction, find the connection between threats, and provide practical insights. In the end, users will be more confident and faster to respond to threats. IBM QRader Advisor with Waston can automatically generate daily SOC tasks, discover commonalities in the investigation, and provide analysts with practical feedback, allowing them to have more time focusing on the more important factors in the investigation, while improving the efficiency of the analysts.

2.6.2.2 FortiSandbox

Today's modern malware entails new techniques such as the use of exploits. Exploiting a vulnerability in a legitimate application can cause anomalous behaviors, and attackers can take advantage of this behavior to compromise computer

Table 2.6 Summary of security management products.

Company	Product	Type
IBM	QRader Advisor with Wastom	SIEM
Fortinet	FortiSIEM	SIEM
	FortiSandbox	Sandbox
	FortiEDR	Endpoint detection and response software
	FortiClient	Endpoint software
H3C	SecCenter CSAP	Threat discovery and operation management platform

systems. The process of an attack by exploiting an unknown software vulnerability is what is known as a zero-day attack, and before sandboxing, there was no effective means to stop it. A malware sandbox, within the computer security context, is a system that confines the actions of an application, such as opening a word document, to an isolated environment. Within this safe environment, the sandbox analyzes the dynamic behavior of an object and its various application interactions in a pseudo-user environment and uncovers any malicious intents. Therefore, if something unexpected happens, it affects only the sandbox and not the other computers and devices on the network. In parallel, any malicious intent is captured, leading to an alert and relevant threat intelligence generated to stop this zero-day attack. FortiSandbox is an AI-powered, top-rated, and integrated sandbox. Below are the FortiSandbox's solutions:

- First-in-the-industry patent-pending ML-based static analysis, and ML-based dynamic analysis.
- MITRE ATT&CK standards-based reporting.
- Automated zero-day breach protection with integration to both Fortinet and non-Fortinet solutions.

2.6.2.3 FortiSIEM

As digital transformation sweeps through every industry, the attack surface grows dramatically (and constantly), making security management increasingly difficult. Security teams struggle to keep up with the deluge of alerts and other information generated by their multitude of security devices. Cybersecurity skills gap only makes this more difficult. Infrastructure, applications, and endpoints (including IoT devices) must all be secured. This requires visibility of all devices and all the infrastructure in real time. Organizations also need to know what devices represent a threat and where.

FortiSIEM UEBA leverages ML and statistical methodologies to baseline normal behaviors and incorporate real-time, actionable insights into anomalous user behaviors regarding business-critical data. By combining telemetry that is pulled from endpoint sensors, network device flows, server and applications logs, and cloud APIs, FortiSIEM is able to build comprehensive profiles of users, peer groups, endpoints, applications, files, and networks. FortiSIEM UEBA behavioral anomaly detection is a low-overhead but high-fidelity way to gain visibility of end-to-end activity, from endpoints, to on-premises servers, and from network activity, to cloud applications.

2.6.2.4 FortiEDR

An advanced attack may only take a few minutes or even a few seconds to break the endpoint. The first generation of endpoint detection and response (EDR) tools simply cannot handle it. They require manual classification and response. Faced with ever-changing threats, this method is not only inefficient, but also generates a large number of indicators, which is undoubtedly worse for the already overwhelmed security team. In addition, traditional EDR tools will increase security operating costs and reduce operating efficiency, which will have a negative impact on the business. FortiEDR uses a ML-powered antivirus engine to prevent pre-execution of malware. This cross-operating system next-generation antivirus (NGAV) function can be configured and built into a single lightweight agent, allowing users to provide antimalware protection for any endpoint group without additional installation.

2.6.2.5 FortiClient

FortiClient is a Fabric Agent that delivers protection, compliance, and secure access in a single, modular lightweight client. A Fabric Agent is a bit of endpoint software that runs on an endpoint, such as a laptop or mobile device, that communicates with the Fortinet Security Fabric to provide information, visibility, and control to that device. It also enables secure, remote connectivity to the Security Fabric. The EPP/APT Edition of FortiClient expands on the capabilities of the Zero Trust Network Access Edition by adding AI-based NGAV, endpoint quarantine, and application firewall, as well as support for cloud sandbox.

2.6.2.6 H3C SecCenter CSAP

H3C SecCenter CSAP is a security threat discovery and operation management platform. It introduces AI-based intelligent threat analysis. Below are its features:

- According to different usage scenarios, it actively adjusts the model algorithm parameters to make the security analysis results more suitable for the actual network conditions.
- Based on existing security incidents, it relies on the experience of offensive and defensive experts, correlate assets, intelligence, and other multidimensional information to provide "expert-level" reasoning analysis.
- It introduces AI algorithms such as supervised learning and RL, uses the "knowledge brain" to detect complex attacks of known and unknown types and fully grasps the infection path of large-scale mass incidents.
- It establishes a behavioral baseline and judges various abnormal behaviors based on the deviation of asset/user traffic, actions, and other behaviors.

2.7 Standards on Network and Security Management

2.7.1 Network Management

Standards on network management in recent years cover Cognitive Network Management, E2E 5G Beyond, Software-Defined Radio Access Network (SD-RAN), Architectural Framework for machine learning in future networks, etc. They are shown in Table 2.7.

Table 2.7 Standards on network management.

Standardization body	Working group/Project	Outcome	Release date
ETSI	Working group: Experimental Networked Intelligence (ENI) Industry Specification Group (ISG)	A series of specifications for Cognitive Network Management systems	2019.09-2021.03
NGMN	—	Requirements for a 5G End-to-End (E2E) Architecture Framework	2020-10
ONF	Project: Software Defined Radio Access Network (SD-RAN)	Support for mobile 4G and 5G RAN deployments	2020-08
ITU	Working group: ITU-T Study Group 13	Recommendation ITU-T Y.3172 specifies an architectural framework for ML in future networks including IMT-2020	2019-06

2.7.1.1 Cognitive Network Management

The ETSI Industry Specification Group on Experimental Networked Intelligence (ISG ENI) develops specifications for a Cognitive Network Management system with the aim of introducing a metric for the optimization and adjustment of the operator experience over time by taking advantage of AI techniques like ML and reasoning. It focuses on improving the operator experience to more quickly recognize and incorporate new and changed knowledge, and hence, make actionable decisions, in day-to-day-operations. The specifications are shown in Table 2.8.

ISG ENI's approach employs the "observe-orient-decide-act" control model which enables the system to adjust the offered services based on the changes in user needs, environmental conditions, and business goals. ISG ENI has specified a set of use cases and the derived requirements for a generic technology independent architecture of a network supervisory assistant system. The introduction of technologies such as SDN, NFV, and network slicing, means that networks are becoming more flexible, powerful, and configurable. ISG ENI will make the deployment more intelligent and efficient.

2.7.1.2 End-to-End 5G and Beyond

The Next Generation Mobile Networks (NGMN) Alliance announced the latest requirements for a 5G E2E Architecture Framework in November 2020. It aims

Table 2.8 ISG ENI's specifications on Cognitive Network Management.

Name	Topic	Release date
ETSI GR ENI 008 V2.1.1	InTent Aware Network Autonomicity (ITANA)	2021-03
ETSI GR ENI 010 V1.1.1	Evaluation of categories for AI Application to Networks	2021-03
ETSI GR ENI 001 V3.1.1	ENI use cases	2020-12
ETSI GR ENI 002 V3.1.1	ENI requirements	2020-12
ETSI GR ENI 006 V2.1.1	Proof of Concepts Framework	2020-05
ETSI GR ENI 007 V1.1.1	ENI Definition of Categories for AI Application to Networks	2019-11
ETSI GR ENI 004 V2.1.1	Terminology for Main Concepts in ENI	2019-10
ETSI GR ENI 001 V2.1.1	ENI use cases	2019-09
ETSI GR ENI 005 V1.1.1	System Architecture	2019-09
ETSI GR ENI 002 V2.1.1	ENI requirements	2019-09

to advance the 5G ecosystem to enable heterogeneous access, virtualization, autonomic capabilities, forward-looking service enablers, and emerging usage scenarios that support 5G's full potentials. The content of this publication builds on the architectural concepts and directions described in the first NGMN 5G White Paper and further related NGMN publications. Essential to an evolving 5G ecosystem, the latest requirements from NGMN describe the next steps needed to advance forward-looking technologies and use cases that will enable network service providers to offer new capabilities and enhance the customer experience. With many new 5G use cases to deliver, diverse service deployment from an E2E perspective is a challenge. NGMN addresses this by looking at agile service deployment as one of the objectives of a cognitive Platform as a Service, with a focus on AI and ML data models.

This White Paper outlines the requirements in terms of entities and functions that characterize the capabilities of an E2E framework. Architectural perspectives and considerations underscore the definition of the E2E framework requirements. This goes in hand with the service categories – Enhanced Mobile Broadband, Massive IoT, and Ultra-Reliable Low Latency Communications – envisioned for 5G. Furthermore, the document analyzes in detail autonomic networking, which provides a scalable, customizable, and self-organizing model for system-wide automation. Here, virtualization and programmability are adopted in an E2E manner. Self-organization is an integral aspect of autonomic networking for automation that dynamically learns and adapts to changing conditions in the system and its environment, while satisfying service KPIs and the QoS experience.

2.7.1.3 Software-Defined Radio Access Network

In August 2020, the Open Networking Foundation (ONF) announced the formation of the SD-RAN project (Software-Defined Radio Access Network) to pursue the creation of open-source software platforms and multivendor solutions for mobile 4G and 5G RAN deployments. Initially, the project focused on building an open-source Near Real-Time RAN Intelligent Controller (nRT-RIC) compatible with the O-RAN architecture. The new SD-RAN project is backed by a consortium of leading operators and aligned technology companies and organizations that together are committed to creating a truly open RAN ecosystem. Founding members include AT&T, China Mobile, China Unicom, Deutsche Telekom, Facebook, Google, Intel, NTT, Radisys, and Sercomm.

ONF has a track record of building open-source platforms deployed in Tier-1 operator networks worldwide. ONF's cloud-native solutions all leverage disaggregation and whitebox hardware, utilizing SDN, NFV, and the latest cloud technologies to build flexible, performant, highly available solutions where intelligence and control is moved from proprietary vendor specific devices up into the cloud. To date, the ONF has addressed a wide array of operator use cases, including data center, fixed access, backhaul, optical transport, and the mobile core domains. Mobile RAN is one of the most challenging use cases, and it has yet to benefit from disaggregation, multivendor interoperability, and SDN-ization. Now that the industry is aligning behind the open architecture and interfaces specified by the O-RAN ALLIANCE, the SD-RAN community has formed to help bring the full benefits of ONF's unique approach to the RAN domain. SD-RAN Community is building Open Source RIC Controller and ML/AI-driven xApps Compatible with the O-RAN architecture.

2.7.1.4 Architectural Framework for ML in Future Networks

ML holds great promise to enhance network management and orchestration. Drawing insight from network-generated data, ML can yield predictions to support the optimization of network operations and maintenance. This optimization is becoming increasingly challenging, and increasingly important, as networks gain in complexity to support the coexistence of a diverse range of information and communication technology (ICT) services. Network operators aim to fuel ML models with data correlated from multiple technologies and levels of the network. They are calling for deployment mechanisms able to "future-proof" their investments in ML. They are in need of interfaces to transfer data and trained ML models across ML functionalities at multiple levels of the network. Recommendation ITU Y.3172 specifies an architectural framework to meet these requirements. ITU Y.3172 was proposed in June 2019 and was under the responsibility of ITU-T Study Group 13. ITU Y.3172 has established a basis for the cost-effective integration of ML into 5G and future networks.

2.7.2 Security Management

Standards on security management in recent years are mainly aimed at securing AI. They are shown in Table 2.9.

2.7.2.1 Securing AI

The rapid expansion of AI into new industries with new stakeholders, coupled with an evolving threat landscape, presents a tough challenge for security. AI impacts our lives every day, from local AI systems on our mobile phones suggesting the next word in our sentences to large manufacturers using AI to improve industrial processes. AI has the potential to revolutionize our interactions with technologies, improve our quality of life, and enrich security – but without high-quality technical standards, AI has the potential to create new attacks and worsen security.

The ETSI Industry Specification Group on Securing Artificial Intelligence (ISG SAI) focuses on three key areas: using AI to enhance security, mitigating against attacks that leverage AI, and securing AI itself from attack. The ETSI ISG SAI works alongside a landscape of huge growth in AI, creating standards to preserve and improve the security of AI.

ETSI GR SAI 004 v1.1.1 was published in December 2020. It describes the problem of securing AI-based systems and solutions, with a focus on ML, and the challenges relating to confidentiality, integrity and availability at each stage of the ML lifecycle. It also describes some of the broader challenges of AI systems

Table 2.9 Standards on security management.

Standardization body	Working group	Outcome	Release date
ETSI	Securing Artificial Intelligence (SAI) Industry Specification Group (ISG)	Problem Statement: ETSI GR SAI 004 v1.1.1	2020-12
	Securing Artificial Intelligence (SAI) Industry Specification Group (ISG)	Mitigation Strategy Report: ETSI GR SAI 005 v1.1.1	2021-03

including bias, ethics, and explainability. A number of different attack vectors are described, as well as several real-world use cases and attacks.

ETSI GR SAI 005 v1.1.1 was published in March 2021. It summarizes and analyzes existing and potential mitigation against threats for AI-based systems as discussed in ETSI GR SAI 004 v1.1.1. The goal was to have a technical survey for mitigating against threats introduced by adopting AI into systems. The technical survey shed light on available methods of securing AI-based systems by mitigating against known or potential security threats. It also addresses security capabilities, challenges, and limitations when adopting mitigation for AI-based systems in certain potential use cases.

2.8 Projects on Network and Security Management

As shown in Table 2.10, in recent years, ML technologies have been increasingly used for network security and network management. In this section, some open-source applications will be selected from Github to illustrate the application of ML technologies in the projects.

2.8.1 Poseidon

In order to improve the accuracy of identifying what a node is (based on captured IP header data) and housing ML techniques for additional use cases in SDN environment, Poseidon[1] was implemented by IQTLabs. The project utilizes SDN and ML to automatically capture network traffic, extracts relevant features from that traffic, performs classifications through trained models, conveys results, and provides mechanisms to take further actions, as shown in Figure 2.5.

Poseidon is a platform that can be easily expanded based on python implementation. It can provide context-aware capabilities for items and traffic added

Table 2.10 Projects on network and security management using ML techniques.

Project name	Developer	Application field	Stars
NetworkML	IQTLabs	Functional role classification	89
NetworkML	IQTLabs	Node identification	322
Credential-Digger	SAP	Data protection	156
ART	Trusted-AI	ML security	2500

---

1 https://github.com/IQTLabs/poseidon.

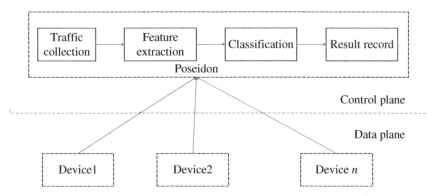

Figure 2.5 The processing flow of Poseidon.

or deleted from the network. It uses ML technologies to check interactive activities on the network, and through learning to track and block various malicious activities-related behaviors. In the preliminary test, Poseidon obtained a malicious activity detection rate of 84%, while the false positive rate was only 2.2%.

2.8.2 NetworkML

In order to classify each device into a functional role, IQTLabs implements NetworkML.[2] "Functional role" refers to the authorized administrative purpose of the device on the network and includes roles such as printer, mail server, and others typically found in an IT environment.

As shown in Figure 2.6, taking the network traffic for a single device as input, NetworkML uses a feedforward neural network from the scikit-learn-package to predict the functional role of network-connected devices. By using network

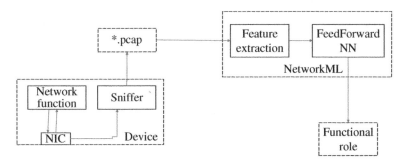

Figure 2.6 The processing flow of NetworkML.

2 https://github.com/IQTLabs/NetworkML.

traffic of a single device, it means all packets sent and received by that device over a given time period. In addition, in its default configuration, NetworkML has 11 roles: active directory controller, administrator server, administrator workstation, confluence server, developer workstation, distributed file share, exchange server, graphics processing unit (GPU) laptop, github server, public key infrastructure (PKI) server, and printer.

The NetworkML in this project can be used via Docker and in a standalone manner on a Linux host. In addition, in order to avoid problems related to data privacy, NetworkNL only uses the packet header to predict the functional role.

2.8.3 Credential-Digger

In the field of data protection, one of the most critical threats is represented by hardcoded (or plaintext) credentials in open-source projects. Although several tools are already available to detect leaks in open-source platforms, but the diversity of credentials (depending on multiple factors such as the programming language, code development conventions, or developers' personal habits) is a bottleneck for the effectiveness of these tools. Their lack of precision leads to a very high number of pieces of code incorrectly detected as leaked secrets. Data wrongly detected as a leak is called false positive data and composes the huge majority of the data detected by currently available tools. As a result, SAP implements Credential-Digger[3] to reduce the amount of false positive on the output of the scanning phase by leveraging ML models.

As shown in Figure 2.7, Credential-Digger takes the path of code as input and determine whether there is a certificate or password leak in the code. It first uses rules, which comprises a regex, to find all possible leaks, then ML models will be used for false positive detection. It has three types of models, i.e. path model, snippet model, and similarity model.

- Path models. The path model classifies a file as false positive according to its file path. The path models first process the path of file in order to extract all the

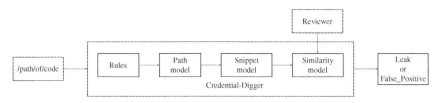

Figure 2.7 The processing flow of Credential-Digger.

---

3 https://github.com/SAP/credential-digger.

worlds contained in the path. Then, each word is converted into its root. Finally, the roots of the words are used for the ML classification.

- Snippet model. The snippet model classifies a discovery as false positive according to its code snippet, i.e. the line of code detected as a possible leak in the commit. The goal of the snippet model is to classify false positive passwords (it can be used also with tokens, but its precision is lower).
- Similarity model. No matter how robust a classifier is, instances of misclassified snippets will always remain a reality. As a result, after files are processed by snippet models, the reviewer will verify that the code snippets are correctly classified. Usually, those misclassified snippets share similarities between each other. Upon manually updating a snippet to a new state, e.g. from "leak" to "false_positive," Similarity models are able to automatically detect similar snippets in the repository and update their state accordingly, which can save the user a lot of time.

In addition to local files and directories, Credential-Digger also supports the scanning of online and local repositories. In addition, this project is very easy to expand, where we can add rules and models according to our needs.

2.8.4 Adversarial Robustness Toolbox

Adversarial Robustness Toolbox (ART[4]) is a Python library for ML Security implemented by Trusted-AI. ART provides tools that enable developers and researchers to defend and evaluate ML models and applications against the adversarial threats of Evasion, Poisoning, Extraction, and Inference. ART supports most popular ML frameworks (e.g. TensorFlow, Keras, PyTorch, MXNet, scikit-learn, XGBoost, LightGBM, CatBoost, GPy), most data types (images, tables, audio, video, etc.), and ML tasks (e.g. classification, object detection, speech recognition, generation, certification).

Although this project is not specifically used in the field of network security and management, due to the large number of noise samples in the network resulting in the difficulties of guaranteeing the reliability of the data, this project can still play a great role in the field of network security. In fact, many researchers have begun to study against malicious samples in the field of network intrusion detection (Madani and Vlajic, 2018).

In addition to the above projects, there are some projects to support the application of ML technologies in the network, such as MIST[5] (a platform to collect, storage and share cyber security indicators and threats), openCTI[6]

---

4 https://github.com/Trusted-AI/adversarial-robustness-toolbox.
5 https://github.com/MISP/MISP.
6 https://github.com/OpenCTI-Platform/opencti.

(an open-source platform allowing organizations to manage their cyber threat intelligence knowledge and observables), etc. We did not introduce them in detail in this section because their focuses are not on the application of ML models.

2.9 Proof-of-Concepts on Network and Security Management

With the continuous development of ML technologies, more researchers have begun to use them to solve network security and network management problems. At the same time, they often open source their experimental code as Proof of Concepts.

2.9.1 Classification

As shown in Figure 2.8, the classification system can classify various data sources according to their characteristics. In the field of network security and network management, data sources can be network data packets, host logs, traffic information, etc. The classification model can be used as the core of malicious URL detection, malicious DAG detection, intrusion detection, and traffic classification systems.

2.9.1.1 Phishing URL Classification

Malicious Web sites are a cornerstone of Internet criminal activities. These Web sites contain various unwanted content such as spam-advertised products, phishing sites, dangerous "drive-by" harness that infect a visitor's system with malware. The most influential approaches to the malicious URL problem are manually constructed lists in which all malicious web page's URLs are listed, as well as users systems that analyze the content or behavior of a Web site as it is visited. The disadvantage of Blacklisting approaches is that we have to do the tedious task of searching the list for presence of the entry. The list can be very large considering the amount of web sites on the Internet. Also the list cannot be kept up to date because of the ever-growing web link over time.

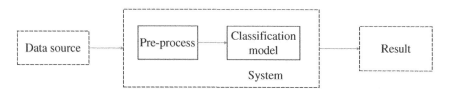

Figure 2.8 The processing flow of classification.

In the given System,[7] the developer is using ML techniques to classify a URL as either Safe or Unsafe in real time without even the need to download the webpage. In this system, Random Forest, Logistic Regression, Decision Trees, and Gradient Boosting are used as classification models. In the experiments, the URL collected from Phishtank[8] is used as data source. Then, Lexical features (mainly include Length of URL, Domain Length, Presence of IP Address in Host Name and Presence of Security Sensitive Words in URL) are extracted from URL.

2.9.1.2 Intrusion Detection

With the continuous updating of network attack technologies, the number of rules in traditional rule-based intrusion detection systems is becoming more judgmental. In addition, in terms of zero-day attack detection, rule-based intrusion detection systems have natural disadvantages. Therefore, in recent years, more researchers have tried to use ML-based intrusion detection systems for security protection.

In the Network Intrusion Detection System,[9] the network traffic collected from NSL-KDD dataset is used as data source. Then, in order to reduce the number of features, ANOVA F-test is used as preprocess method. It analyzes each feature individually to determine the strength of the relationship between the features and labels, using the SecondPercentile method (sklearn.feature_selection) to select features based on percentile of the highest scores. Finally, Decision Tree and Random Forest are used as detection models to classify the intrusion.

In the Web Attacks Detection System,[10] the http logs are used as the data source. Then, the features of each log are extracted by Regular expression rules, and the label of each log is assigned manually. Finally, after being trained by the labeled samples, Decision Tree and Logistic-Regression models are used to detect whether there is an attack on the unlabeled log.

2.9.2 Active Learning

In the process of supervised and semisupervised learning, the training data needs to be labeled. However, in many practical fields, labeling all data will incur a great cost and cause a waste of manpower. For example, in the field of anomaly detection, there is often only a small part of the anomaly data that security experts are interested in. Anaël et al. proposed "ILAB: An Interactive Labelling Strategy for Intrusion Detection" in Beaugnon et al. (2017) and provided an open-source

---

7 https://github.com/surajr/URL-Classification.
8 https://www.phishtank.com/.
9 https://github.com/CynthiaKoopman/Network-Intrusion-Detection.
10 https://github.com/slrbl/Intrusion-and-anomaly-detection-with-machine-learning.

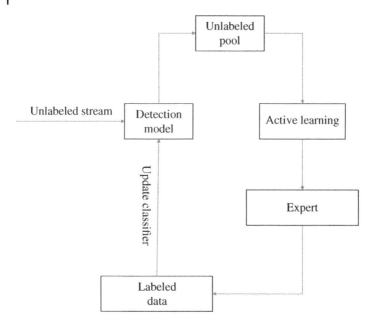

Figure 2.9 The processing flow of active learning.

implementation[11] to allow security experts to label their own datasets and researchers to compare labeling strategies.

The workflow of active learning is shown in Figure 2.9. First, a detection model is trained by initial labeled data. After that, the system starts to work, and the unlabeled data will be placed in the unlabeled pool. Then, active learning is performed to select representative samples from the unlabeled pool and provides them to experts for labeling. Finally, after the expert finishes labeling the selected data, the marked data will be used for training the detection model.

In order to overcome the problem of sampling bias, ILAB considers both uncertainty and rarity when it selects data. Therefore, ILAB can find those rare malicious samples. As a result, when compared with other schemes, ILAB can select samples with more training value.

2.9.3 Concept Drift Detection

With the rapid development of network and information technology, traffic classification has received significant attention and plays an important role in intrusion detection, flow identification, etc. In the standard ML framework, data

---

11 https://github.com/ANSSI-FR/SecuML/.

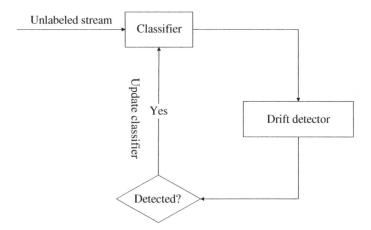

Figure 2.10 The processing flow to overcome concept drift.

are usually processed in an offline way. Since network traffic, logs, and data packets are usually generated continuously, data in the network domain is usually regarded as a stream. Hence, the underlying data distribution may be changed and severely reduce the performance of ML models, which is called concept drift.

In order to overcome the occurrence of concept drift and maintain the performance of ML models, many conceptual drift detectors have been proposed. As shown in Figure 2.10, whenever a concept drift is detected, the model update phase will be triggered. In the prototype system called "concept-drift,"[12] two detectors called Adwin (Bifet and Gavaldà, 2007) and Page–Hinckley Test (Gama et al., 2013) are implemented. Although these two algorithms are not specifically used in the network field and because they are based on full supervision hypothesis which is difficult to achieve in the network field, many variants have been proposed.

2.10 Conclusion

This chapter introduced the current status and situation of network and security management in both academia and industry. We provided the basic classification of AI and ML, and briefly introduced how different types of ML techniques can empower network and security management. Finally, we summarized the related products, standards, and proof-of-concepts for AI and ML in network and security management.

---

12 https://github.com/blablahaha/concept-drift.

References

Anaël Beaugnon, Pierre Chifflier, and Francis Bach. ILAB: An interactive labelling strategy for intrusion detection. In Marc Dacier, Michael Bailey, Michalis Polychronakis, and Manos Antonakakis, editors, *Research in Attacks, Intrusions, and Defenses*, pages 120–140, Cham, 2017. Springer International Publishing. ISBN 978-3-319-66332-6.

M. C. Belavagi and B. Muniyal. Performance evaluation of supervised machine learning algorithms for intrusion detection. *Procedia Computer Science*, 89:117–123, 2016.

A. Bifet and R Gavaldà. Learning from time-changing data with adaptive windowing. In *Proceedings of the 7th SIAM International Conference on Data Mining*, April 26–28, 2007, Minneapolis, Minnesota, USA, 2007.

Alessio Botta, Alberto Dainotti, and Antonio Pescapè. A tool for the generation of realistic network workload for emerging networking scenarios. *Computer Networks*, 56(15):3531–3547, 2012. doi: 10.1016/j.comnet.2012.02.019.

Leo Breiman, J. H. Friedman, R. A. Olshen, and C. J. Stone. *Classification and Regression Trees*. Wadsworth, 1984. ISBN 0-534-98053-8.

Yi-Ren Chen, Amir Rezapour, Wen-Guey Tzeng, and Shi-Chun Tsai. RL-routing: An SDN routing algorithm based on deep reinforcement learning. *IEEE Transactions on Network Science and Engineering*, 7(4):3185–3199, 2020.

Jin Cheng, Runkang He, E Yuepeng, Yulei Wu, Junling You, and Tong Li. Real-time encrypted traffic classification via lightweight neural networks. In *GLOBECOM 2020 - 2020 IEEE Global Communications Conference*, pages 1–6, 2020a. doi: 10.1109/GLOBECOM42002.2020.9322309.

Xiangle Cheng, Yulei Wu, Geyong Min, Albert Y. Zomaya, and Xuming Fang. Safeguard network slicing in 5G: A learning augmented optimization approach. *IEEE Journal on Selected Areas in Communications*, 38(7):1600–1613, 2020b. doi: 10.1109/JSAC.2020.2999696.

Jin Cheng, Yulei Wu, E Yuepeng, Junling You, Tong Li, Hui Li, and Jingguo Ge. MATEC: A lightweight neural network for online encrypted traffic classification. *Computer Networks*, 199:108472, 2021. ISSN 1389-1286. doi: 10.1016/j.comnet.2021 .108472. URL https://www.sciencedirect.com/science/article/pii/ S1389128621004217.

Martin Ester, Hans-Peter Kriegel, Jörg Sander, and Xiaowei Xu. A density-based algorithm for discovering clusters in large spatial databases with noise. In Evangelos Simoudis, Jiawei Han, and Usama M. Fayyad, editors, *Proceedings of the 2nd International Conference on Knowledge Discovery and Data Mining (KDD-96)*, Portland, Oregon, USA, pages 226–231. AAAI Press, 1996. URL http://www.aaai .org/Library/KDD/1996/kdd96-037.php.

Adil Fahad, Zahir Tari, Ibrahim Khalil, Ibrahim Habib, and Hussein M. Alnuweiri. Toward an efficient and scalable feature selection approach for internet traffic classification. *Computer Networks*, 57(9):2040–2057, 2013. doi: 10.1016/j.comnet .2013.04.005.

Mostafa Farshchi, Jean-Guy Schneider, Ingo Weber, and John C. Grundy. Experience report: Anomaly detection of cloud application operations using log and cloud metric correlation analysis. In *26th IEEE International Symposium on Software Reliability Engineering, ISSRE* 2015, Gaithersbury, MD, USA, November 2–5, 2015, pages 24–34. IEEE Computer Society, 2015. doi: 10.1109/ISSRE.2015.7381796.

Jie Feng, F. Richard Yu, Qingqi Pei, Xiaoli Chu, Jianbo Du, and Li Zhu. Cooperative computation offloading and resource allocation for blockchain-enabled mobile-edge computing: A deep reinforcement learning approach. *IEEE Internet of Things Journal*, 7(7):6214–6228, 2019.

Qiang Fu, Jian-Guang Lou, Yi Wang, and Jiang Li. Execution anomaly detection in distributed systems through unstructured log analysis. In Wei Wang, Hillol Kargupta, Sanjay Ranka, Philip S. Yu, and Xindong Wu, editors, *ICDM 2009, The 9th IEEE International Conference on Data Mining, Miami*, Florida, USA, 6–9 December 2009, pages 149–158. IEEE Computer Society, 2009. doi: 10.1109/ICDM .2009.60. URL https://doi.org/10.1109/ICDM.2009.60.

João Gama, Raquel Sebastião, and Pedro Rodrigues. On evaluating stream learning algorithms. *Machine Learning*, 90:317–346, 2013. doi: 10.1007/s10994-012-5320-9.

Katerina Goseva-Popstojanova, Goce Anastasovski, Ana Dimitrijevikj, Risto Pantev, and Brandon Miller. Characterization and classification of malicious web traffic. *Computer Security*, 42:92–115, 2014. doi: 10.1016/j.cose.2014.01.006.

Xuancheng Guo, Hui Lin, Zhiyang Li, and Min Peng. Deep-reinforcement-learning-based QoS-aware secure routing for SDN-IoT. *IEEE Internet of Things Journal*, 7(7):6242–6251, 2019.

Yalan Guo, Yulei Wu, Yanchao Zhu, Bingqiang Yang, and Chunjing Han. Anomaly detection using distributed log data: A lightweight federated learning approach. In *2021 International Joint Conference on Neural Networks (IJCNN)*, pages 1–8, 2021. doi: 10.1109/IJCNN52387.2021.9533294.

Youngjune Gwon and H. T. Kung. Inferring origin flow patterns in Wi-Fi with deep learning. In Xiaoyun Zhu, Giuliano Casale, and Xiaohui Gu, editors, *11th International Conference on Autonomic Computing, ICAC '14*, Philadelphia, PA, USA, June 18–20, 2014, pages 73–83. USENIX Association, 2014. URL https://www .usenix.org/conference/icac14/technical-sessions/presentation/gwon.

Soroush Haeri and Ljiljana Trajković. Virtual network embedding via Monte Carlo tree search. *IEEE transactions on cybernetics*, 48(2):510–521, 2017.

Hossein Hamooni, Biplob Debnath, Jianwu Xu, Hui Zhang, Guofei Jiang, and Abdullah Mueen. LogMine: Fast pattern recognition for log analytics. In Snehasis Mukhopadhyay, ChengXiang Zhai, Elisa Bertino, Fabio Crestani, Javed Mostafa,

Jie Tang, Luo Si, Xiaofang Zhou, Yi Chang, Yunyao Li, and Parikshit Sondhi, editors, *Proceedings of the 25th ACM International Conference on Information and Knowledge Management, CIKM 2016*, Indianapolis, IN, USA, October 24–28, 2016, pages 1573–1582. ACM, 2016. doi: 10.1145/2983323.2983358.

Shilin He, Qingwei Lin, Jian-Guang Lou, Hongyu Zhang, Michael R. Lyu, and Dongmei Zhang. Identifying impactful service system problems via log analysis. In Gary T. Leavens, Alessandro Garcia, and Corina S. Pasareanu, editors, *Proceedings of the 2018 ACM Joint Meeting on European Software Engineering Conference and Symposium on the Foundations of Software Engineering, ESEC/SIGSOFT FSE 2018*, Lake Buena Vista, FL, USA, November 04–09, 2018, pages 60–70. ACM, 2018. doi: 10.1145/3236024.3236083.

Ying He, Yuhang Wang, Chao Qiu, Qiuzhen Lin, Jianqiang Li, and Zhong Ming. Blockchain-based edge computing resource allocation in IoT: A deep reinforcement learning approach. *IEEE Internet of Things Journal*, 8:2226–2237 2020.

Chengqiang Huang, Geyong Min, Yulei Wu, Yiming Ying, Ke Pei, and Zuochang Xiang. Time series anomaly detection for trustworthy services in cloud computing systems. *IEEE Transactions on Big Data*, 8(1) 60–72, 2022. doi: 10.1109/TBDATA .2017.2711039.

Chengqiang Huang, Yulei Wu, Yuan Zuo, Ke Pei, and Geyong Min. Towards experienced anomaly detector through reinforcement learning. *Proceedings of the AAAI Conference on Artificial Intelligence*, 32(1), 2018. URL https://ojs.aaai.org/ index.php/AAAI/article/view/12130.

Nikita Jalodia, Shagufta Henna, and Alan Davy. Deep reinforcement learning for topology-aware VNF resource prediction in NFV environments. In *2019 IEEE Conference on Network Function Virtualization and Software Defined Networks (NFV-SDN)*, pages 1–5. IEEE, 2019.

Heng Li, Weiyi Shang, and Ahmed E. Hassan. Which log level should developers choose for a new logging statement? (journal-first abstract). In Rocco Oliveto, Massimiliano Di Penta, and David C. Shepherd, editors, *25th International Conference on Software Analysis, Evolution and Reengineering, SANER 2018*, Campobasso, Italy, March 20–23, 2018, page 468. IEEE Computer Society, 2018a. doi: 10.1109/SANER.2018.8330234.

Zhuo Li, Xu Zhou, Junruo Gao, and Yifang Qin. SDN controller load balancing based on reinforcement learning. In *2018 IEEE 9th International Conference on Software Engineering and Service Science (ICSESS)*, pages 1120–1126. IEEE, 2018b.

Y. Liang, Y. Zhang, X. Hui, and R. Sahoo. Failure prediction in IBM BlueGene/L event logs. In *ICDM*, 2007.

Qingwei Lin, Hongyu Zhang, Jian-Guang Lou, Yu Zhang, and Xuewei Chen. Log clustering based problem identification for online service systems. In Laura K. Dillon, Willem Visser, and Laurie A. Williams, editors, *Proceedings of the 38th International Conference on Software Engineering, ICSE 2016*, Austin, TX, USA,

May 14–22, 2016 - Companion Volume, pages 102–111. ACM, 2016. doi: 10.1145/2889160.2889232.

Dapeng Liu, Youjian Zhao, Haowen Xu, Yongqian Sun, Dan Pei, Jiao Luo, Xiaowei Jing, and Mei Feng. Opprentice: Towards practical and automatic anomaly detection through machine learning. In Kenjiro Cho, Kensuke Fukuda, Vivek S. Pai, and Neil Spring, editors, *Proceedings of the 2015 ACM Internet Measurement Conference, IMC 2015*, Tokyo, Japan, October 28–30, 2015, pages 211–224. ACM, 2015. doi: 10.1145/2815675.2815679.

Xun Liu, Junling You, Yulei Wu, Tong Li, Liangxiong Li, Zheyuan Zhang, and Jingguo Ge. Attention-based bidirectional GRU networks for efficient https traffic classification. *Information Sciences*, 541:297–315, 2020. ISSN 0020-0255. doi: 10.1016/j.ins.2020.05.035. URL https://www.sciencedirect.com/science/article/pii/S002002552030445X.

J. B. Macqueen. Some methods for classification and analysis of multivariate observations. 1966.

Pooria Madani and Natalija Vlajic. Robustness of deep autoencoder in intrusion detection under adversarial contamination. In *Proceedings of the 5th Annual Symposium and Bootcamp on Hot Topics in the Science of Security*, HoTSoS '18, New York, NY, USA, 2018. Association for Computing Machinery. ISBN 9781450364553. doi: 10.1145/3190619.3190637.

Weibin Meng, Ying Liu, Shenglin Zhang, Dan Pei, Hui Dong, Lei Song, and Xulong Luo. Device-agnostic log anomaly classification with partial labels. In *2018 IEEE/ACM 26th International Symposium on Quality of Service (IWQoS)*, pages 1–6, Banff, AB, Canada, 2018. IEEE. doi: 10.1109/IWQoS.2018.8624141.

C. Mu, X. Tian, X. H. Huang, and Y. Ma. FlowAntEater: network traffic automatic signature generator. *Journal of China Universities of Posts & Telecommunications*, 20(Suppl. 1):69–74, 2013.

Neeraj Namdev, Shikha Agrawal, and Sanjay Silakari. Recent advancement in machine learning based internet traffic classification. In Liya Ding, Charles Pang, Mun-Kew Leong, Lakhmi C. Jain, and Robert J. Howlett, editors, *19th International Conference in Knowledge Based and Intelligent Information and Engineering Systems, KES 2015*, Singapore, 7–9 September 2015, volume 60 of *Procedia Computer Science*, pages 784–791. Elsevier, 2015. doi: 10.1016/j.procs.2015.08.238.

Lizhi Peng, Bo Yang, Yuehui Chen, and Zhenxiang Chen. Effectiveness of statistical features for early stage internet traffic identification. *International Journal of Parallel Programming*, 44(1):181–197, 2016. doi: 10.1007/s10766-014-0337-2.

J. Ross Quinlan. Induction of decision trees. *Machine Learning*, 1(1):81–106, 1986. doi: 10.1023/A:1022643204877.

J. Ross Quinlan. *C4.5: Programs for Machine Learning*. Morgan Kaufmann, 1993. ISBN 1-55860-238-0.

Shahbaz Rezaei and Xin Liu. How to achieve high classification accuracy with just a few labels: A semisupervised approach using sampled packets. In Petra Perner, editor, *Advances in Data Mining - Applications and Theoretical Aspects, 19th Industrial Conference, ICDM 2019, New York, USA, July 17 - July 21, 2019*, pages 28–42. ibai Publishing, 2019a.

Shahbaz Rezaei and Xin Liu. Deep learning for encrypted traffic classification: An overview. *IEEE Communications Magazine*, 57(5):76–81, 2019b. doi: 10.1109/MCOM.2019.1800819.

Justus Rischke, Peter Sossalla, Hani Salah, Frank H. P. Fitzek, and Martin Reisslein. QR-SDN: Towards reinforcement learning states, actions, and rewards for direct flow routing in software-defined networks. *IEEE Access*, 8:174773–174791, 2020.

S. Shaikh, A. P. Khan, and V. S. Mahajan. Implementation of dbscan algorithm for internet traffic classification, 2013.

Keiichi Shima. Length matters: Clustering system log messages using length of words. *CoRR*, abs/1611.03213, 2016. URL http://arxiv.org/abs/1611.03213.

O. Soualah, I. Fajjari, N. Aitsaadi, and A. Mellouk. A batch approach for survivable virtual network embedding based on Monte–Carlo tree search. *IEEE*, 36–43 2015.

Murat Soysal and Ece Guran Schmidt. Machine learning algorithms for accurate flow-based network traffic classification: Evaluation and comparison. *Performance Evaluation*, 67(6):451–467, 2010. doi: 10.1016/j.peva.2010.01.001.

Peijie Sun, E Yuepeng, Tong Li, Yulei Wu, Jingguo Ge, Junling You, and Bingzhen Wu. Context-aware learning for anomaly detection with imbalanced log data. In *2020 IEEE 22nd International Conference on High Performance Computing and Communications; IEEE 18th International Conference on Smart City; IEEE 6th International Conference on Data Science and Systems (HPCC/SmartCity/DSS)*, pages 449–456, 2020. doi: 10.1109/HPCC-SmartCity-DSS50907.2020.00055.

Penghao Sun, Zehua Guo, Julong Lan, Junfei Li, Yuxiang Hu, and Thar Baker. ScaleDRL: A scalable deep reinforcement learning approach for traffic engineering in SDN with pinning control. *Computer Networks*, 190:107891, 2021.

Yulei Wu. Cloud-edge orchestration for the internet-of-things: Architecture and AI-powered data processing. *IEEE Internet of Things Journal*, 8(16):12792–12805, 2021. doi: 10.1109/JIOT.2020.3014845.

Yulei Wu, Hong-Ning Dai, and Haina Tang. Graph neural networks for anomaly detection in industrial internet of things. *IEEE Internet of Things Journal*, 9(12):9214–9231, 2022. doi: 10.1109/JIOT.2021.3094295.

Yulei Wu, Zehua Wang, Yuxiang Ma, and Victor C.M. Leung. Deep reinforcement learning for blockchain in industrial IoT: A survey. *Computer Networks*, 191:108004, 2021. ISSN 1389-1286. doi: 10.1016/j.comnet.2021.108004. URL https://www.sciencedirect.com/science/article/pii/S1389128621001213.

Yikai Xiao, Qixia Zhang, Fangming Liu, Jia Wang, and Zhao. NFVdeep: Adaptive online service function chain deployment with deep reinforcement learning.

In *Proceedings of the International Symposium on Quality of Service*, pages 1–10, 2019.

Wei Xu, Ling Huang, Armando Fox, David A. Patterson, and Michael I. Jordan. Detecting large-scale system problems by mining console logs. In Jeanna Neefe Matthews and Thomas E. Anderson, editors, *Proceedings of the 22nd ACM Symposium on Operating Systems Principles 2009, SOSP 2009*, Big Sky, Montana, USA, October 11–14, 2009, pages 117–132. ACM, 2009. doi: 10.1145/1629575 .1629587.

Z. Yan, J. Ge, Y. Wu, L. Li, and T. Li. Automatic virtual network embedding: A deep reinforcement learning approach with graph convolutional networks. *IEEE Journal on Selected Areas in Communications*, 38(99):1040–1057, 2020.

Le Yang, Meng Li, Pengbo Si, Ruizhe Yang, Enchang Sun, and Yanhua Zhang. Energy-efficient resource allocation for blockchain-enabled industrial internet of things with deep reinforcement learning. *IEEE Internet of Things Journal*, 8:2318–2329 2020.

Haipeng Yao, Bo Zhang, Peiying Zhang, Sheng Wu, Chunxiao Jiang, and Song Guo. RDAM: A reinforcement learning based dynamic attribute matrix representation for virtual network embedding. *IEEE Transactions on Emerging Topics in Computing*, 9:901–914 2018.

Xu Zhang, Yong Xu, Qingwei Lin, Bo Qiao, Hongyu Zhang, Yingnong Dang, Chunyu Xie, Xinsheng Yang, Qian Cheng, Ze Li, Junjie Chen, Xiaoting He, Randolph Yao, Jian-Guang Lou, Murali Chintalapati, Furao Shen, and Dongmei Zhang. Robust log-based anomaly detection on unstable log data. In Marlon Dumas, Dietmar Pfahl, Sven Apel, and Alessandra Russo, editors, *Proceedings of the ACM Joint Meeting on European Software Engineering Conference and Symposium on the Foundations of Software Engineering, ESEC/SIGSOFT FSE 2019*, Tallinn, Estonia, August 26–30, 2019, pages 807–817. ACM, 2019. doi: 10.1145/3338906.3338931.

Junjie Zhang, Minghao Ye, Zehua Guo, Chen-Yu Yen, and H. Jonathan Chao. CFR-RL: Traffic engineering with reinforcement learning in SDN. *IEEE Journal on Selected Areas in Communications*, 38(10):2249–2259, 2020.

G. Zheng, C. Wang, W. Shao, Y. Yuan, and S. Mumtaz. A single-player Monte Carlo tree search method combined with node importance for virtual network embedding. *Annals of Telecommunications - Annales des Télécommunications*, 76(8), 297–312 2020.

Yuan Zuo, Yulei Wu, Geyong Min, Chengqiang Huang, and Ke Pei. An intelligent anomaly detection scheme for micro-services architectures with temporal and spatial data analysis. *IEEE Transactions on Cognitive Communications and Networking*, 6(2):548–561, 2020. doi: 10.1109/TCCN.2020.2966615.

3

Learning Network Intents for Autonomous Network Management*

3.1 Introduction

Nowadays, the network carries a large number of applications related to important fields, such as government services, online payment, live broadcast, virtual reality, augmented reality. Due to the extremely demanding performance, network and service providers propose intents to the network, hoping that the network can meet their requirements by deploying network policies (Ujcich et al., 2020, Szyrkowiec et al., 2018). From the perspective of the network, it prioritizes the intent of applications according to different service levels and does its best to realize the intent of low-service-level applications. From the perspective of applications, it hopes that its network intent can be timely and accurately realized. In order to reconcile the contradiction between the network and the application, the Internet Service Provider and the Cloud Service Vendor raise equipment investment, hire more service maintenance operators, or design complex scheduling algorithms. However, this leads to more complex network architectures and unpredictable behaviors of network applications.

Network applications can be a simple path selection task (Hassani et al., 2020) or a complex computational offloading task (Xia et al., 2014). The network environment may be a static local area network or a dynamic edge computing network. When a simple network task runs on a static network environment, the behavior of tasks fits the intentions and can be predictable in general. When a complex network task is running in a dynamic and time-varying network environment, the behavior of the network task is often unpredictable, so that we need to do extra work to determine whether the behavior of the network task is consistent with the operator's intention. For example, when a mobile device offloads tasks to the edge network, it is expected that these tasks can achieve the lowest latency and the highest completion rate. However, the network environment often changes

---

* This chapter is written based on our previous publication (Lin et al., 2021).

AI and Machine Learning for Network and Security Management, First Edition.
Yulei Wu, Jingguo Ge, and Tong Li.

due to the movement of the device so that the network cannot continue providing enough resources. Inevitably, it has to sacrifice the completion rate of the task to ensure the low latency of the task. This results in the status of the task being inconsistent with the intention of the operator. The contradiction becomes more prominent when the task is more complex and the network environment changes over time, e.g. in the 5G network (Saha et al., 2016).

In order to deal with a series of new challenges, for example, the applications' intent may not be accurately realized and the behavior of the network task is unpredictable, and it is necessary to propose an automated solution that can automatically infer the intentions of network behavior. It is convenient for judging whether the intention is consistent with that of the operator's. The behavioral intents of network applications are abstract, which are independent of the specific network environment, such as finding a shortest path. It is transferable across different network environments.

The first step of the automated solution is to infer the intent of the network behavior from the network measurement data. For example, for the task offloading of the Internet of Vehicles (Sonmez et al., 2021), there are multiple offloading strategies to achieve different optimization goals for different types of applications. It is not easy to infer its intentions. Even a simple network application, such as finding a connected and loop-free path between two points, it implies two intentions. One is connectivity, and the other is acyclic. It is very common that a network behavior includes multiple intentions. In order to fully reveal the intentions of a network behavior, the representation method of the intentions should be a structured model composed of multiple atomic intentions.

The issue can be greatly inspired by symbolism. The meaningful symbol refers to an abstract concept with a certain practical significance. Some of the concepts can be regarded as intentions and are widely used in different tasks and environments to form new concepts. For example, for the concept of "connectivity" and "shortest," they can be combined into the concept of "finding the shortest path." If we can learn the basic symbols that express intents from measurement data, through the combination of these symbols, we can get a structured expression that represents the intentions of a meaningful network behavior.

It is important to figure out what a symbol is and how it can express a concept. British scholars Charles Kay Ogden and Ivor Armstrong Richards proposed the semantic triangle in the important semantics work "The Meaning of Meaning" published in 1923 (Odgen and Richards, 1923). This theory refers to the mutual restriction and interaction between symbols, concepts, and objective things. As shown in Figure 3.1, the semantic triangle contains the following meanings: (i) There is a solid line connection between concept/reference and thing/referent. Concepts are generalized on the basis of objective things, which mean a concept refers to a thing. (ii) There is also a solid line connection between

Figure 3.1 The semantic triangle.

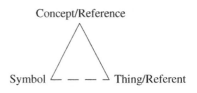

Figure 3.2 The triangle theory of intention symbol semantics.

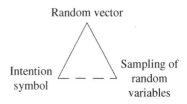

concept/reference and symbols. Concepts are expressed through symbols, which mean a symbol symbolizes a concept. (iii) There is a dashed connection between a symbol and a thing/referent. A symbol stands for a thing/referent, and there is no inherent necessary connection between the two. For example, we can use the symbol L or other symbols to represent the link. The concept of link and its role will emerge in the mind of the network and service operators, which is a concept/reference in the semantic triangle. The thing/referent in the semantic triangle is a link of the specific network in reality.

With the help of the semantic triangle theory, we propose a triangle theory of intention symbol semantics. As shown in Figure 3.2, the intention symbol is to indicate a random vector. Every element of a random vector is a random variable, which represents a certain concept such as bandwidth. Sampling from the probability distribution of each random variable, we can get the concrete examples of abstract bandwidth concepts represented by random vectors, such as a bandwidth threshold.

As shown in the left part of Figure 3.3, the symbol A is used to indicate the concept of connectivity, which is described by a random vector containing three

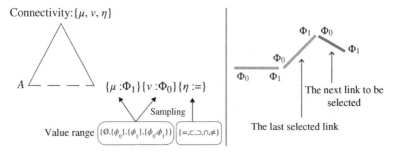

Figure 3.3 Examples of intention symbol semantics.

random variables: μ, υ, and η. The first variable represents the last selected link, the second variable denotes the next link to be selected, and the third variable means the relationship between the two variables μ and υ. As shown in the right part of Figure 3.3, Φ_0 and Φ_1 represent two nodes of a link. Intuitively, we know that in order to ensure that the next link to be selected is connected to the current path, Φ_1 of the last selected link and Φ_0 of the next link must be equal, which means that they are connected to the same switch. Therefore, on the left side of Figure 3.3, the three random variables of the concept connectivity are most likely to be sampled to "Φ_1," "Φ_0," and "=," respectively, according to their probability distributions. The above is about using the triangle theory of intention symbol semantics to describe a concept of connectivity intention from the perspective of random vectors.

The intention symbol semantics theory defines the relationship between symbols, concepts, and instantiated things. In the rest of this chapter, we will focus on inferring intention symbols from the perspective of statistical learning, and what kind of structures these symbols form to completely describe the intent of a network behavior. Finally, we will introduce how the symbolic structure is transferable.

3.2 Motivation

On the way to realize automated network management, it is inefficient and infeasible to artificially equip a tool with various intentions for network management. Artificial intentions are either very abstract and do not have the ability to be directly executed, or require users to have comprehensive network knowledge to express a correct intention. This chapter uses the behavioral data of network applications to explore a way to mine intentions from data and uses symbols to express intentions. It is a direction worth exploring. These symbols can form a structure to express the complete intent. They can replace artificial management intentions. The intention symbol semantics theory guides the inference of network intentions. The inference of the network intention is transformed into the problem of fitting the probability distribution represented by the symbol. It is motivated to solve two important problems: one is the inference of network intent. It can not only allow network operators to judge whether the current network behavior meets the requirements but also learn the basic knowledge of the network, which provides a basis for automatically expressing network intents. The second is to solve the computational problem of using symbols to express intents. It expresses intents as probability distributions.

3.3   The Hierarchical Representation and Learning Framework for Intention Symbols Inference

This section will take the path selection task as an example to explain how to use the framework we designed to infer the intention of the network application through data and express it as a symbolic structure. The proposed framework is devised with two components: symbolic semantic learning (SSL) and symbolic structure inferring (SSI). The SSL is about learning symbols that represent intent. The SSI is about inferring the structural form of the intention symbol, so as to fully express the intention of a network behavior. The SSL and the SSI will be introduced in detail below.

3.3.1   Symbolic Semantic Learning (SSL)

The premise of inferring intention symbols is to judge the possibility of symbol existence according to prior knowledge, that is, the place where intention will appear. Taking path selection as an example, according to the prior knowledge of network management, we can intuitively judge that the task will have intention in three places. We use symbols *A*, *B*, and *C* as marks, respectively. The path must satisfy the intention of connectivity, so as shown in Figure 3.4, the connectivity intention represented by symbol *A* will appear in the dark gray box. It means that only when two links are connected to the same switch can they satisfy the connectivity. In addition, the path also needs to satisfy the deadlock free intention,

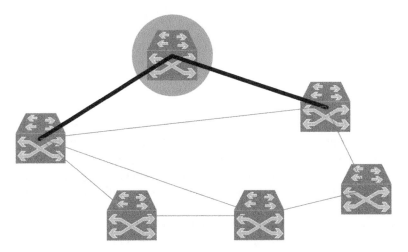

Figure 3.4   Connectivity intention symbol.

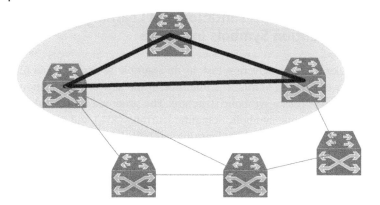

Figure 3.5 Deadlock free intention symbol.

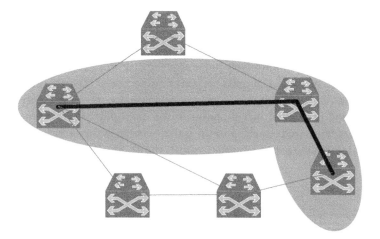

Figure 3.6 Whole path intention symbol.

so as shown in Figure 3.5, the symbol *B* representing the deadlock free intention appears in the dark gray box. It means a path needs to avoid loops. Finally, there is an intention about the performance. For example, the path is required to be the shortest or guaranteed by deterministic delay. As shown in Figure 3.6, the symbol *C* representing the performance intention on the path appears in the gray part.

The above is the first step of symbols inference, which uses prior knowledge to judge the possible intention of a network task. This is a kind of preliminary judgment of possible intention symbols by means of operators' prior knowledge. It can also be determined by artificial intelligence (AI), which is an open question.

3.3.1.1 Connectivity Intention

The triangle theory of intention symbol semantics mentioned in Section 3.1 puts forward the view that each intention symbol needs to be given a random vector to express its meaning. Each element of a random vector is a random variable. The symbol A expressing connectivity occurs between two links, so it was endowed with a random vector of length three. The first and the second random variables represent two links, respectively, and the third random variable expresses the relationship between the two links. We mark them as μ_a, υ_a, η_a, respectively.

In most cases, intent is a description of the state of one or more attributes. For example, the shortest path is the description of the path length attribute; deterministic delay guarantee is the description of delay; deadlock free path is the description of the nodes that the path passes through. Therefore, it is a natural and sensible idea that the sampling range of random variables with intention symbols is the attribute. The network attributes involved in path selection include node index. A link is described by node indexes at both ends, marked as ϕ_0 and ϕ_1, respectively. The power set of these two signs can be regarded as the sampling range of random variables μ_a and υ_a. In other words, the possible values of μ_a and υ_a are the set of signs as the set elements: (ϕ_0), (ϕ_1), (ϕ_0, ϕ_1) and $\emptyset$. In addition, η_a describes the relationship between μ_a and υ_a, that is, the relationship between two sets. In most instances, there are equality, inequality, true inclusion, inclusion, intersection, and nonintersection. These five relationships are used as the sampling range of random variables η_a.

After completing the design of symbol A in the three aspects of symbol, random vector, and network attribute as the sampling range, as discussed in the triangle theory of intention symbol semantics, the next step is to obtain the instantiation of intention by means of statistical learning. That is, the sampling of the intent random vector.

Assume that the random vector $A = (\mu_a, \upsilon_a, \eta_a)$ follows a probability model as follows:

$$A \sim P(A) \tag{3.1}$$

Its elements are not independent of each other. μ_a and υ_a depend on η_a. By observing η_a to take a certain relationship, we determine which combination modes of μ_a and υ_a have significant probabilities. The model can be further expressed as follows:

$$P(A) = P\left(\mu_a, \upsilon_a, \eta_a\right) = P\left(\mu_a, \upsilon_a \mid \eta_a\right) P\left(\eta_a\right) \tag{3.2}$$

$$\begin{aligned} \mu_a, \upsilon_a &\sim P\left(\mu_a, \upsilon_a \mid \eta_a\right) \\ \eta_a &\sim P\left(\eta_a\right) \end{aligned} \tag{3.3}$$

where $P\left(\mu_a, \upsilon_a \mid \eta_a\right)$ and $P\left(\eta_a\right)$ can be any probability distribution model. In the following, $P\left(\eta_a\right)$ is assumed to be uniformly distributed, and $P\left(\mu_a, \upsilon_a \mid \eta_a\right)$ is discussed simply as multinomial distributions. The formula is as follows:

$$P\left(\mu_a, \upsilon_a \mid \eta_a\right) = Multinomial(\mu_a, \upsilon_a; \theta_{\mu_a})$$
$$P\left(\eta_a\right) = Uniform(\eta_a; \theta_{\eta_a}) \tag{3.4}$$

where θ_{μ_a} and θ_{η_a} are the parameter vectors of the probability model. The purpose of statistical learning is to use the measurement data to fit these parameters.

3.3.1.2 Deadlock Free Intention

Similar to the previous connectivity intention, the design of deadlock free intention symbol B also includes a random vector, the value range of the random vector, and the probability distribution of the random vector. As shown in Figure 3.5, the deadlock free intent involves multiple nodes. When selecting a path, deadlock can be avoided as long as the current link does not intersect with the previously selected paths. Therefore, the length of random vector of symbol B is four. The first and the second random variables describe the previously selected paths and the link to be selected, respectively. The third random variable denotes the relationship between the first and the second random variables. The fourth random variable means the number of occurrences of the relationship. These four random variables are recorded as μ_b, υ_b, η_b, and γ_b, respectively. Assume that the random vector $B = (\mu_b, \upsilon_b, \eta_b, \gamma_b)$ follows a probability model as follows:

$$B \sim P\left(B\right) \tag{3.5}$$

Like the previous symbol A, its elements are not independent of each other. μ_b and υ_b depend on η_b and γ_b. By observing η_b to take a certain relationship and γ_b to take the number of occurrences, we need to determine which combination modes of μ_b and υ_b have significant probabilities. The model can be further expressed as follows:

$$P\left(B\right) = P\left(\mu_b, \upsilon_b, \eta_b, \gamma_b\right) = P\left(\mu_b, \upsilon_b \mid \eta_b, \gamma_b\right) P\left(\eta_b\right) P\left(\gamma_b\right) \tag{3.6}$$
$$\mu_b, \upsilon_b \sim P\left(\mu_b, \upsilon_b \mid \eta_a, \gamma_b\right)$$
$$\eta_b \sim P\left(\eta_b\right) \tag{3.7}$$
$$\gamma_b \sim P\left(\gamma_b\right)$$

where $P\left(\mu_b, \upsilon_b \mid \eta_a, \gamma_b\right)$, $P\left(\eta_b\right)$ and $P\left(\gamma_b\right)$ can be any probability distribution model. In the following, $P\left(\eta_b\right)$ and $P\left(\gamma_b\right)$ are assumed to be uniformly distributed, and $P\left(\mu_b, \upsilon_b \mid \eta_b, \gamma_b\right)$ is discussed simply as multinomial distributions. The formula is as follows:

$$P\left(\mu_b, \upsilon_b \mid \eta_b, \gamma_b\right) = Multinomial(\mu_b, \upsilon_b; \theta_{\mu_b})$$
$$P\left(\eta_b\right) = Uniform(\eta_b; \theta_{\eta_b}) \tag{3.8}$$
$$P\left(\gamma_b\right) = Uniform(\gamma_b; \theta_{\gamma_b})$$

θ_{μ_b}, θ_{η_b} and θ_{γ_b} are the parameter vectors of the probability model.

3.3.1.3 Performance Intention

Performance intent is to describe the performance of a path in some aspect. The length of random vector of symbol C is two. One describes the performance object, such as path length, path bandwidth, and the other shows the performance, such as the longest, shortest, maximum. The two random variables are recorded as μ_c and v_c, respectively. Assume that the random vector $C = (\mu_c, v_c)$ follows a probability model as follows:

$$C \sim P(C) \tag{3.9}$$

It can be further expressed as follows:

$$P(C) = P(\mu_c, v_c) \tag{3.10}$$

$$\mu_c, v_c \sim P(\mu_c, v_c) \tag{3.11}$$

where $P(\mu_c, v_c)$ can be any probability distribution model. In the following, they are discussed simply as multinomial distributions. The formula is as follows:

$$P(\mu_c, v_c) = Multinomial(\mu_c, v_c; \theta_{\mu_c}) \tag{3.12}$$

where θ_{μ_c} is the parameter vector of the probability model.

3.3.1.4 Discussion

In the previous part, we give three examples to discuss the design of intention symbols which express the requirements of network and service operators for some aspects of the network. In order to give semantics to symbols, it is necessary to endow random vectors for each symbol to represent some concepts and relationships. The specific semantic of intention is the sampling values or the expectation of random vectors, which are inferred from the data. These symbols obtained during the inference are to translate into the network policies and deployed to the network automatically.

3.3.2 Symbolic Structure Inferring (SSI)

Symbols A, B, and C can be regarded as atomic intentions, expressing the ability of the network in a certain aspect. They need to be combined into a structure to express an accurate application intention. For example, the shortest path contains the intention of connectivity, the intention of shortest length, and the intention of deadlock free. Only the combination of these three intentions can express the intention that the application hopes the network to provide the shortest path. However, it is an important challenge to develop a mechanism to ensure that flow entries can satisfy all intents at the same time. As shown in Figure 3.7, when looking for the path from node 1 to node 7, the "paths" with the length of two satisfy the intention of shortest, as shown in the bold links,

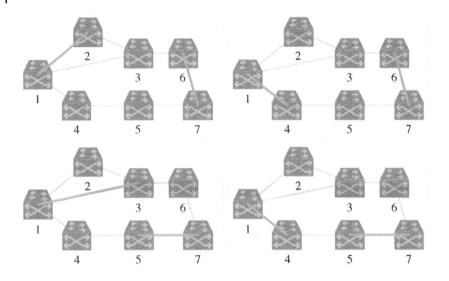

Figure 3.7 "Paths" satisfying the shortest intention.

but these "paths" do not meet the intention of connectivity. This means that the flow entry corresponding to the intention of shortest does not satisfy the intent of connectivity. The correct approach should be to find the flow table entries between node 1 and node 7 that meet the intent of connectivity, as shown in Figure 3.8, and then find the flow table entries corresponding to the shortest path

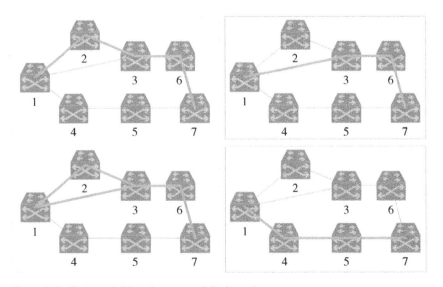

Figure 3.8 Paths satisfying the connectivity intention.

Figure 3.9 Three priority
modes of intention symbols.

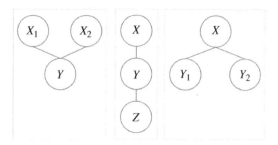

among them. As shown in the dark gray box in the figure. A reasonable shortest path that meets the user's intention is obtained.

These two cases show that there is a priority between atomic intentions, rather than a simple parallel relationship. The symbolic structure is based on priority between intents. Determining the priority between intention symbols is an important step. This step is called SSI.

The purpose of SSI is to determine the precedence between intention symbols. First, the path sets satisfying the high-priority intention are obtained, and then the paths satisfying the lower-priority intention are further filtered on the set. The precedence between intention symbols has three modes, as shown in Figure 3.9. The X, Y and Z represent three priorities from high to low, respectively. The same layer indicates that they have the same priority. Only the paths that meet the high-priority intention can further judge whether these paths meet the next level intention.

3.4 Experiments

Two specific experiments are carried out to verify the feasibility of the framework discussed above. They are SSL and SSI. Then, we migrate the learned symbolic structure to four new networks with different network topologies, and let it find the shortest paths and the load-balancing paths between all pairs of nodes. This is to verify the symbolic structure's ability of transferring knowledge across different networks.

3.4.1 Datasets

The experiment is divided into the training phase and the testing phase. In the training phase, we implement the classic shortest path routing algorithm in the network with a given topology to collect the target path between any pair of nodes[1]

---

[1] For the sake of clarity of illustration, we choose classic algorithms as examples for evaluation. It is worth noting that the proposed model framework can be applicable to learn knowledge of any network protocols and algorithms.

denoted as D_{target}. At the same time, we implement a common path finding algorithm (Garcia-Luna-Aceves and Li, 2005) in the network with the same topology to obtain all simple paths between any pair of nodes, denoted by D_{sp}. That is, D_{sp} contains D_{target}, i.e. $D_{target} \subset D_{sp}$. In addition, in order to introduce noisy data to assess the robustness of the proposed framework, we implement a random path selection algorithm and obtain the noisy "path" data, denoted by D_{noise}. The paths in D_{noise} have loops and even false paths composed of disconnected links. In brief, the training process is as follows. First, the agent receives the data of D_{target}, D_{sp} and D_{noise}. Second, it analyzes the characteristics of D_{target} in the background data $D_{sp} \cup D_{noise}$ and infers the intention symbol semantic. Third, it learns the symbolic structure. This symbolic structure is the generation model that can generate D_{target} from $D_{sp} \cup D_{noise}$. In the testing phase, we migrate the symbolic structure to another four new network environments to evaluate the framework's ability of transferring the learned symbolic structure across different networks.

3.4.2 Experiments on Symbolic Semantic Learning

In order to evaluate the effectiveness of the proposed triangle theory of intention symbol semantics for autonomously achieving the intentions for path selection tasks, we conduct extensive experiments to verify the learning performance on intention symbols. The previous section mentioned three different intentions, namely the symbol A for connectivity, the symbol B for deadlock-free, and the symbol C for path performance.

Regarding the experiment of symbol A, the $A = (\mu_a, \upsilon_a, \eta_a)$ follows the probability distribution as follows:

$$A \sim P(A) \tag{3.13}$$

$$P(A) = P(\mu_a, \upsilon_a, \eta_a) = P(\mu_a, \upsilon_a \mid \eta_a) P(\eta_a) \tag{3.14}$$

In the experiment, we set η_a to follow a uniform distribution, so the distribution of $P(A)$ mainly depends on $P(\mu_a, \upsilon_a \mid \eta_a)$. As shown in Figure 3.10, it is the probability distribution $P(\mu_a, \upsilon_a \mid \eta_a)$ under the condition that η_a takes the equal relationship after the training phase. It can be seen from the figure that when the value of μ_a is (ϕ_1) and the value of υ_a is (ϕ_0), the probability is significantly greater than those in other cases. In other words, $\mu_a : (\phi_1) = \upsilon_a : (\phi_0)$ is a significant pattern in the path selection process. Its interpretation is that if two links are connected, the end node of one link must be equal to the end node of the other link. This mode is the semantic expression form of the intention of the symbol A.

The intention symbol B obeys the following probability distribution:

$$B \sim P(B) \tag{3.15}$$

$$P(B) = P(\mu_b, \upsilon_b, \eta_b, \gamma_b) = P(\mu_b, \upsilon_b \mid \eta_b, \gamma_b) P(\eta_b) P(\gamma_b) \tag{3.16}$$

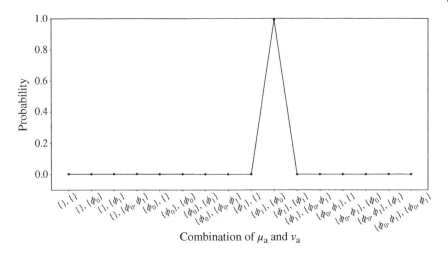

Figure 3.10 The probability distribution $P\left(\mu_a, v_a \mid \eta_a\right)$ under the condition that η_a takes the equal relationship.

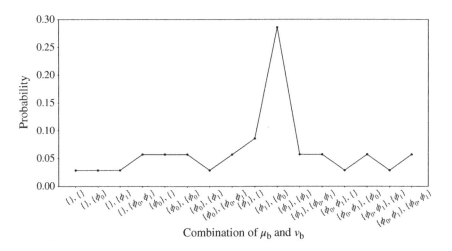

Figure 3.11 The probability distribution $P\left(\mu_b, v_b \mid \eta_b, \gamma_b\right)$ under the condition that η_b takes the equal relationship and γ_b equals 1.

We set η_b and γ_b to follow a uniform distribution, so we only look at the probability distribution $P\left(\mu_b, v_b \mid \eta_b, \gamma_b\right)$. As shown in Figure 3.11, it is the probability distribution $P\left(\mu_b, v_b \mid \eta_b, \gamma_b\right)$ under the condition that η_b takes the equal relationship, and γ_b equals 1 after the training phase. It can be seen

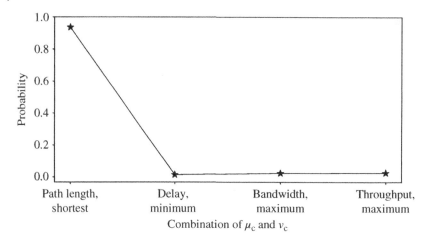

Figure 3.12 The probability distribution $P\left(\mu_c, v_c\right)$.

from the figure that when the value of μ_b is $\left(\phi_1\right)$ and the value of v_b is $\left(\phi_0\right)$, the probability is significantly greater than those in other cases. $\mu_b: \left(\phi_1\right) = v_b: \left(\phi_0\right), \gamma_b = 1$ is a significant pattern in the path selection process. Its interpretation is that if the path is deadlock free, the current link to be selected will only be connected to one end of the path, and not to the other parts of the path. This mode is the semantic expression form of the intention of the symbol B.

The intention symbol C follows the probability distribution below:

$$C \sim P\left(C\right) \tag{3.17}$$

$$P\left(C\right) = P\left(\mu_c, v_c\right) \tag{3.18}$$

As shown in Figure 3.12, it is the probability distribution $P\left(\mu_c, v_c\right)$ after the training phase. It can be seen from the figure that the value of shortest path is significantly greater than those in other cases. μ_c: path length, v_c: shortest is a significant pattern in the path selection process. Its interpretation is to choose the shortest path between two nodes. This mode is the semantic expression form of the intention of the symbol C.

3.4.3 Experiments on Symbolic Structure Inferring

Although the intention semantics of the three symbols have been calculated through statistical learning, the precedence among them has not been calculated yet. This part of the experiment mainly calculates the priority relationship among the three intent symbols and constructs the symbol structure based on the priority

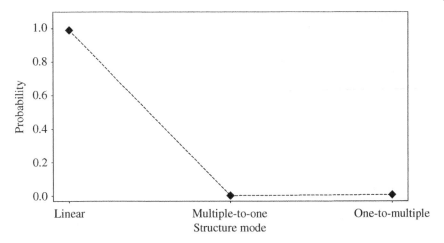

Figure 3.13 The probability distribution of three structure modes.

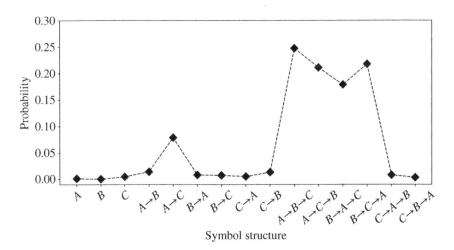

Figure 3.14 The probability distribution of symbol structures.

relationship. As shown in Figure 3.13, the linear structure mode has the highest probability. This means that the three intention symbols A, B, C will follow a linear arrangement as shown on the leftmost side of Figure 3.9. However, which of the three is the highest priority and which is the lowest priority have not been evaluated. The priority information is shown in Figure 3.14. The structure of the form $[1, 2, 3]$ has the highest probability. It means that the highest priority of the three intent symbols is A, followed by B, and the lowest priority is C.

3.4.4 Experiments on Symbolic Structure Transferring

The previous experiments obtained the structure of the three intention symbols involved in the path selection task. In order to verify the accuracy of the symbols structure, they need to be transferred to different network topologies to test whether they can correctly complete the path selection task. The experimental results of this part are shown in Figures 3.15–3.18. The abscissa of each graph is A, $A \rightarrow B$, $A \rightarrow B \rightarrow C$. They respectively represent the experimental results when the path selection task only satisfies the intention A, the intentions A and B, and the intentions of A, then B, and finally C. The ordinate of each graph is the value of P and R, which are light gray and dark gray columns, respectively. They are indicators to measure the correctness of the symbol structure. As mentioned

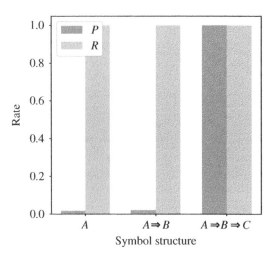

Figure 3.15 IBM network topology.

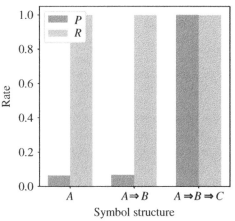

Figure 3.16 CWIX network topology.

Figure 3.17 BT Europe network topology.

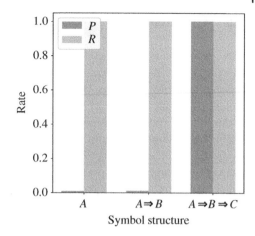

Figure 3.18 Darkstrand network topology.

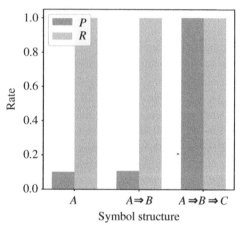

earlier, the symbolic structure is the generation model that can generate D_{target} from $D_{sp} \cup D_{noise}$. If according to the symbolic structure with the precedence order of the three intents inferred above, D_{target} can finally be obtained completely. It proves that this structure is the correct intent structure of the shortest path selection task. The P value indicates what percentage of D_{target} is obtained when the intent corresponding to the abscissa is satisfied. The R value indicates the proportion of the obtained path that also belongs to D_{target} when the intent of the corresponding abscissa is satisfied. Therefore, we can see that in the four experimental results graphs, the P value is gradually equal to 1, and the R value is always 1. It shows that the paths obtained by satisfying the intention are all in D_{target}, and there is no invalid path. Finally, both P and R are equal to 1, indicating that the symbolic structure of the corresponding abscissa has obtained a complete D_{target}.

3.5 Conclusion

This chapter mainly discussed learning the intentions behind network tasks based on symbolism and statistical learning, and inferring the priority relationship between multiple intentions. We regarded intention as a meaningful symbol and proposed a triangle theory of intention symbol semantics. Under the guidance of the triangle theory, the algorithm learned that the semantics of an intention symbol is to sample a random vector. The result of sampling made the intention symbol have a clear meaning. When a network task involves multiple intents, it is also necessary to infer the priority relationship between the intents. The intents symbol structure is constructed based on this priority. Experiments showed that the framework of SSL and SSI is feasible.

References

J. Garcia-Luna-Aceves and Z. Li. Solving the multi-constrained path selection problem by using depth first search. In *2005 2nd International Conference on Quality of Service in Heterogeneous Wired/Wireless Networks*, page 15, Los Alamitos, CA, USA, August 2005. IEEE Computer Society. doi: 10.1109/QSHINE.2005.57. URL https://doi.ieeecomputersociety.org/10.1109/QSHINE.2005.57.

A. E. Hassani, A. Sahel, and A. Badri. A new objective function based on additive combination of node and link metrics as a mechanism path selection for RPL protocol. *International Journal of Communication Networks and Information Security*, 12(1):63, 2020.

Guozhi Lin, Jingguo Ge, Yulei Wu, Hui Li, Tong Li, Wei Mi, and Yuepeng E. Network automation for path selection: A new knowledge transfer approach. In *2021 IFIP Networking Conference (IFIP Networking)*, pages 1–9, 2021. doi: 10.23919/IFIPNetworking52078.2021.9472841.

C. K. Odgen and I. A. Richards. *The Meaning of Meaning A Study of the Influence of Language upon Thought and of the Science of Symbolism*. Routledge & Kegan Paul Ltd., London, 10th edition, 1923.

R. K. Saha, P. Saengudomlert, and C. Aswakul. Evolution toward 5G mobile networks - a survey on enabling technologies. *Engineering Journal*, 20(1):87–119, 2016.

Cagatay Sonmez, Can Tunca, Atay Ozgovde, and Cem Ersoy. Machine learning-based workload orchestrator for vehicular edge computing. *IEEE Transactions on Intelligent Transportation Systems*, 22(4):2239–2251, 2021. doi: 10.1109/TITS.2020.3024233.

Thomas Szyrkowiec, Michele Santuari, Mohit Chamania, Domenico Siracusa, Achim Autenrieth, Victor Lopez, Joo Cho, and Wolfgang Kellerer. Automatic intent-based secure service creation through a multilayer SDN network orchestration. *Journal of Optical Communications and Networking*, 10(4):289–297, 2018. doi: 10.1364/JOCN .10.000289.

Benjamin E. Ujcich, Adam Bates, and William H. Sanders. Provenance for intent-based networking. In *2020 6th IEEE Conference on Network Softwarization (NetSoft)*, pages 195–199, 2020. doi: 10.1109/NetSoft48620.2020.9165519.

Q. Xia, W. Liang, Z. Xu, and B. Zhou. Online algorithms for location-aware task offloading in two-tiered mobile cloud environments. In *IEEE/ACM International Conference on Utility & Cloud Computing*, 2014.

4

Virtual Network Embedding via Hierarchical Reinforcement Learning[1]

4.1 Introduction

As one of the most promising technologies for the future Internet, network virtualization decouples the virtual network services from the underlying substrate network, which offers a great solution to evaluate new protocols and services (Anderson et al., 2005, Cheng et al., 2018). Besides, network virtualization techniques have been widely applied in many research testbeds, such as 4WARD (Feamster et al., 2007) and CABO (Endo et al., 2011). Today, as a key enabling technology for 5G network softwarization (Cheng et al., 2018, 2020), network virtualization has been successfully used in the telecommunication market. It can be exemplified by OpenFlow (McKeown et al., 2008), which is supported by the industry within the Open Networking Foundation (Open Networking Foundation, 2010). In general, the process of embedding virtual networks into a substrate network is called virtual network embedding (VNE) (Cheng et al., 2021, Yan et al., 2020a).

Nowadays, a business model called Infrastructure as a Service (IaaS) (Bhardwaj et al., 2010) has been widely accepted by the market, where the role of Internet Service Providers (ISPs) is decoupled into two parts: the infrastructure provider (InP) and the service provider (SP). In this model, the InP is responsible for deploying and maintaining the network resources, and the SP takes charge of end-to-end services of users. As shown in Figure 4.1, the function of SP can be divided into three lines: (1) Virtual Network (VN) provider that mounts the virtual resources into the InPs, (2) VN operator that manages the VNs according to the requests, (3) User service provider that focuses on business models by abstracting customized services. By embedding virtual resources into the physical network dynamically, the ISPs can reap large gains through effective VNE algorithms, which aim to optimize the dynamic resource allocation and offer various

1 This chapter is written based on our previous publication (Cheng et al., 2021).

AI and Machine Learning for Network and Security Management, First Edition.
Yulei Wu, Jingguo Ge, and Tong Li.

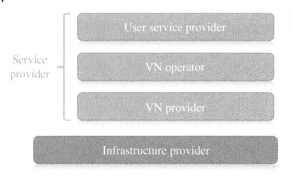

Figure 4.1 IaaS business model.

end-to-end customized services to users. In practice, the measurement criteria of an VNE algorithm cover many different objectives, including quality of service (QoS), economic profit, resource cost, embedding efficiency, and energy efficiency.

In VNE, the primary entity is a virtual network (VN) consisting of a set of network elements (network nodes and network links). Virtual nodes are joined by virtual links according to a virtual topology. By virtualizing both nodes and links, virtual topologies with varying features can be cohosted on the same substrate network hardware through network-embedding algorithms. Besides, due to such an abstraction of virtual networks and substrate networks, network operators can manage networks in a centralized and dynamic way. Generally, the process of VNE consists of two steps, virtual node mapping and virtual link mapping (Chowdhury and Boutaba, 2010). For virtual network mapping, a virtual node is allocated in a physical node, and with regard to virtual link mapping, a virtual network link between two virtual nodes has to be mapped into a sequence of physical network links which can connect the corresponding two physical nodes.

4.2 Motivation

Recall that the VNE problem is known to be NP-hard (Yu et al., 2008) due to the huge search space of the substrate network. Traditional VNE algorithms are divided into two categories: the exact and the heuristic solutions. Using the exact optimization strategies (Wolsey, 1998), the methods aim to find the optimal solution through, e.g. integer linear programming (ILP) and mixed-integer linear programming (MILP) (Chowdhury et al., 2009, Shanbhag et al., 2015). Due to the high complexity, such exact methods take considerable time on calculating feasible solutions, which means that they can only be used to solve small-size instances of VNE problems. Instead of being fixed on getting the optimal embedding solution, the heuristic solutions manage to find a feasible solution with lower execution time (Cormen et al., 2009). However, one of the problems of the heuristic methods is that they are easily stuck in a local optimum that may be far away from the global optimum (Cao et al., 2019). It is obvious that in practice, traditional techniques for solving online problems are impractical because of the unpredictability and the general huge search space of the substrate network.

With the fast development of artificial intelligence (AI), machine learning (ML) and deep learning (DL) have been put into use in the field of VNE (He et al., 2021, Xiao et al., 2019). Due to the high fitting ability and flexible adjustment of network parameters, AI-based algorithms can obtain the global optimal solution and make embedding strategies within an acceptable time (Yao et al., 2018b). In addition, due to the outstanding performance of automatic exploration and quick development, reinforcement learning (RL) (Kaelbling et al., 1996, Sutton and Barto, 2018) has also been taken into account. In RL, an agent starts from scratch and gradually learns the optimal VNE policy, by exploring the external environment, to maximize the accumulated reward. However, there are three major drawbacks of the existing RL-based methods. First, existing approaches (Yao et al., 2018a,b, Xiao et al., 2019) make embedding algorithms focus on the current virtual network request (VNR), which may waste resources on embedding the infeasible VNRs. Second, existing methods treat all VNRs equally and independently, which loses long-time horizons. Third, in the real scenario, the extrinsic reward is usually sparse, which is returned only when a VNR is embedded completely. Existing methods, however, decompose the extrinsic reward in an implicit way and cannot ensure the globally optimal solution (Yao et al., 2018a).

Hierarchical reinforcement learning (HRL) has been proved excellent at speeding up the learning process (Song et al., 2019) and solving the task with long-time horizons in playing games like Go (Silver et al., 2016) and Atari (Mnih et al., 2013). Typically, to get long-time horizons, HRL is implemented as a high-level agent that periodically assigns subgoals to low-level agents that learns from experience at different temporal abstraction levels simultaneously. Besides, by dividing the reward into extrinsic reward and intrinsic reward, HRL works well in the sparse reward problem (Bacon et al., 2017) in comparison with the general reinforcement learning (RL).

In this chapter, based on HRL, a proactive VNE algorithm is proposed, which considers both the long-term impact of a VNR and the short-term effect of an embedding action. We call this proactive algorithm as VNE-HRL. In this algorithm, a high-level agent first selects the currently feasible VNR that has the greatest long-term return from a window-based batch, which ensures long-term benefits. Then, a low-level agent embeds the selected VNR on the substrate network according to a low-level policy, which treats a VNR embedding as a sequence of virtual nodes embedding. Meanwhile, the extrinsic and intrinsic rewards are returned to the high-level agent and the low-level agent, respectively, which encourage the agents to improve the embedding policies in order to achieve better performance in the future instead of maximizing the current revenue. Both high-level and low-level policies are trained with the double deep Q network (DDQN) algorithm (Van Hasselt et al., 2016), which can achieve the stable convergence. With the help of DDQN, agents can gradually optimize the policy from scratch without much manual intervention.

The rest of this chapter is constructed as follows: Section 4.3 introduces the preliminaries of the work, including the definitions and mathematical description of VNE, RL, and HRL. The framework of the model is presented in Section 4.4. Performance evaluation results are shown and analyzed in Section 4.5. Section 4.6 presents related works. Finally, Section 4.7 concludes this chapter.

4.3 Preliminaries and Notations

In this section, we will introduce the following lines: mathematical formulation of the VNE problem (Section 4.3.1), reinforcement learning (Section 4.3.2), and hierarchical reinforcement learning (Section 4.3.3).

4.3.1 Virtual Network Embedding

4.3.1.1 Substrate Network and Virtual Network

VNE is a process of embedding virtual networks to the substrate network according to VNRs. A substrate network (SN) can be defined as a weighted undirected graph $G^S = (N^S, L^S, A_N^S, A_L^S)$, where N^S and L^S denote the sets of substrate nodes and links, respectively, and A_N^S and A_L^S represent the attributes of substrate nodes and links, respectively. In this chapter, for the sake of clarity of illustration, CPU processing capability and the bandwidth of each substrate link are considered as the node attribute and the substrate link attribute, respectively.

Similarly, a virtual network (VN) can be described as a weighted undirected graph $G^V = (N^V, L^V, R_N^V, R_L^V)$, where N^V and L^V are virtual nodes and links, and R_N^V and R_L^V are the requirements of virtual nodes and links, respectively. Therefore, a VNR can be denoted as $VNR = (G^V, t_a, t_d)$, where t_a is the arrival time of a VNR. It is worth noting that when embedding takes place online, the departure time t_d of VNR is uncertain.

4.3.1.2 The VNE Problem

The VNE problem can be defined as a mapping process from G^V to a subgraph G^S:

$$G^V(N^V, L^V) \rightarrow G^S(N^S, L^S) \tag{4.1}$$

The embedding of VNR involves two mapping process: (1) the node mapping procedure, in which the available computing resources of the substrate node should be larger than the requested resources from the mapping virtual node.

Figure 4.2 A typical scene of a VNE problem. The edge weights and node weights of VNR represent the bandwidth and the CPU requests, respectively. Besides, the edge and node weights of the substrate node stand for the bandwidth and CPU resources, respectively.

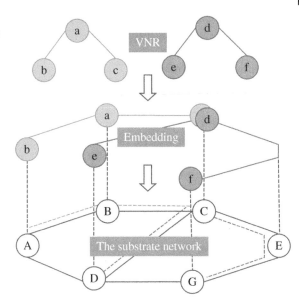

(2) The link mapping procedure, in which a virtual link can be embedded onto several physical links. The available resources of substrate links should be larger than the requirement of the virtual link. Besides, there are two points to note. First, the virtual nodes from different VNRs may be embedded into the same substrate node. Second, a virtual link may consist of several physical links on the substrate network, which may result in the use of more resources than requested.

To clarify, we describe the embedding procedure in Figure 4.2. Node c shares the same substrate node C with the Node d. In addition, the virtual link between d and f, $R^V(d,f)$, crosses over two substrate links, including $L^S(C,E)$ and $L^S(E,G)$.

4.3.1.3 Evaluation Metrics

In the VNE field, three key metrics have been widely used to measure the effectiveness of a VNE algorithm (Thakkar et al., 2020), including acceptance ratio, long-time average revenue, and rev2cost.

- Acceptance Ratio: The VNR acceptance ratio of the substrate network at time T can be defined as

$$Acp = \lim_{T \to \infty} \frac{\sum_{t=0}^{T} Accept(G_t^V)}{\sum_{t=0}^{T} All(G_t^V)} \tag{4.2}$$

where $Accept(G_t^v)$ and $All(G_t^v)$ denote the number of successful VNR embeddings and the number of total arrival VNRs at time t.

- Long-time Average Revenue: From the ISPs' point of view, the more resources are demanded, the more infrastructure resources can be leased, and in turn, the more profit will be made. Therefore, the revenue of a successful VNR embedding can be formulated by

$$Rev(G^v) = w_c \sum_{n^V \in N^V} CPU(n^V) + w_b \sum_{l^V \in L^V} BW(l^V) \tag{4.3}$$

where $CPU(n^V)$ and $BW(l^V)$ are the CPU and network bandwidth requests from the virtual nodes and links, respectively. Specifically, w_c and w_b are the unit prices of CPU and bandwidth, respectively. The long-term average revenue over an infinite period evaluates the overall performance of a VNE algorithm. Therefore, we have

$$Ave\_Rev = \lim_{T \to \infty} \frac{\sum_{t=0}^{T} Rev(G_t^V)}{T} \tag{4.4}$$

where T denotes the overall time, and G_t^V represents the successful VNR embedding at time t.

- Rev2Cost Ratio: Similarly, the cost of a successful VNR embedding can be defined as follows:

$$Cost(G^v) = \sum_{n^V \in N^V} CPU(n^V) + \sum_{l^V \in L^V} \sum_{l^S \in P^S} BW(l^S) \tag{4.5}$$

where the definition of P^S represents a sequence of substrate links in which a virtual link l^V is embedded. The fewer physical links a virtual link crosses over, the more it saves the cost. The long-term revenue to cost ratio, $Rev2Cost$, aims to reflect the efficiency of VNE and can be calculated by

$$Rev2Cost = \lim_{T \to \infty} \frac{\sum_{t=0}^{T} Rev(G_t^V)}{\sum_{t=0}^{T} Cost(G_t^V)} \tag{4.6}$$

where $Cost(G_t^V)$ denotes the cost of all the VNR embedding at time t.

4.3.2 Reinforcement Learning

In the standard reinforcement learning (RL) framework, an agent interacts with an environment and learns from the sequential exploration (Wang et al., 2019). RL follows a Markov Decision Process (MDP) formulated as (S, A, P, r, γ), where S denotes the environment state space, A denotes the action space, $P : S \times A \times S \to [0, 1]$ denotes the transition function to generate the next state according to the current state and action, $r : S \times A \times S \to \mathbb{R}$ denotes the reward function, and $\gamma \in [0, 1]$ is a discount factor. According to the policy $\pi : S \times A \to [0, 1]$, a trajectory $\tau = s_0, a_0, r_0, s_1 \cdots$ is sampled. The objective of RL is to find an optimal policy π^* which can maximize the expected cumulative reward $R_{t_0} = E\left[\sum_{t=t_0}^{\infty} \gamma^t r_t\right]$, where $\gamma^t r_t$ is the discount reward at time t.

As we can see, instead of defining an explicit objective function in linear programming or labeling the data in supervised machine learning, the RL agent improves its policy according to the expected cumulative reward. Therefore, the agent may sacrifice the best current reward to obtain a better long-term performance.

4.3.3   Hierarchical Reinforcement Learning

HRL has been successfully used in many fields, such as robotics and games (Sutton et al., 1999). Typically, to solve tasks with long time horizons, HRL is implemented as a high-level agent, which periodically assigns subgoals to low-level agents. It has been proved that different levels of abstraction implemented by this hierarchy consider different long-term planning and achieve different performance (Sutton et al., 1999). The *options framework* (Sutton et al., 1999) is one of the most popular HRL architectures, where an MDP endowed with a set of options is extended to a Semi-Markov Decision Process (SMDP) (Du et al., 2020). At the high level of the hierarchy, an option $(\pi, I, \beta) \in \mathcal{O}$ includes a policy π over actions, an initial state I, and a terminate function β. In the options framework, a high-level agent chooses an option o according to the high-level policy to execute until being terminated by β. At the low level of the hierarchy, according to the low-level policy, a low-level agent selects a set of actions $a_{i,j}$ to complete the task indicated by the chosen option.

4.4   The Framework of VNE-HRL

4.4.1   Overview

It is important to handle the VNRs as they arrive rather than handling a large batch of requests at once (Yu et al., 2008), because VNRs may arrive dynamically and stay in the substrate network for an arbitrary period. Therefore, we are inspired to apply the *time window* and *request queue* mechanisms to handle VNRs on time (Yu et al., 2008). The time window spans a short period, and the VNRs in the current time window will be processed. The processed VNRs may be deferred because of the lack of bandwidth or CPU resources and will be put into the request queue. As shown in Figure 4.3, a window-based batch that consists of the VNRs in the time window and the request queue is the input of the algorithm.

According to the definition of HRL, we model the VNE problem as a Semi-Markov Decision Process (SMDP). First, we encode the state of VNRs and SNs as the environment state where the agents will be used to make decisions. For each process, a high-level agent selects a feasible option (i.e. a VNR from a window-based batch) with the greatest long-term rewards according to a

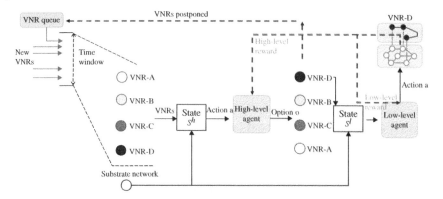

Figure 4.3   The architecture of the VNE-HRL.

high-level policy. Instead of treating all VNRs equally and independently, the high-level agent (HEA) process described above ensures that the algorithm is proactive. Then, a low-level agent performs a sequence of actions to embed the VN according to a low-level policy. After an option or action terminates, the environment will give feedback (i.e. rewards) to encourage the agents to improve the policies. Next, the state of the environment is updated. This process repeats until all VNRs are processed. Based on the above settings, we propose a novel HRL-based VNE framework as shown in Figure 4.3, including a high-level VNE agent (HEA) and a low-level agent (LEA).

To express the ideas clearly, first we define the required terms.

- **High-level State Space** S^H: A high-level state $s^h \in S^H$ is a hidden vector representing the high-level environment state, which is extracted from VNRs in the window and the underlying SN.
- **Low-level State Space** S^L: A low-level state $s^l \in S^L$ is a hidden vector denoting the low-level environment state, which is extracted from the selected VNR and the underlying SN.
- **Option Space** $\mathcal{O}$: An option $o \in \mathcal{O}$ is a VNR selected from a window-based batch, which can be regarded as an implementation of admission control.
- **Action Space** $\mathcal{A}$: An action $a \in \mathcal{A}$ is the valid embedding process that allocates a virtual network node onto a substrate network node.
- **High-level Reward** r^h: A high-level reward r^h is a scalar returned to the HEA and is also called an extrinsic reward, which evaluates the short-term benefits of an option.
- **Low-level Reward** r^l: A low-level reward r^l is a scalar returned to the LEA and is also called an intrinsic reward, which evaluates the short-term benefits of an action.
- **Discount Factor** γ: $\gamma \in [0, 1]$ defines the discounting factor to measure the expect value of future rewards.

4.4.2 The High-level Agent

HEA aims to select a feasible option (i.e. a VNR from a window-based batch) with the greatest long-term reward according to a high-level policy. Instead of treating all VNRs equally and independently, the selection process ensures that the algorithm is proactive, including two steps: (1) The environment states are encoded by extracting the high-level state features through a state encoder. (2) According to the encoded states, HEA estimates the long-term cumulative reward of options and executes an ϵ-soft strategy (Bacon et al., 2017) to select a VNR. Then, HEA assigns LEA to embed the selected VNR. When the selected VNR embedding completes, a high-level reward is returned and a new VNR will be selected from the window-based batch, while the VNRs that have been handled in the current batch will be masked. This process continues repeatedly.

In what follows, the details of the state encoder, the estimated long-term cumulative reward, and the short-term high-level reward will be illustrated.

4.4.2.1 State Encoder for HEA

The high-level environment states include the VNRs in the window-based batch, and the underlying SN. Obviously, the spatial features of network topology are vital for the VNE problem. Instead of using the explicit link features, we choose an alternative method to extract more useful features in an efficient way. Inspired by the work Yan et al. (2020b), we apply graph convolutional network (GCN) to extract the spatial features of VN and SN. The state of SN can be encoded as follows:

$$E^S = GCN(SN) \tag{4.7}$$

The i-th VNR can be formulated by,

$$e_i^V = GCN(VNR_i) \tag{4.8}$$

In practice, the number of VNRs in a time window is usually unpredictable, and we set a fixed value M to indicate the size of the window-based batch. If the number of VNRs in the current window and queue exceeds M, the excess VNRs will be added into the current batch gradually to cover the processed VNRs. Otherwise, the batch will be filled up to M with empty VNRs. Thus, the embedding of all the VNRs can be formulated by adding up all the VNRs as follows:

$$E^V = \sum_{i=0}^{M-1} e_i^V \tag{4.9}$$

As last, the high-level environment state for HEA can be encoded by adding up the embeddings of VNRs and SN:

$$s^h = E^V + E^S \tag{4.10}$$

where s^h is a vector with length N^S and represents the global state.

4.4.2.2 Estimated Long-term Cumulative Reward

Typically, a multilayer neural network with parameter θ is utilized to estimate the long-term cumulative reward of an option. Given an n-dimensional state s^h, it outputs a vector of estimated long-term rewards over options.

In HEA, we apply a two-layer fully connected network, and the estimated long-term rewards R_h can be calculated by

$$R_h(s^h; \theta) = FullConnectLayer^2(s^h; \theta) \tag{4.11}$$

where s^h is the encoded global state as defined in Eq. (4.10). Thus, we obtain the estimated long-term cumulative reward of each VNR. Based on the results, we can select the option with maximum estimated long-term cumulative reward with a probability of $1 - \epsilon$ or randomly select an option with a probability of ϵ. Then, we manage to embed the corresponding VNR into the SN by a low-level agent.

4.4.2.3 Short-term High-level Reward

A high-level reward indicates the real effectiveness of an option o_t, which is extrinsic and closely related to ISP pricing strategies. To get a high-yield ratio, we should encourage successful VNR embeddings. A positive reward is returned if the selected VNR is embedded completely and otherwise, a negative one returns. Besides, HEA takes the extrinsic factor into consideration, and the agent should not only consider the profit but also the cost. In this way, the high-level reward is expressed as follows:

$$r^g = \begin{cases} \dfrac{Rev_t^2(G^V)}{Cost_t(G^V)} & o_t \text{ is successful} \\ -Cost_t(G^V) & \text{otherwise} \end{cases} \tag{4.12}$$

where the meanings of $Rev(G^V)$ and $Cost(G^V)$ have been explained in Eqs. (4.3) and (4.5), respectively, in Section 4.3.1.3.

4.4.3 The Low-level Agent

After HEA selects an option (i.e. VNR) at a high level, LEA performs a sequence of actions to embed the VN according to the low-level policy π. However, as the size of nodes increases, the number of subgraphs of the network grows exponentially. It is impossible to consider every subgraph as embedding actions, as the action space will be enormous. Thus, it is not fit for the RL agent to search every possible subgraph of the SN to host the VN. In this work, the VNR embedding process is decomposed into a sequence of virtual node embeddings following the work (Yao et al., 2018a).

The embedding process of a virtual node includes node mapping and link mapping. With respect to the node mapping, LEA chooses a certain substrate network node to host a virtual network node. The selection process involves two steps: (1) The environment states are encoded by extracting the low-level state features through a state encoder, and (2) According to the encoded states, LEA estimates the long-term rewards of all actions through a multilayer neural network and executes an ϵ-soft strategy to select a substrate node to host the current VNR. If the chosen substrate node has enough spare resources for the current virtual node, we will map the virtual links between the current virtual node and the other already embedded virtual node. However, it is NP-hard to find an optimal mapping from a virtual link to a set of substrate paths (Kolliopoulos and Stein, 1997). Therefore, for each virtual link, *the k-shortest paths* for increasing k are searched until we find a substrate path that has sufficient bandwidth to embed the corresponding virtual link. *The k-shortest paths* algorithm can be solved in $O(m + n\log n + k)$ time in an SN with n nodes and m links (Eppstein, 1998). In consideration of computational efficiency, k should be kept small.

Next, the details of the state encoder, the estimated long-term cumulative reward, and the short-term low-level reward will be illustrated.

4.4.3.1 State Encoder for LEA

The low-level environment states include the current virtual node and the underlying SN. Thus, the local state can be formulated by adding up the vectors of the current virtual node and the SN as follows:

$$s^l = e^V_{selected} + E^S \tag{4.13}$$

where e^V and E^S have already been declared in Section 4.4.2.1.

4.4.3.2 Estimated Long-term Cumulative Reward

Typically, a multilayer neural network with parameter ξ is utilized to estimate the long-term cumulative reward of an action. Given an n-dimensional state s^l, it outputs a vector of estimated long-term rewards over actions.

In LEA, we apply a two-layer fully connected network and the estimated long-term cumulative rewards R_l can be formulated by

$$R_l(s^l; \xi) = FullConnectLayer^2(s^l; \xi) \tag{4.14}$$

where s^l is the encoded local state as defined in Eq. (4.13). Thus, we obtain the estimated long-term cumulative reward of each substrate node. Based on the results, we can select the action with maximum estimated long-term cumulative reward with the probability of $1 - \epsilon$ or randomly select an action with the probability of ϵ. Then, we use the abovementioned *The k-shortest paths* for link mapping.

4.4.3.3 Short-term Low-level Reward

A low-level reward reveals the real short-term feedback of an action a_t. A positive reward is returned if the selected substrate node hosts the current virtual node successfully and otherwise, a negative one returns. To ensure the availability of SN, LEA should embed every virtual node in a cost-efficient way and maximize the resource utilization. Therefore, the low-level reward can therefore be expressed as follows:

$$r^l = \begin{cases} 10 \times \dfrac{Cost_{t-1}(G^V)}{Cost_t(G^V)} & a_t \text{ is successful} \\ -10 \times \rho_t & \text{otherwise} \end{cases} \qquad (4.15)$$

where ρ_t is a discount factor that gradually rises from $\frac{1}{Size(N^V)}$ to 1. It means that virtual nodes that are embedded at the end are more important, and the failure of embedding the last few nodes will result in greater losses.

4.4.4 The Training Method

In this work, the neural network with a set of trainable parameters is utilized for feature extraction and policy generation. To get the optimal policies, we should optimize the neural network iteratively. Here, to decrease the possibility of divergence or oscillations during the training process, we adopt a dual policy learning method, called DDQN (Van Hasselt et al., 2016), which updates parameters by gradient descent in an efficient way.

4.5 Case Study

4.5.1 Experiment Setup

To verify the effectiveness of the proposed model, we set up a simulated environment as most previous works (Yao et al., 2018a,2020, Yan et al., 2020b) have done. An SN of 100 nodes and about 500 links are generated, which can represent a medium-sized ISP. The CPU of the substrate node satisfies the uniform distribution from 50 to 100 units, while the bandwidth of links satisfies the uniform distribution from 20 to 50 units. The expected arrival rate is 4 VNRs per 100 time units. Each VNR has an exponentially distributed lifetime with an average of 500 time units. Following many previous works (Yao et al., 2020, Yan et al., 2020b), every VNR has 2–10 nodes and each pair of virtual nodes has a 50% chance to form a link. The initial virtual node and link resources in a VNR are uniformly distributed from 0 to 40 units. A time window includes 500 time units and about 20 VNRs, which is suitable for the agent to process without considerable consumption of computing resources and achieve proactive performance. Besides, the lengths of the time window and the request queue are set to 25 and 10, respectively. In the testing phase, we build a timeline with a length of 50 000 time units, which means that every episode lasts 50,000 time units, and about 2000 VNRs are generated.

4.5.2 Comparison Methods

In the evaluation, the VNE-HRL algorithm will be compared with four selected algorithms including NodeRank (Cheng et al., 2011), MCViNE (Haeri and Trajković, 2017), and seq2seqRL (Yao et al., 2020). NodeRank is a traditional algorithm, which was developed based on mixed-integer programs and PageRank (Page et al., 1999). In addition, MCViNE and seq2seqRL are two representative RL-based algorithms, which are implemented through Monte-Carlo Tree Search and Recurrent Neural Networks, respectively. We utilize the public VNE simulator VNE-Sim (Haeri and Trajković, 2016) to collect the performance of these algorithms.

4.5.3 Evaluation Results

In the testing phase, the VNRs with maximum long-term revenue are selected from a window-based batch by HEA and embedded by LEA, which makes the method proactive. To assess the performance of the algorithm, the comparison experiments with other algorithms are conducted in terms of the evaluation metrics presented in Section 4.3.1.3. Besides, to avoid interference caused by random initialization of neural network parameters, the seq2seqRL and VNE-HRL algorithms need to run for 15 different initialization settings, and the error bar is added to represent the performance under different initialization settings.

4.5.3.1 Performance Over Time

For the first group of tests, we evaluate the performance of four algorithms over time. As we can see from Figure 4.4, the long-term average revenue and acceptance ratio are relatively high in early epochs, because there are more available resources in the SN at the beginning of the embedding. As the testing process continues, more VNRs are embedded and the available substrate resources are gradually occupied, which leads to the decrease in the long-term average revenue and acceptance ratio. However, VNE-HRL algorithm keeps leading, which can accurately identify the long-term benefits of the current VNR, embed the VNR with a low cost, and leave plenty of room for the coming VNRs. The long-term revenue to cost ratio has not experienced significant variations throughout the simulation time, which shows that this metric is independent of the available resources. At last, as shown in Figures 4.4a and 4.4c, VNE-HRL

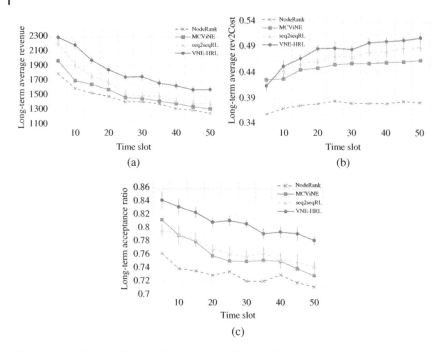

Figure 4.4 The algorithm performance over time on the test dataset. (a) The long-term average revenue, (b) The long-term average Rev2Cost, and (c) The long-term average acceptance ratio.

algorithm outperforms NodeRank, MCViNE, and seq2seqRL with a gap of 26.78%, 21.42%, and 14.69% on average revenue and 6.62%, 5.19%, and 3.73% on average acceptance ratio. Significantly, there is a big gap between the traditional algorithms (i.e. NodeRank) and the other three methods (i.e. MCViNE, seq2seqRL, and VNE-HRL) in Figure 4.4b, which indicates that RL agents perform well in the event of automatically exploring the embedding strategy with a low cost. According to the metric figures and error bars, we can draw a conclusion that the VNE-HRL algorithm has maintained a relatively better performance over the long term due to proactive planning.

4.5.3.2 Performance of Various VNRs with Diverse Resource Requirements

For the second group of tests, we observe the performance of these four algorithms under various resource request modes. Due to the different resource requirements, the VNRs can be divided into two types: computation-intensive and communication-intensive. To simulate these cases, the node resource request distribution varies from the [0, 40] uniform distribution to a [0, 100] uniform distribution, and a higher upper bound denotes a more intensive computation mode. In each step, we raise the upper bound by 10. According to the results shown

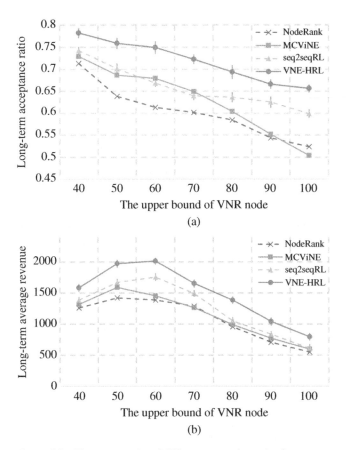

Figure 4.5 The test results of different upper bounds of resource requests of VNR nodes. (a) The long-term average acceptance ratio and (b) The long-term average revenue.

in Figure 4.5, the VNE-HRL algorithm outperforms NodeRank, MCViNE, and seq2seqRL with an average of 43.84%, 33.48%, and 29.58% on average revenue, and 14.84%, 15.91%, and 4.47% on acceptance ratio. In addition, as the resource request of VNRs increases, the acceptance ratio of each algorithm drops. This is because the SN components gradually become harder to host virtual networks and a VNR with large resource requests is likely to fail in the steps of embedding. Besides, the average revenue of these algorithms rises first before going down. This is because a VNR with large resource requests can bring a higher revenue. However, as the resource demands of VNRs become bigger, the average revenue descends due to the quick drop in the acceptance ratio of these VNRs. Through comparison, we can conclude that the VNE-HRL method again outperforms the other algorithms in a wide range of different resource request distributions.

4.6 Related Work

Research on VNE problems has drawn tremendous attention. In this section, we will introduce the traditional methods (Section 4.6.1) and the ML-based algorithms (Section 4.6.2).

4.6.1 Traditional Methods

Due to the differences in optimization strategies, traditional VNE algorithms are usually classified into two categories, the exact and the heuristic.

As for the exact algorithms, each VNR is embedded by an exact optimization strategy (Wolsey, 1998), such as ILP (Schrijver, 1998) and MILP (Bénichou et al., 1971). Shahriar et al. (2018) transformed VNE into an ILP problem, which jointly optimized spare capacity location and request survivability. Although an auxiliary algorithm was proposed to optimize the execution time, it was still unacceptable to embed a VNR due to the high-computation complexity of the node-mapping algorithm. Chowdhury et al. (2011) formulated the VNR problem as an MILP through SN augmentation, which relaxed the integer constraints to obtain a linear program and devised two embedding algorithms. However, this approach suffered from the requirement of considerable computational resources for a linear programming solution. To sum up, the exact algorithms aim at achieving an optimal embedding solution yet with high-computational complexity, which only can be used to solve small-sized VNE problems.

The heuristic methods manage to find a feasible VNR embedding solution with less execution time (Cormen et al., 2009). Inspired by the Pagerank algorithm (Page et al., 1999, Cheng et al., 2011) ranked the network node based on its resource and topological attributes and mapped virtual nodes to substrate nodes according to their ranks. However, due to the fixed node ranking, the embedding policy was hard to be optimized. The authors in Haeri and Trajković (2017) proposed a multicommodity flow and shortest-path approach to embedding VNRs into SNs to maximize the profit of the infrastructure provider. However, they did not consider the future resource demand and historical information, leading to the restriction of profit maximization up to a certain extent. To sum up, the heuristic methods usually suffer from the issue of local optimum that may be far away from the global optimum.

4.6.2 ML-based Algorithms

Recently, several research works explored the utilization of ML in VNE problems. Xiao et al. (2019) introduced a Markov decision process (MDP) model to capture the dynamic network state and automatically deployed service function chains for requests. However, this work did not take the admission control into account, which wasted many resources on infeasible VNRs and disregarded the long-term effects of a VNR. Based on Hopfield neural network, He et al. (2021) established an energy-efficient virtual network embedding model to provide a candidate set for virtual network embedding. In Alsarhan et al. (2017), an RL-based framework automatically acclimatized itself to the system changes, such as service cost, resource capability, and resource requests. However, it only aims to meet the demand of service-level agreement (SLA) but treat all VNRs equally. Yao et al. (2018b) applied the policy-based RL with historical request data to the node mapping, of which the overall objective is to maximize the revenue by embedding nodes and links with a convolutional neural network. To sum up, most existing ML-based approaches focus on the current VNR and treat all VNRs equally, which waste resources when the infeasible VNRs present and disregard the long-term impacts of the embedding.

4.7 Conclusion

In this chapter, we proposed a proactive VNE algorithm relying on HRL, which takes the long-term impact of VNR embedding into consideration. Within the VNE-HRL framework, the task of embedding a sequence of VNRs has been performed by a two-level agent. For each process, the high-level agent aims to select a currently feasible VNR with maximum long-term reward, and the low-level agent is designed to embed the selected VNR on the substrate network. Extensive simulation results have shown that the VNE-HRL algorithm possesses good effectiveness and robustness when the type of VNR changes.

References

Ayoub Alsarhan, Awni Itradat, Ahmed Y. Al-Dubai, Albert Y. Zomaya, and Geyong Min. Adaptive resource allocation and provisioning in multi-service cloud environments. *IEEE Transactions on Parallel and Distributed Systems*, 29(1):31–42, 2017.

Thomas Anderson, Larry Peterson, Scott Shenker, and Jonathan Turner. Overcoming the internet impasse through virtualization. *Computer*, 38(4):34–41, 2005.

Pierre-Luc Bacon, Jean Harb, and Doina Precup. The option-critic architecture. In *31st AAAI Conference on Artificial Intelligence*, 2017.

Michel Bénichou, Jean-Michel Gauthier, Paul Girodet, Gerard Hentges, Gerard Ribière, and O Vincent. Experiments in mixed-integer linear programming. *Mathematical Programming*, 1(1):76–94, 1971.

Sushil Bhardwaj, Leena Jain, and Sandeep Jain. Cloud computing: A study of infrastructure as a service (IAAS). *International Journal of Engineering and Information Technology*, 2(1):60–63, 2010.

Haotong Cao, Shengchen Wu, Yue Hu, Yun Liu, and Longxiang Yang. A survey of embedding algorithm for virtual network embedding. *China Communications*, 16(12):1–33, 2019.

Xiang Cheng, Sen Su, Zhongbao Zhang, Hanchi Wang, Fangchun Yang, Yan Luo, and Jie Wang. Virtual network embedding through topology-aware node ranking. *ACM SIGCOMM Computer Communication Review*, 41(2):38–47, 2011.

Xiangle Cheng, Yulei Wu, Geyong Min, and Albert Y. Zomaya. Network function virtualization in dynamic networks: A stochastic perspective. *IEEE Journal on Selected Areas in Communications*, 36(10):2218–2232, 2018. doi: 10.1109/JSAC.2018.2869958.

Xiangle Cheng, Yulei Wu, Geyong Min, Albert Y. Zomaya, and Xuming Fang. Safeguard network slicing in 5G: A learning augmented optimization approach. *IEEE Journal on Selected Areas in Communications*, 38(7):1600–1613, 2020.

Jin Cheng, Yulei Wu, Yeming Lin, Yuepeng E, Fan Tang, and Jingguo Ge. VNE-HRL: A proactive virtual network embedding algorithm based on hierarchical reinforcement learning. *IEEE Transactions on Network and Service Management*, 18(4):4075–4087, 2021. doi: 10.1109/TNSM.2021.3120297.

N. M. Mosharaf Kabir Chowdhuryand Raouf Boutaba. A survey of network virtualization. *Computer Networks*, 54(5):862–876, 2010.

N. M. Mosharaf Kabir Chowdhury, Muntasir Raihan Rahman, and Raouf Boutaba. Virtual network embedding with coordinated node and link mapping. In *IEEE INFOCOM 2009*, pages 783–791. IEEE, 2009.

Mosharaf Chowdhury, Muntasir Raihan Rahman, and Raouf Boutaba. ViNEYard: Virtual network embedding algorithms with coordinated node and link mapping. *IEEE/ACM Transactions on Networking*, 20(1):206–219, 2011.

Thomas H. Cormen, Charles E. Leiserson, Ronald L. Rivest, and Clifford Stein. *Introduction to Algorithms*. MIT press, 2009.

J. Du, J. Futoma, and F. Doshi-Velez. Model-based reinforcement learning for semi-Markov decision processes with neural odes. *Advances in Neural Information Processing Systems* 33: 19805–19816, 2020.

Patricia Takako Endo, Andre Vitor de Almeida Palhares, Nadilma Nunes Pereira, et al. Resource allocation for distributed cloud: Concepts and research challenges. *IEEE Network*, 25(4):42–46, 2011.

David Eppstein. Finding the K shortest paths. *SIAM Journal on Computing*, 28(2):652–673, 1998.

Nick Feamster, Lixin Gao, and Jennifer Rexford. How to lease the internet in your spare time. *ACM SIGCOMM Computer Communication Review*, 37(1):61–64, 2007.

Soroush Haeri and Ljiljana Trajković. VNE-SIM: A virtual network embedding simulator. In *Proceedings of the 9th EAI International Conference on Simulation Tools and Techniques*, pages 112–117, 2016.

Soroush Haeri and Ljiljana Trajković. Virtual network embedding via Monte Carlo tree search. *IEEE Transactions on Cybernetics*, 48(2):510–521, 2017.

Mengyang He, Lei Zhuang, Sijin Yang, Jianhui Zhang, and Huiping Meng. Energy-efficient virtual network embedding algorithm based on Hopfield neural network. *Wireless Communications and Mobile Computing*, 2021:8889923:1–8889923:13, 2021.

Leslie Pack Kaelbling, Michael L. Littman, and Andrew W. Moore. Reinforcement learning: A survey. *Journal of Artificial Intelligence Research*, 4:237–285, 1996.

Stavros G. Kolliopoulos and Clifford Stein. Improved approximation algorithms for unsplittable flow problems. In *Proceedings 38th Annual Symposium on Foundations of Computer Science*, pages 426–436. IEEE, 1997.

Nick McKeown, Tom Anderson, Hari Balakrishnan, Guru Parulkar, et al. OpenFlow: Enabling innovation in campus networks. *ACM SIGCOMM Computer Communication Review*, 38(2):69–74, 2008.

Volodymyr Mnih, Koray Kavukcuoglu, David Silver, Alex Graves, Ioannis Antonoglou, Daan Wierstra, and Martin Riedmiller. Playing Atari with deep reinforcement learning. *arXiv preprint arXiv:1312.5602*, 2013.

Open Networking Foundation. ONF, "Open networking foundation", 2010. https://www.opennetworking.org/.

Lawrence Page, Sergey Brin, Rajeev Motwani, and Terry Winograd. The PageRank citation ranking: Bringing order to the web. Technical report, Stanford InfoLab, 1999.

Alexander Schrijver. *Theory of Linear and Integer Programming*. John Wiley & Sons, 1998.

Nashid Shahriar, Shihabur Rahman Chowdhury, Reaz Ahmed, Aimal Khan, Siavash Fathi, Raouf Boutaba, Jeebak Mitra, and Liu Liu. Virtual network survivability through joint spare capacity allocation and embedding. *IEEE Journal on Selected Areas in Communications*, 36(3):502–518, 2018.

Shashank Shanbhag, Arun Reddy Kandoor, Cong Wang, Ramgopal Mettu, and Tilman Wolf. VHub: Single-stage virtual network mapping through hub location. *Computer Networks*, 77:169–180, 2015.

David Silver, Aja Huang, Chris J. Maddison, Arthur Guez, Laurent Sifre, George Van Den Driessche, Julian Schrittwiese, et al. Mastering the game of Go with deep neural networks and tree search. *Nature*, 529(7587):484–489, 2016.

Yuhang Song, Jianyi Wang, Thomas Lukasiewicz, Zhenghua Xu, and Mai Xu. Diversity-driven extensible hierarchical reinforcement learning. In *Proceedings of the AAAI Conference on Artificial Intelligence*, volume 33, pages 4992–4999, 2019.

Richard S. Sutton and Andrew G. Barto. *Reinforcement Learning: An Introduction*. MIT press, 2018.

Richard S. Sutton, Doina Precup, and Satinder Singh. Between MDPs and semi-MDPs: A framework for temporal abstraction in reinforcement learning. *Artificial Intelligence*, 112(1–2):181–211, 1999.

Hiren Kumar Thakkar, Chinmaya Kumar Dehury, and Prasan Kumar Sahoo. MUVINE: Multi-stage virtual network embedding in cloud data centers using reinforcement learning-based predictions. *IEEE Journal on Selected Areas in Communications*, 38(6):1058–1074, 2020.

Hado Van Hasselt, Arthur Guez, and David Silver. Deep reinforcement learning with double Q-learning. In *Proceedings of the AAAI Conference on Artificial Intelligence*, Volume 30, 2016.

Haozhe Wang, Yulei Wu, Geyong Min, Jie Xu, and Pengcheng Tang. Data-driven dynamic resource scheduling for network slicing: A deep reinforcement learning approach. *Information Sciences*, 498:106–116, 2019.

Laurence A. Wolsey. *Integer Programming*, volume 52. John Wiley & Sons, 1998.

Yikai Xiao, Qixia Zhang, Fangming Liu, Jia Wang, and Miao Zhao. NFVdeep: Adaptive online service function chain deployment with deep reinforcement learning. In *Proceedings of the International Symposium on Quality of Service*, pages 1–10, 2019.

Zhongxia Yan, Jingguo Ge, Yulei Wu, Liangxiong Li, and Tong Li. Automatic virtual network embedding: A deep reinforcement learning approach with graph convolutional networks. *IEEE Journal on Selected Areas in Communications*, 38(6):1040–1057, 2020a. doi: 10.1109/JSAC.2020.2986662.

Zhongxia Yan, Jingguo Ge, Yulei Wu, Liangxiong Li, and Tong Li. Automatic virtual network embedding: A deep reinforcement learning approach with graph convolutional networks. *IEEE Journal on Selected Areas in Communications*, 38(99):1040–1057, 2020b.

Haipeng Yao, Xu Chen, Maozhen Li, Peiying Zhang, and Luyao Wang. A novel reinforcement learning algorithm for virtual network embedding. *Neurocomputing*, 284:1–9, 2018a.

Haipeng Yao, Bo Zhang, Peiying Zhang, Sheng Wu, Chunxiao Jiang, and Song Guo. RDAM: A reinforcement learning based dynamic attribute matrix representation for virtual network embedding. *IEEE Transactions on Emerging Topics in Computing* 9 (2): 901–914, 2018b.

Haipeng Yao, Sihan Ma, Jingjing Wang, Peiying Zhang, and Song Guo. A continuous-decision virtual network embedding scheme relying on reinforcement learning. *IEEE Transactions on Network and Service Management* 17 (2): 864–875, 2020.

Minlan Yu, Yung Yi, Jennifer Rexford, and Mung Chiang. Rethinking virtual network embedding: Substrate support for path splitting and migration. *ACM SIGCOMM Computer Communication Review*, 38(2):17–29, 2008.

5

Concept Drift Detection for Network Traffic Classification

5.1 Related Concepts of Machine Learning in Data Stream Processing

5.1.1 Assumptions and Limitations

With the rapid development of network and information technologies, traffic classification has received significant attention and plays an important role in intrusion detection (Roshan et al., 2017, Zhang et al., 2021, Wang et al., 2021), flow identification (Zou et al., 2018, Lotfollahi et al., 2017), just to name a few. However, standard machine-learning frameworks, in which data are processed in an offline way, become limited in network traffic processing due to exponential increase of the available data. In order to deal with the large amounts of data, more studies started to research on the processing of network data as a stream and used machine-learning methods to classify the traffic online. In terms of machine learning, several types of assumptions and constraints can be identified which are related to the data and to the type of concept to be learned. In the remainder of this chapter, x, y, and $P(x, y)$ denote the given input feature, the given label, and the concept (i.e. the data distribution), respectively (Lemaire et al., 2015).

5.1.1.1 Availability of Learning Examples

In the context of this chapter, models are learned from representative examples coming from a classification problem. In practice the availability and the access to these examples can vary, e.g. all examples have been stored in a database, all examples are stored in memory, examples are partially stored in memory, examples are available one by one in a stream. Several types of algorithms for different types of availability of the examples have been reported in the literature (Lemaire et al., 2015). However, in some fields such as network traffic classification, data are continuously available from a data stream and, over time, the amount of data will become too large to be stored. According to the "data streams"

AI and Machine Learning for Network and Security Management, First Edition.
Yulei Wu, Jingguo Ge, and Tong Li.

paradigm, the representative examples can be seen only once and in their order of arrival (without storage) (Lemaire et al., 2015). In this case, the learning algorithm must be incremental and needs to have an efficient processing capability due to the potentially high-data arrival rate from data stream.

5.1.1.2   Availability of the Model

Data mining is a two-step process: (1) train and learn the model, and (2) deploy the model to predict on the new data. In the case of regular batch learning, these two steps are carried out one after the other. But in the case of an incremental algorithm, the training and learning stages are triggered as soon as a new example arrives. In the cases of time-critical applications, the training and learning steps require a low-latency algorithm (i.e. with a low-time complexity).

5.1.1.3   Concept to be Learned

The concept to be learned is the joint probability $P(x, y)$, where x and y is the given input feature and the given label, respectively. Traditional traffic classification is carried out by learning an underlying data distribution $P(x, y)$ from a static data set. However, in real network environment, the concept, i.e. the joint probability, of traffic always changes because of the changing user interests and time-varying network status, e.g. network congestion. In this chapter, we mainly consider the problem of concept drift in network traffic classification, where the labeling of network traffic is significantly hindered by its nature of streaming applications.

5.1.2   Concept Drift and Its Solution

The change of concept is called "concept drift." Although network traffic classification algorithms based on machine learning can alleviate the limitations imposed by traditional techniques, most of them still cannot address concept drift problems (Qu et al., 2019), which will bring a devastating blow to the performance of the classifier. For example, in the intrusion detection field, the F1-score of Artificial Neural Networks (ANN) will drop from 99.24% to 9.59% when the distribution of traffic (i.e. concept) changes (Al-Riyami et al., 2018). Therefore, in order to perform online traffic classification, it is of paramount importance to give in-depth research on concept drift. According to the changing speed of drift, concept drift can be either abrupt, when the concept is changed suddenly, or gradual, when the concept evolves slowly over time (Wang et al., 2018). In addition, based on the definition of "concept," i.e. $P(x, y) = P(x) * P(y|x) = P(y) * P(x|y)$, concept drift can manifest four fundamental forms of changes corresponding to the four major variables in Bayes' theorem (Wang et al., 2018). In order to solve the problem of classifier's performance degradation caused by concept drift, two types of solutions have been proposed: passive versus active approaches, according to whether an explicit

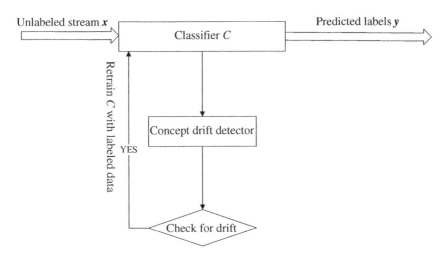

Figure 5.1 Main processes of the active approach-addressing concept drift.

drift detection mechanism is employed (Wang et al., 2018, Singh et al., 2015). The passive approach (also known as the adaptive classifier) refers to the continuous training of the classifier without an explicit trigger reporting the drift. The active approach, whose main processes are shown in Figure 5.1, evolves the classifier after determining whether the concept drift occurs. Compared with the passive approach, the active approach can effectively reduce the times of classifier retraining, which is useful under the condition of limited computing resources (Charyyev and Gunes, 2020). As the core component of active approaches, concept drift detection has become the main research topic (Wang et al., 2018, Hu et al., 2020). Existing methods of detecting concept drift assume one among three situations according to the availability of data labels (Hu et al., 2020), including full access, no access, and limited access to labels of the data streams. They correspond to the supervised, unsupervised, and semisupervised learning approaches, respectively. The semisupervised learning mechanism is a compromise between the label cost and the detection rate. Although supervised detector can detect all types of drift, it is unrealistic to label every network traffic due to its streaming nature. Therefore, in real network environment, a sensible semisupervised concept drift detection scheme is more practical and efficient. In order to obtain the drift indicator, the current semisupervised concept drift detection scheme mainly needs to measure and evaluate the confidence score (Kim and Park, 2017, Sriwatanasakdi et al., 2017, Haque et al., 2016a,b) or the accuracy score (Lughofer et al., 2016) of the classifier. However, approaches based on the confidence score (Kim and Park, 2017, Sriwatanasakdi et al., 2017, Haque et al., 2016a,b) only focus on the change of decision boundaries, namely $P(y|x)$.

Therefore, only a small subset of all concept drift types can be detected (Hu et al., 2020). Although the indicator based on the accuracy score can no longer detect changes in decision boundaries, the drift analysis method proposed in Lughofer et al. (2016) assumed that the previously obtained indicators follow the Gaussian distribution, which is not always true. In order to efficiently detect both sudden drifts and gradual drifts, Zhang et al. (2020) proposed an ensemble drift analysis method. However, true drifts need to be labeled in this method, which is very difficult to achieve in real-world environment. In order to efficiently complete concept drift detection under the semisupervised learning, we propose a concept drift detector based on CVAE, which is elaborated in Section 5.3.

5.2 Using an Active Approach to Solve Concept Drift in the Intrusion Detection Field

In order to show the process of concept drift detection more intuitively, we use an example in intrusion detection to illustrate.

5.2.1 Application Background

The explosive growth of computer systems and networks has led to a heightened importance to protect them from attacks or intrusions. As one of the important network security technologies, Intrusion Detection System (IDS) continuously collects different kinds of data about the operating system calls and the network traffic which may show abnormalities caused by malicious attacks or policy violations. In order to overcome disadvantages of traditional IDS, such as time consumption and insensitiveness to emerging types of intrusions, more researchers have made their efforts to utilize machine learning and data mining techniques to automatically detect and classify the abnormalities. However, the real-world network is a nonstationary environment, in which the characteristics of continuous data stream is time varying and, more importantly, various new types of networks have been emerging endlessly. In this case, it is necessary to retrain the classifier when it does not match the current concept, i.e. the concept drift occurs. In this section, we use two real-world datasets in the intrusion detection field, i.e. Gure–KDD and NSL–KDD, to simulate the concept drift. NSL–KDD is an improved version of KDD99, which is the data set used for The Third International Knowledge Discovery and Data Mining Tools Competition to build a network intrusion detector. Both NSL–KDD and Gure–KDD contain 5 attacks and 41-dimensional input features. In this scenario, we use the full training set of NSL–KDD to train the classifier. The testing set is composed of the testing set of NSL–KDD and the full set of Gure–KDD, with the proportion of 1:7. Once the concept drift is detected, we use 5000 labeled data to train the classifier online.

5.2.2 System Workflow

As shown in Figure 5.1, after classifying the unlabeled stream x, the detector takes x as input to determine whether concept drift occurs or not. The detailed operation process of the semisupervised detector is shown in Figure 5.2. For online traffic classification, it is unrealistic for experts to continuously perform timely and reliable labeling of data. In practice, as shown in Figure 5.2, only a small number of samples selected by the **Active Learning** method can be labeled by, e.g. Oracle (Lughofer et al., 2016). Oracle can process the selected input feature **X** and obtain their true labels **Y**, and then it uses the [**X, Y**] as the input of the **Drift Indicator** to calculate the current value of loss function as the indicator. The **Drift Analyzer** then analyzes the loss and generates a signal to determine whether the concept drift occurs. Since the innovations of this research are mainly reflected in the Drift Indicator and Drift Analyzer, in what follows we will mainly introduce these two parts. In the rest of this chapter, random sampling with sampling rate r is used in the Active Learning method. We use the most intuitive value, that is, the accuracy of the classifier as the indicator of the detector. Then, setting the sampling rate $r = 1$ and using the method in Gama et al. (2004) as the analyzer, when the accuracy of the classifier drops beyond a certain threshold, a drift signal is sent. After receiving the drift signal, the classifier will be retrained. The result is shown in Figure 5.3. As we can see from the figure, if we do not deal with the problem of concept drift, the accuracy of classifier will drop sharply. However, if we use drift detector and retrain the classifier whenever the drift occurs, the classifier will have better performance. In this way, the problem of concept drift can be basically solved. Next, we will describe how to achieve a better performance of concept drift detectors with less sampling rate based on CVAE under the semisupervised learning.

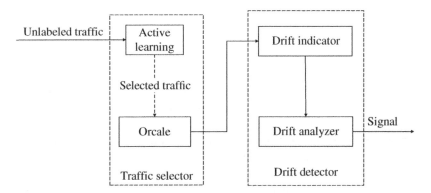

Figure 5.2 Overview of the semisupervised methodology.

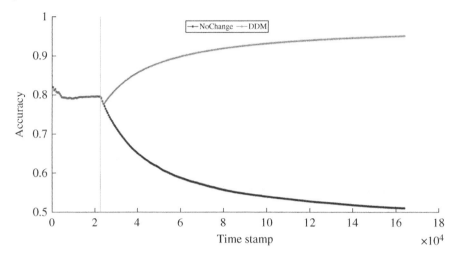

Figure 5.3 Results of the active approach to solve concept drift.

5.3 Concept Drift Detector Based on CVAE

According to Section 5.2, there are two main components in concept drift detector, i.e. **Drift Indicator** and **Drift Analyzer**. In the following, we will carefully introduce how to complete these two parts based on CVAE.

5.3.1 CVAE-based Drift Indicator

As a generative neural network, variational autoencoder (VAE) is able to model the distribution of observed data, i.e. $P(\mathbf{X})$. CVAE extends VAE by taking labels into consideration, aiming to model the relationship between features and labels, which means that the loss value of CVAE is highly related to the current concept, i.e. $P(\mathbf{X}, \mathbf{Y})$.

The structure of CVAE is shown in Figure 5.4. It can be seen that the CVAE is composed of an encoder and a decoder. The encoder takes $[\mathbf{X}, \mathbf{Y}]$ as input to generate the variable $\mathbf{z}$. Formally, the goal of encoder is to estimate the parameters of the latent data distribution $q(\mathbf{z}|\mathbf{X}, \mathbf{Y})$ that approximates the prior distribution of the latent vector $p(\mathbf{z}|\mathbf{Y})$. Taking label $\mathbf{Y}$ as input, the decoder then samples $\mathbf{z}$ from the approximate distribution and attempts to reconstruct the original feature $\mathbf{X}$ back, i.e. using the decoder output $f(\mathbf{z}, \mathbf{Y})$ to approximate the input $\mathbf{X}$. Both the encoder and decoder parameters can be trained using a deep learning framework (Agrawal and Ganapathy, 2019).

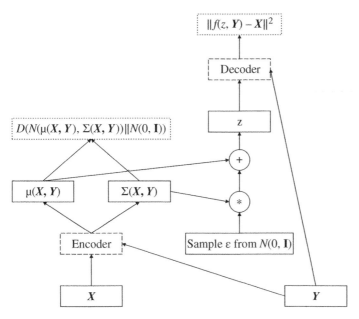

Figure 5.4 The structure of CVAE.

If the input feature $\mathbf{X}$ is reconstructed from distribution $p(\mathbf{X}|\mathbf{z}, \mathbf{Y})$, the target function of CVAE can be written by Eq. (5.1), where $D(.)$ is Kullback–Leibler Divergence.

$$L = D(q(\mathbf{z}|\mathbf{X}, \mathbf{Y}) \,\|\, p(\mathbf{z}|\mathbf{Y})) - E_{\mathbf{z} \sim q(\mathbf{z}|\mathbf{X}, \mathbf{Y})}(\log p(\mathbf{X}|\mathbf{z}, \mathbf{Y})) \qquad (5.1)$$

Generally, the prior distribution of latent vector $p(\mathbf{z}|\mathbf{Y})$ is assumed to be a standard normal distribution, and $q(\mathbf{z}|\mathbf{X}, \mathbf{Y})$ is assumed to be a normal distribution with mean $\mu(\mathbf{X}, \mathbf{Y})$ and variance $\Sigma(\mathbf{X}, \mathbf{Y})$ (Doersch, 2016). In addition, the second term in Eq. (5.1) can be substituted by the negative of mean square error (MSE) (Agrawal and Ganapathy, 2019). Finally, the loss function of CVAE for every sample can be rewritten as Eq. (5.2).

$$L_C = D(q(\mathbf{z}|\mathbf{X}, \mathbf{Y}) \| N(0, \mathbf{I})) + \|f(\mathbf{z}, \mathbf{Y}) - \mathbf{X}\|^2 \qquad (5.2)$$

The stochastic gradient descent technique can be used to minimize Eq. (5.2). After the training process of CVAE, the **CVAE-based drift indicator** will take the kth sample $[\mathbf{X}_k, \mathbf{Y}_k]$, where $k = 1, 2, 3, \ldots$, as input and output the value of loss function l_k according to Eq. (5.2).

5.3.2 Drift Analyzer

Based on the output value of **CVAE-based drift indicator**, we can determine whether concept drift happens by using the following theorem.

Theorem 5.1 The mean of L_C is stable if the concept $P(\mathbf{X}, \mathbf{Y})$ is constant.

Proof: We can get the mean of L_C, which is denoted by $E(L_C)$, through Eqs. (5.3) ~ (5.5).

$$E(L_C) = \iiint_{X,Y,z} L_C P(\mathbf{X}, \mathbf{Y}, \mathbf{z}) d\mathbf{X} d\mathbf{Y} d\mathbf{z} \tag{5.3}$$

$$= \iiint_{X,Y,z} L_C P(\mathbf{z}|\mathbf{X}, \mathbf{Y}) P(\mathbf{X}, \mathbf{Y}) d\mathbf{X} d\mathbf{Y} d\mathbf{z} \tag{5.4}$$

$$= \iiint_{X,Y,z} L_C q(\mathbf{z}|\mathbf{X}, \mathbf{Y}) P(\mathbf{X}, \mathbf{Y}) d\mathbf{X} d\mathbf{Y} d\mathbf{z} \tag{5.5}$$

As we can see in Eq. (5.5), if the concept $P(\mathbf{X}, \mathbf{Y})$ is constant, the L_C and $q(\mathbf{z}|\mathbf{X}, \mathbf{Y})$ are stable after the training process of CVAE, so $E(L_C)$ is stable. In other words, if there is a significant change in $E(L_C)$, a concept drift occurs. ∎

Suppose **CVAE-based drift indicator** has output N values since the last concept drift occurs, which is denoted as $Loss_{CVAE} = \begin{bmatrix} l_1 & l_2 & \cdots & l_N \end{bmatrix}$, where M is the size of the window in which we detect whether a concept drift occurs. The mean of loss function value of the concept before the drift happens is $E(Loss_1)$, and $E(Loss_2)$ is the mean value after concept drift occurs. According to Theorem 5.1, $E(Loss_1) \neq E(Loss_2)$, it is easy to find that Eq. (5.6) holds if a concept drift occurs.

$$\min(E(Loss_1), E(Loss_2)) < E([l_1, l_2, ..., l_N])$$
$$< \max(E(Loss_1), E(Loss_2)) \tag{5.6}$$

The changed value of current loss function is shown in Eq. (5.7).

$$\delta_N = E([l_1, l_2, ..., l_N]) - E([l_{N-M+1}, l_{N-M+2}, ... l_N]) \tag{5.7}$$

If $\delta_N \cdot \delta_{N-1} < 0$, it means that the data in the Nth window and the $(N-1)$th window no longer belong to the same concept, and the **Drift Analyzer** will generate a drift signal $s_N = 1$; otherwise, $s_N = 0$. In practice, we can predefine a small value m to improve robustness of the detection scheme. In other words, when the absolute value of δ_N is less than m, the drift signal can be ignored.

5.3.3 The Performance of CVAE-based Concept Drift Detector

In this section, artificial datasets are used to verify the performance of the proposed solution. To demonstrate the performance of the proposed CVAE-based concept drift detector, we compare it with the following three related schemes.

5.3.3.1 Comparison Drift Detectors

- The drift detector proposed in Lughofer et al. (2016) is based on Faded Page–Hinkley test (referred as to PH_test in the rest of this chapter). Similar with our proposed solution, it has limited access to class labels. The drift indicator of PH_test is based on the accuracy score of the classifier. However, the drift analysis method, i.e. Faded Page–Hinkley test, assumes that the indicator follows Gaussian distribution, which is not always realistic in many real-world settings.
- The drift detection method based on the Hoeffding's Bound (referred as to HDDM) was proposed in Frías-Blanco et al. (2015). Although the hypothesis of the HDDM has full access to class labels, to make it comparable with our proposed solution, we limit the sample rate and measure the performance of the supervised concept drift detection scheme under limited access of sample labels. We use output of **CVAE-based drift indicator** as the drift indicator of HDDM.
- A drift indicator based on Restricted Boltzmann Machine (RBM) was proposed in Jaworski et al. (2018). To compare the indicator based on other generative models such as RBM, we modify the drift analysis method proposed in Jaworski et al. (2018) and incorporate it into our method proposed in Section 5.3.2.

5.3.3.2 Experiment Settings

In this section, the well-known artificial data generator, SINE (Wang et al., 2018) is adopted. In SINE (Wang et al., 2018), each generated point has two features (x_1, x_2) and one label y. The feature is uniformly distributed in [0, 1]. Starting from the first data, a concept drift occurs every 100 data. A total of 99 drifts are generated in the artificial dataset. To measure the performance of the proposed solution in the context of gradual drift in the concept, we generate the SINEg dataset. The details of the generated datasets are provided in Table 5.1. In this section, the hidden layer of CVAE consists of 10 neurons and the dimension of **z** is 2. To improve the robustness of the proposed method, we set the predefined value $m = 0.25$. In addition, the windows size M is set to 10. The following widely used performance metrics are considered to evaluate our proposed solution (Wang et al., 2018):

Table 5.1 Database description.

Generator	Concept	Speed	Name
SINE	Concept 1: if $x_1 < sin(x_2), y = 0$, else $y = 1$	Within one time step	SINE
	Concept 2: if $x_1 < sin(x_2), y = 1$, else $y = 0$	Within ten time steps	SINEg

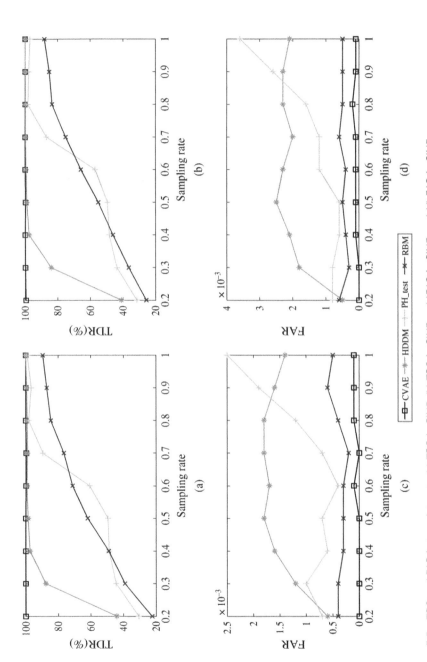

Figure 5.5 TDR and FAR in two datasets. (a) TDR in SINE, (b) TDR in SINE_g, (c)FAR in SINE_g, and (d) FAR in SINE_g

- True Detection Rate (TDR): It is the probability of detecting the true concept drift, as shown in Eq. (5.8), where N_p is the number of true concept drift, and D_p is the number of detected true drift. In this section, we define that the drift is detected as $\exists C_{end} < i \leq C'_{end}, s_i = 1$, where C_{end} and C'_{end} are the end index of the last concept and the current concept, respectively.
- False Alarm Rate (FAR): It is the probability of reporting a concept drift that does not exist, as shown in Eq. (5.9), where N_s is the number of samples, and R_F is the number of false alarms. Drift signal $s_j = 1$ is the false alarm if the corresponding drift does not exist or is repeatedly alarmed.

$$TDR = \frac{D_p}{N_p} \tag{5.8}$$

$$FAR = \frac{R_F}{N_s} \tag{5.9}$$

We use logistic regression implemented by Scipy to classify the data and sample the data stream S at a certain sampling rate r, where $0.2 \leq r \leq 1$, while detecting the drift in the data stream. For example, the Oracle only labels 20% of the data when the sampling rate is 0.2. Figure 5.5 depicts the results of TDR and FAR obtained from our proposed solution (denoted by CVAE) and the three related schemes, using the two artificial datasets *SINE* and *SINEg* (see Table 5.1). It can be seen from Figure 5.5(a) and (b), when the data sampling rate is low (such as 0.2), the TDR of the RBM and PH_test are much lower than the drift detector based on CVAE. The main reason for this phenomenon is that the drift indicator based on the loss value of CVAE is more sensitive to the changes of concept. As shown in Figure 5.5, detector based on CVAE can find all drifts with only 20% labels.

In addition, as shown in Figure 5.5(c) and (d), the FAR of CVAE is much lower than HDDM and PH_test, because the proposed drift analyzer uses a predefined value m to improve the robustness of CVAE-based detector, i.e. it will ignore the drift signal when the change of indicator is less than m.

5.4 Deployment and Experiment in Real Networks

In this section, we systematically describe the deployment methods of data collection, feature extraction, and other steps in the field of network flow recognition and the results of concept drift detection.

5.4.1 Data Collection and Feature Extraction

In order to collect the network traffic data, we deploy the network topology shown in Figure 5.6. As show in the figure, we generate network traffic in our server. In

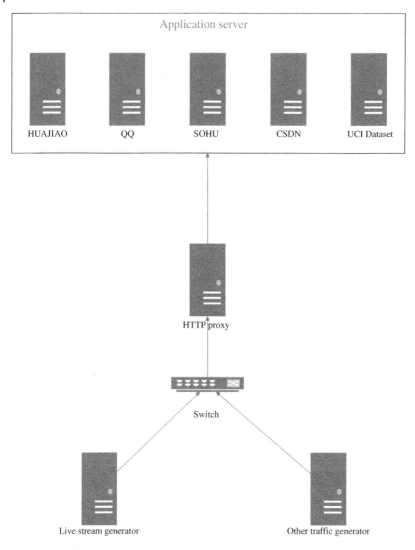

Figure 5.6 The network topology in experiments.

order to generate live stream traffic, we use streamlink to download live stream on Huajiao[1]. In order to generate other traffic, we download data from https://www.qq.com/, https://news.sohu.com, https://blog.csdn.net/ and http://archive.ics.uci.edu. All of them are commonly used in our network environment. All traffic between our server and application server will be forwarded through HTTP

---

1 https://www.huajiao.com/

Table 5.2 Feature selection.

Feature	Description
pkt_len_mean	Mean size of packet
fwd_pkt_len_mean	Mean size of packet in forward
bwd_pkt_len_mean	Mean size of packet in backward
flow_rate	The average rate
fwd_flow_rate	The average rate in forward
bwd_flow_rate	The average rate in backward
flow_pit	Average of packet interval time
fwd_flow_pit	Average of packet interval time in forward
bwd_flow_pit	Average of packet interval time in backward

Proxy. Then, on HTTP Proxy, we use the tcpdump to capture the traffic generated by the two servers. The extracted features are provided in Table 5.2 to form the datasets. All of these features can be generated online.

5.4.2 Data Analysis and Parameter Setting

The traffic collected between 9 a.m. and 9 p.m. is the dataset for working hours ("working dataset" for short) and the traffic collected between 9 p.m. and 9 a.m. is the dataset for after work ("relaxing dataset" for short). In addition, we further split the working dataset into two sub-datasets: the training dataset ("working-train") and the testing dataset ("working-test") with the proportion of 3:1, respectively. We use the Jensen–Shannon divergence to measure the difference of the three datasets (working-train, working-test, and relaxing dataset). The maximum value of the distribution gap between working-train and working-test is 0.0368, and the maximum value of the distribution gap between working-train and relaxing dataset is 0.4659, which means that there is a concept drift between working-train dataset and relaxing dataset.

In this scenario, we use working-train as the training dataset. The working-test, along with the relaxing dataset, is used as the testing dataset. Once the concept drift is detected, we use 2500 labeled data to train the classifier online. The hidden layer of CVAE consists of 20 neurons, and the dimension of z is 5. In addition, the windows size is $M = 20$, and we set the predefined value m to 1.

5.4.3 Result Analysis

Since there are currently no real-world datasets specifically used in the concept drift detection field, to test on the real-world datasets, the performance of the concept drift detection scheme can be indirectly affected by the accuracy of the classifier. In other words, a good concept drift detection scheme should promptly find the concept drift and let the classifier training on the data to improve the accuracy of the classifier.

We use the adaptive classifier (referred as to Online Learner in the following) as the upper limit because they directly train the data model online without concept drift detection and can obtain the most information. Further, we use the offline classifier (referred as to NoChange in the following) as the lower limit because the classifier does not perform any online training. In addition to the three comparison drift detectors illustrated in Section 5.3.3.1, to fully utilize the advantages of our solution in concept drift detection, in this section, we also compare it with the fully supervised Drift Detection Method proposed in Gama et al. (2004) (referred as to DDM in the following).

In this section, we set the sampling rate of semisupervised schemes (including CVAE-based detector, PH-test, HDDM, and RBM) to 0.2, and the sampling rate of DDM and Onliner Learner is set to 1. The performance of the classifier combined with different detectors, including our proposed detector CVAE and the other four related detectors (i.e. PH_test, DDM, HDDM, and RBM), are shown in Figure 5.7. The blue vertical line is the change point of the dataset. All detectors can find one drift in this real-world dataset. However, according to Figure 5.7, it can be seen that the classifier combined with the proposed CVAE-based detector has a higher accuracy rate than the classifier combined with other detectors, and the drift can

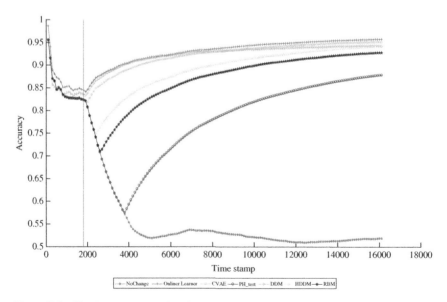

Figure 5.7 The improvement of various schemes of the classifier on real-world dataset.

be detected earlier by our proposed CVAE-based detector, with even smaller sampling rate. Therefore, we can find that the concept drift discovered by CVAE-based detectors has higher training value.

5.5 Future Research Challenges and Open Issues

5.5.1 Adaptive Threshold *m*

In this chapter, we propose a drift detection method based on the loss of CVAE. As shown in Section 5.3.2, we introduce predefined threshold m to improve robustness of the detection scheme. However, in fact, the value of m will significantly affect the TDR and FAR of the drift detector. Thus, it is important to adaptively correct the value of m according to the changing characteristics of the program running time and CVAE.

5.5.2 Computational Cost of Drift Detectors

Although, with fewer labeling cost, the TDR and FAR of the drift detector based on the CVAE are much better than the detector based on the accuracy rate (i.e. HDDM and DDM), it also requires greater computational and resource overhead. The larger number of hidden nodes in CVAE, the greater computational and resource overhead is required for the training and testing processes. Therefore, it is very important to optimize the calculation and resource management process from the aspects of architecture and model.

5.5.3 Active Learning

The concept drift detection scheme based on semisupervised hypothesis needs to seek a compromise between concept detection performance and labeling cost. Therefore, in order to be able to find the data with most labeling value, active learning, which assumes that there is a large amount of unlabeled data but only a fraction of them can be labeled by human efforts, needs to be more carefully designed so that concept drift can be found with as little labeled data as possible.

5.6 Conclusion

In this chapter, we briefly introduced the concepts of data stream processing and concept drift. In addition, we implemented a concept drift detector based on CVAE. Through experiments, we can prove that our concept drift detector is more efficient. However, because the traditional CVAE can only be trained offline and does not have the ability to train online, it is difficult to adapt to the current concept in real time. Our solution still has room for improvement.

References

Purvi Agrawal and Sriram Ganapathy. Deep variational filter learning models for speech recognition. In *ICASSP 2019 - 2019 IEEE International Conference on Acoustics, Speech and Signal Processing (ICASSP)*, pages 5731–5735, 2019. doi: 10.1109/ICASSP.2019.8682520.

Said Al-Riyami, Frans Coenen, and Alexei Lisitsa. A re-evaluation of intrusion detection accuracy: Alternative evaluation strategy. In *Proceedings of the 2018 ACM SIGSAC Conference on Computer and Communications Security*, CCS '18, page 2195-2197, New York, NY, USA, 2018. Association for Computing Machinery. ISBN 9781450356930. doi: 10.1145/3243734.3278490.

B. Charyyev and M. H. Gunes. IoT traffic flow identification using locality sensitive hashes. In *ICC 2020 - 2020 IEEE International Conference on Communications (ICC)*, 2020.

Carl Doersch. Tutorial on variational autoencoders, 2016.

Isvani Frías-Blanco, José del Campo-Ávila, Gonzalo Ramos-Jiménez, Rafael Morales-Bueno, Agustín Ortiz-Díaz, and Yailé Caballero-Mota. Online and non-parametric drift detection methods based on Hoeffding's bounds. *IEEE Transactions on Knowledge and Data Engineering*. 27:810–823, 2015. doi: 10.1109/TKDE.2014.2345382.

Joo Gama, P. Medas, G. Castillo, and P. Rodrigues. Learning with drift detection. In *Brazilian Symposium on Artificial Intelligence*, 2004.

Ahsanul Haque, Latifur Khan, and Michael Baron. SAND: Semi-supervised adaptive novel class detection and classification over data stream. In *Proceedings of the Thirtieth AAAI Conference on Artificial Intelligence*, AAAI'16, page 1652-1658. AAAI Press, 2016a.

Ahsanul Haque, Latifur Khan, Michael Baron, Bhavani Thuraisingham, and Charu Aggarwal. Efficient handling of concept drift and concept evolution over stream data. In *2016 IEEE 32nd International Conference on Data Engineering (ICDE)*, pages 481–492, 2016b. doi: 10.1109/ICDE.2016.7498264.

Hanqing Hu, Mehmed Kantardzic, and Tegjyot S. Sethi. No free lunch theorem for concept drift detection in streaming data classification: A review. *WIREs Data Mining and Knowledge Discovery*, 10(2):e1327, 2020. doi: 10.1002/widm.1327.

Maciej Jaworski, Piotr Duda, and Leszek Rutkowski. Concept drift detection in streams of labelled data using the restricted Boltzmann machine. In *2018*

International Joint Conference on Neural Networks (IJCNN), pages 1–7, 2018. doi: 10.1109/IJCNN.2018.8489053.

Youngin Kim and Cheong Park. An efficient concept drift detection method for streaming data under limited labeling. *IEICE Transactions on Information and Systems*, E100.D:2537–2546, 2017. doi: 10.1587/transinf.2017EDP7091.

V. Lemaire, C. Salperwyck, and A. Bondu. *A Survey on Supervised Classification on Data Streams. Lecture Notes in Business Information Processing*. Springer, 2015.

M. Lotfollahi, Rsh Zade, M. J. Siavoshani, and M. Saberian. Deep packet: A novel approach for encrypted traffic classification using deep learning. *Soft Computing* 24:1999–2012, 2017.

Edwin Lughofer, Eva Weigl, Wolfgang Heidl, C. Eitzinger, and Thomas Radauer. Recognizing input space and target concept drifts in data streams with scarcely labelled and unlabelled instances. *Information Sciences*, 355, 2016. doi: 10.1016/j.ins.2016.03.034.

H. Qu, J. Jiang, J. Zhao, and Y. Zhang. A semi-supervised clustering algorithm for real network traffic with concept drift. *IOP Conference Series: Materials Science and Engineering*, 569(5):052045 (9pp), 2019.

Setareh Roshan, Yoan Miche, Anton Akusok, and Amaury Lendasse. Adaptive and online network intrusion detection system using clustering and extreme learning machines. *Journal of the Franklin Institute*, 355, 2017. doi: 10.1016/j.jfranklin.2017.06.006.

Raman Singh, Harish Kumar, and R.K. Singla. An intrusion detection system using network traffic profiling and online sequential extreme learning machine. *Expert Systems with Applications*, 42(22):8609–8624, 2015. ISSN 0957-4174. doi: 10.1016/j.eswa.2015.07.015. URL https://www.sciencedirect.com/science/article/pii/S0957417415004753.

Noppayut Sriwatanasakdi, Masayuki Numao, and Ken-ichi Fukui. Concept drift detection for graph-structured classifiers under scarcity of true labels. In *2017 IEEE 29th International Conference on Tools with Artificial Intelligence (ICTAI)*, pages 461–468, 2017. doi: 10.1109/ICTAI.2017.00077.

Shuo Wang, Leandro L. Minku, and Xin Yao. A systematic study of online class imbalance learning with concept drift. *IEEE Transactions on Neural Networks and Learning Systems*, 29(10):4802–4821, 2018. doi: 10.1109/TNNLS.2017.2771290.

Z. Wang, Y. Zeng, Y. Liu, and D. Li. Deep belief network integrating improved kernel-based extreme learning machine for network intrusion detection. *IEEE Access*, PP(99):1, 2021.

Shuxiang Zhang, David Tse Jung Huang, Gillian Dobbie, and Yun Sing Koh. SLED: Semi-supervised locally-weighted ensemble detector. In *2020 IEEE 36th International Conference on Data Engineering (ICDE)*, pages 1838–1841, 2020. doi: 10.1109/ICDE48307.2020.00183.

Hao Zhang, Jie-Ling Li, Xi-Meng Liu, and Chen Dong. Multi-dimensional feature fusion and stacking ensemble mechanism for network intrusion detection. *Future Generation Computer Systems*, 122:130–143, 2021. ISSN 0167-739X. doi: 10.1016/j.future.2021.03.024. URL https://www.sciencedirect.com/science/article/pii/S0167739X2100114X.

Zhuang Zou, Jingguo Ge, Hongbo Zheng, Yulei Wu, Chunjing Han, and Zhongjiang Yao. Encrypted traffic classification with a convolutional long short-term memory neural network. In *2018 IEEE 20th International Conference on High Performance Computing and Communications; IEEE 16th International Conference on Smart City; IEEE 4th International Conference on Data Science and Systems (HPCC/ SmartCity/DSS)*, pages 329–334, 2018. doi: 10.1109/HPCC/SmartCity/ DSS.2018.00074.

6

Online Encrypted Traffic Classification Based on Lightweight Neural Networks*

6.1 Introduction

As a crucial tool for network management, traffic classification plays an important role in congestion control and quality-of-service (QoS) guarantees (Dai et al., 2019, Liu et al., 2020, Yao et al., 2020, Zou et al., 2018). Nowadays, due to growing concerns about privacy and security, many applications have adopted various encryption technologies.[1] However, it brings significant challenges for network management. For example, Voice over Internet Protocol (VoIP) applications bypass firewalls and proxies by encrypting the payload, which challenges the intrusion detection systems (Khatouni and Zincir-Heywood, 2019). Meanwhile, the nontransparency of encrypted traffic data leads to high-computational overheads for efficient traffic classification (Rezaei and Liu, 2019). Currently, heavyweight models for encrypted traffic classification cannot be applicable in real-time scenarios due to the considerable growth of encrypted network traffic.

6.2 Motivation

Existing traffic classification approaches sacrifice efficiency to guarantee the high precision of classification results. Most existing machine learning (ML) methods are based on the extraction of the hand-crafted statistical features (Niu et al., 2019, Meng et al., 2015, Alshammari and Zincir-Heywood, 2015), such as mean packet length, flow duration, and the mean interarrival time of the packet. Observing the entire or large part of a flow is necessary to obtain these statistical features. Therefore, these methods can only apply to offline scenarios. Although traffic classification methods based on deep learning (DL) can eliminate the

---

* This chapter is written based on our previous publication (Cheng et al., 2021).
1 https://letsencrypt.org/stats/#percent-pageloads.

AI and Machine Learning for Network and Security Management, First Edition.
Yulei Wu, Jingguo Ge, and Tong Li.

disadvantage of manual feature construction, some problems still exist. For example, most existing studies either use packet-level features or flow-level features, which overlook important information (i.e. these two kinds of features are not used together). Meanwhile, most existing models lack the consideration of model efficiency, where huge overhead of memory and runtime in the complex neural networks leads to high-energy consumption (Rezaei and Liu, 2019, Cheng et al., 2020, 2021).

To address the above issues, in this chapter, we propose a lightweight neural network for online-encrypted traffic classification, which takes three consecutive packets at a random location of a flow as the input. To clarify, we call the proposed model LightNet. Based on the principle "maximizing the reuse of thin modules," the features at global (flow) and local (packet) levels are extracted by using a thin module, which adopts multihead attention and 1D convolutional neural networks (1D-CNNs). Generally, global features come from the interactions between packets in a flow, and local features are included in the bytes from a few raw packets. At the global level, with the multihead attention, each packet interacts with all the other packets in one step to calculate the packet weights by multiplying matrices, greatly reducing the number of parameters and the running time. Additionally, a packet is projected into multiple subspaces, and thus different feature interactions in different subspaces can be captured in parallel by the multihead attention. Therefore, the parameters of the multihead attention mainly come from the projection matrix and are usually low. At the local level, 1D-CNN focuses on the packet bytes and is utilized to extract packet-level features, which has been proved with high effectiveness and efficiency in traffic classification (Rezaei and Liu, 2018).

The rest of this chapter is structured as follows: The preliminaries are presented in Section 6.3, and the proposed model LightNet is elaborated in Section 6.4. Section 6.5 conducts the analysis of experimental results. Section 6.6 shows the related work of the traffic classification. Finally, Section 6.7 draws conclusion of this chapter.

6.3 Preliminaries

6.3.1 Problem Definition

The problem this chapter aims to address is to classify the encrypted traffic into corresponding applications in an effective and efficient way. In this field, two types of granularity are generally used in both industry and academia, packet and flow (Zou et al., 2018). In this chapter, we choose the flow granularity, which can contain both packet and flow information. A flow refers to all packets with the same values of the quintuple,

$$[TransportLayerProtocol, SourceIP, SourcePort, DestinationIP, DestinationPort]$$
$$(6.1)$$

where source and destination can be swapped (Wang et al., 2017c). For any flow f_i in the flow set, we have

$$F = \{f_1, f_2, \dots\} \tag{6.2}$$
$$f_i = \{p_1^i, p_2^i, \dots, p_N^i\} \tag{6.3}$$

where f_i contains N packets, and p_j^i is the jth packet in f_i. Formally, a classifier is trained to recognize the category to which a flow belongs (i.e. classifier: $f_i \rightarrow$ class).

6.3.2 Packet Interaction

Efficient global information can be extracted with high-order interaction between packets (He and Chua, 2017). Given N packets as the input, the packet interaction can be defined as follows:

$$g(x_1, x_2, \dots, x_N) \tag{6.4}$$

where x_i is the unified representation of packet p_i, and $g(\cdot)$ is a nonadditive interactive function, such as outer product (Lian et al., 2018, Wang et al., 2017a) and multiplication (Rendle, 2011). For instance, $x_1 \times x_2$ is an interactive feature concerning packet x_1 and packet x_2. Traditionally, the meaningful high-order interactive features are extracted by recurrent neural network (RNN). However, it is very time-consuming to wait for the pairwise interactions between the joint packets. Besides, the limited hidden unit structure in the RNN cannot efficiently show the interpretability of the high-order features. Hence, we propose to explore an approach that can efficiently discover the meaningful high-order interactive features, and meanwhile, all packet features can be projected into many subspaces, where each packet can interact with all packets in one step.

6.4 The Proposed Lightweight Model

As shown in Figure 6.1, the proposed model will be illustrated in this section. The input of the proposed model comes from either online or offline traffic traces captured on the router. After preprocessing, N consecutive packets in a flow are captured. Then, the initial features of each packet are extracted and embedded into vectors that will be concatenated to represent the flow. The attention encoder is employed to extract the local and global features. At last, a fully connected

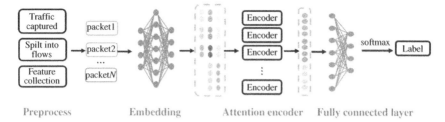

Figure 6.1 The preprocessing and architecture of LightNet. The structure of the embedding and attention encoder layers is fixed, and the structure of fully connected layer varies with different tasks.

layer with softmax is employed to output the probability distribution of labels. To enhance the stability of the lightweight model, a series of training optimization methods are adopted, including ResNet (He et al., 2016), layer normalization (Ba et al., 2016), and the learning rate warmup (He et al., 2016).

6.4.1 Preprocessing

As a crucial encryption technology for network management, the hypertext transfer protocol secure (HTTPS) over secure socket layer is based on transmission control protocol (TCP) (Naylor et al., 2014). In recent years, more and more applications use HTTPS (Liu et al., 2020). In this chapter, we will therefore classify HTTPS traffic. The three-way handshake in TCP connections is skipped because it contains less information that is useful for traffic classification (Este et al., 2009).

For the traffic data, we split it into flows according to the quintuple of a flow. The N consecutive raw packets in a flow are extracted as the only inputs for our model.

6.4.2 Feature Extraction

6.4.2.1 Embedding

The embedding layer is used to extract the shallow features of a packet. In this chapter, both flow-level and packet-level features are leveraged. As a result, the feature representation of each packet is unified in the same format, which includes multiple feature fields in our model.

For packet x_i, the original feature fields can be represented as follows:

$$x_i = \{x_{i_1}, x_{i_2}, \ldots, x_{i_M}\} \tag{6.5}$$

where M is the number of feature fields, and x_{i_j} is the feature value of the jth field. For example, x_{i_1} represents the packet position (e.g. 1, 2, $\ldots$, N), x_{i_2} could denote the packet length, and x_{i_3} could be the first 784 bytes after removing the Ethernet header. The effectiveness of the mentioned features has been validated in many works (Wang et al., 2017c), (Lotfollahi et al., 2020). It is worth noting that even for encrypted traffic, the information in the packet headers can be exploited for traffic classification (Rezaei and Liu, 2019). Not only do we leverage the header of the packet, but a portion of the packet payload is also used. For the number of packet bytes, the features are normalized to [0, 1] by dividing by 255, where the original bytes range from 0 to 255. Then, we unify these features. For a vectorial feature x_{i_j}, the dimension change can be expressed as follows:

$$e_{i_j} = U_j x_{i_j} \tag{6.6}$$

where i represents a packet and j denotes a feature field. U_j is an embedding matrix for field j, which can be predefined or trained. Otherwise, for a scalar feature x_{i_j}, the dimension change can be expressed as follows:

$$e_{i_j} = u_j x_{i_j} \tag{6.7}$$

where u_j is an embedding vector for field j. The above processing applies to all feature fields in each packet. It is worth noting that both parameters U_j and u_j are trainable.

Then, the vectoral and scalar features are transformed into a unified representation, and the packet vector e_i (take packet i as an example) can be represented as follows:

$$e_i = W_{map}[e_{i_1}, e_{i_2}, \dots, e_{i_M}] \tag{6.8}$$

where $[e_{i_1}, e_{i_2}, \dots, e_{i_M}] \in \mathbb{R}^m$ is the result of concatenating all feature fields and $W_{map} \in \mathbb{R}^{d \times m}$ is the mapping matrix. Therefore, the packet can be expressed as a vector of d dimensions. The flow can be represented as a matrix with a shape of $N \times d$ by stacking the packet vectors, where N is the number of packets in a flow.

6.4.2.2 Attention Encoder

The attention encoder is designed to extract packet-level and flow-level features at a deeper level. Inspired by the literature (Vaswani et al., 2017), we apply thin modules with multihead attention mechanism and 1D-CNN feed-forward layers. Specifically, in our model, the thin module is reused T times to model the T-order interactions between the packets, and the number of parameters of the model is significantly reduced.

For the attention encoder, four lines of works are contained (see Figure 6.2): (i) multihead attention, (ii) add & norm, (iii) feed-forward layer and (iv) flatten layer. In what follows, the detailed design of each component will be explained.

Multihead Attention The multihead attention block is utilized to extract the flow-level features, as it can model the interactions between packets. In the field of traffic classification, multihead attention has not been verified for its effectiveness. We find that it can be one of the most effective and efficient blocks to

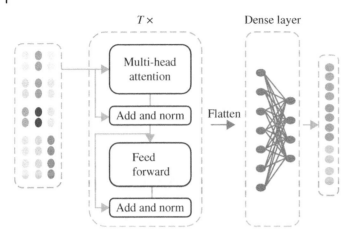

Figure 6.2 The construct of attention encoder.

extract flow-level features, as shown by the experimental results in Section 6.5.4. With the help of multihead attention, each packet is allowed to interact with all the other packets in one step as shown in (6.9), greatly reducing the number of parameters and shortening the running time. Moreover, a packet is projected into multiple subspaces, and therefore the multihead attention can capture different feature interactions in different subspaces. By stacking the module with multihead attention, we can model different orders of feature interactions.

Take packet m as an example, and we explain the extraction method for high-order features. According to the work by Vaswani et al. (2017), the attention weight under head h between packet m and k is calculated as $\alpha_{m,k}^h$ with the value of $\boldsymbol{e}_m$ and $\boldsymbol{e}_k$ and the weight of head h. Then, a temporary representation of packet m is defined as follows:

$$\tilde{\boldsymbol{e}}_m^h = \sum_{i=1}^{N} \alpha_{m,i}^h \boldsymbol{e}_i \tag{6.9}$$

by combining all the packets in the same flow with corresponding attention weights. After computing all the $\tilde{\boldsymbol{e}}_m^h$ in all heads, the packet vector can be expressed as follows:

$$\tilde{\boldsymbol{e}}_m = Concat(\tilde{\boldsymbol{e}}_m^1, \dots, \tilde{\boldsymbol{e}}_m^H) \tag{6.10}$$

where H is the number of heads.

Remarkably, the computation of all the heads is parallelized, providing a benefit to the model running speed.

Add & Norm This layer is designed to speed up the training and prevent network degradation of the model. The add & norm module includes residual network (ResNet) and layer normalization, where "add" corresponds to ResNet and "norm" corresponds to layer normalization.

Expressed as $y = F(x) + x$, a ResNet block can prevent network degradation with few parameters. After the multihead attention and feed-forward layer, we add a standard ResNet to save the raw and previously learned information.

Moreover, layer normalization is a technique to normalize the distributions of intermediate layers, which enables smoother gradients, faster training, and better generalization accuracy (Xu et al., 2019).

Feed Forward Layer In the feed forward layer, the deployment of 1D-CNN helps to extract the packet-level features, as it focuses on a single packet. In our work, a 1D-CNN layer with kernel size 1 is applied. For each packet, the inner products with each kernel constitute the deeper representation of the packet.

The combination of the three modules above (i.e. multihead attention, add & norm, and feed-forward) makes up the loop block as shown in Figure 6.2, with consistent dimensions of input and output.

Flatten Layer In the flatten layer, the final vector of the flows is integrated. All the packet vectors e_i of the flow f are concatenated into the flatten vector E_f to represent the flow f, shown in (6.11).

$$E_f = Concat(e_1, \ldots, e_N) \tag{6.11}$$

6.4.2.3 Fully Connected Layer
Fully connected layer with softmax function converts the flow feature E_f into the probability distribution of labels. Finally, we choose the label with maximum probability as the output label.

6.5 Case Study

6.5.1 Evaluation Metrics

To evaluate the effectiveness of the proposed model, we adopt four well-known metrics, namely accuracy, precision, recall, and F1-score. *Accuracy* represents the proportion of correctly classified flows. With respect to the other three metrics, we obtain the true positive (TP), false positive (FP), and false negative (FN) by comparing the output classification results with the labeled ground truth. Take class i as an example, the information above can be used to calculate the index of $Precision_i$, $Recall_i$, and $F1$-$score_i$ as Eqs. (6.12)–(6.14) show. The *Precision*, *Recall*, and *F1-score* can be obtained by averaging the corresponding metrics of each class.

$$Precision_i = \frac{TP_i}{TP_i + FP_i} \tag{6.12}$$

$$Recall_i = \frac{TP_i}{TP_i + FN_i} \tag{6.13}$$

$$F1\text{-}score_i = \frac{2 \times Precision_i \times Recall_i}{Precision_i \times Recall_i} \tag{6.14}$$

Additionally, to evaluate the efficiency of LightNet, we measure the training time and testing time per 100 batches, and the batch size is set to 32, where the word "batch" can be interpreted as a set of flows processed each time.

6.5.2 Baselines

To confirm the effectiveness of our model, we compare the model with the following baselines in terms of accuracy, precision, recall, and F1-score. For model efficiency, our model is compared with the baseline models in terms of average training time and average testing time.

- 1D-CNN model This model was proposed in Wang et al. (2017c). This method integrated feature selection, feature extraction, and classifier into a unified end-to-end framework with 1D-CNN, intending to automatically learn the nonlinear relationship between raw input and expected output. To the best of our knowledge, it was the first time to develop an end-to-end method for encrypted traffic classification.
- CNN with LSTM model This model was introduced in Zou et al. (2018) and employed to compare the effectiveness of multihead attention and RNN for flow feature extraction. It should be noted that in Zou et al. (2018), the convolutional network was utilized to extract the packet features for a single packet. Long short-term memory (LSTM) units were trained to extract the flow features, and the model also took three consecutive packets of a flow as the input.
- Bi-GRU model with transfer learning The work was shown in Liu et al. (2020), which also utilized bidirectional gate recurrent unit (Bi-GRU) to model the packet interactions. With respect to the input, the model selected three packets in a flow, where each packet contained 900 bytes. Besides, the attention mechanism was adopted to assign weights to features according to their contributions to the classification. The Bi-GRU network in Liu et al. (2020) has been proved to be the state-of-art deep learning method for encrypted traffic classification.

6.5.3 Datasets

Two datasets are employed to validate the performance of LightNet. Dataset A contains flows in all directions (i.e. from client to server and from servers to clients). Dataset B only contains the flow from clients to servers.

- Dataset A (Shbair, 2016) was published by the University of Lorraine, constructed by crawling HTTPS websites over two weeks. The details of Dataset A are shown in Table 6.1. The dataset contains PCAP files of crawling top 779 accessed HTTPS websites by Google Chrome and Mozilla Firefox Web browsers.

Table 6.1 The details of Dataset A.

Applications	Flows	Applications	Flows
nexus.ensighten.com	7035	r.nexac.com	3699
s.amazonaws.com	4770	pixel.quantserve.com	9420
mc.yandex.ru	7443	usu.openx.net	3855
tpc.googlesyndication.com	3825	bat.bing.com	5898
t.co	3030	www.google.fr	6720
adserver.adtechus.com	3405	ads.yahoo.com	4665
pbs.twimg.com	4389	d.adroll.com	15 786
connect.facebook.net	3552	beacon.krxd.net	6084
batr.msn.com	5310	www.google-analytics.com	3285
tags.tiqcdn.com	8517	www.googletagmanager.com	3390
coupang.com	4329	statsg.doubleclick.net	3459
bam.nr-data.net	4002	ascii.jp	9132
fonts.googleapis.com	3627	sb.scorecardresearch.com	5385
dnxstfruwz.cloudfront.net	3615	fonts.gstatic.com	3987
ib.adnxs.com	6717	secure.adnxs.com	17 760
cdnjs.cloudflare.com	3690	cdn.optimizely.com	3522
www.facebook.com	5127	optimizedby.rubiconproject.com	4545
ssl.gstatic.com	6282	s.adroll.com	5265
www.livepartners.com	4557	selfrepair.mozilla.org	3195
googleadsg.doubleclick.net	4152	ssl.google-analytics.com	3357
www.vcommission.com	4368	scontentxx.fbcdn.net	3234
api.mixpanel.com	4995	assets.adobedtm.com	7830
www.google.com	5727	spanalytics.yahoo.com	3750
analytics.twitter.com	3405		

To simplify the training process, we remove the special characters (e.g. dashes and numbers). At last, the applications with more than 1000 flows were chosen to use in the experiment, which contains 47 classes and 84 245 flows.

- Dataset B (Liu et al., 2020) was collected by ourselves from the backbone of China Science and Technology Network (CSTNET), an Internet service provider in China. This dataset only contains unidirectional traffic flows, from clients to servers. In the end, the top 16 services with the most traffic flows were selected as the experimental data, which contain more than 49K flows.

It is important to note that all the original data is raw, and it is necessary to label the data manually. To label the data, we adopt an advanced method proposed in Liu et al. (2018). The process can be summarized as (i) getting the value of server name indication (SNI), which is the domain's substring of applications, (ii) comparing the IP address resolution with the SNI field for the credibility enhancement, and (iii) discarding the flow if the SNI filed is null or the IP cannot be parsed into a domain name.

6.5.4 Evaluation on Datasets

6.5.4.1 Evaluation on Dataset A

- Effectiveness analysis

As mentioned above, a new embedding approach for packet representation is explored, which can enhance the efficiency of extracting high-order features. Both the statistical features (e.g. the packet length and packet position) and the packet byte features are embedded into a vector uniformly to represent the packet. In the three comparison baseline works, packet bytes are the only original features as the input into the model. As presented in Figure 6.3, a comparative experiment of the two embedding methods is conducted on Dataset A. The experimental results are generated from a 10-fold cross-validation. As shown in Figure 6.3a, when the embedding method we illustrated in Section 6.4.2.1 is adopted, it is obvious that our model outperforms the baseline models on all metrics. The accuracy, precision, recall, and F1-score rate reach 99.76%, 98.84%, 98.74%, and 98.79%, respectively. Improvements of 15.01%, 2.89%, and 1.38% on F1-score compared to the 1D-CNN, CNN with LSTM, and Bi-GRU models demonstrate the great performance of our model. As shown in Figure 6.3b, when only the packet bytes are embedded as the original features such as the three baseline works, the performance of all models degrades due to less information available. The experimental results show that our embedding method improves the precision of LightNet by 1.7%. To summarize, the model performs better when our proposed embedding method is applied.

The model which employs 1D-CNN to classify flows performs worst due to the oversimplified model structure, which focuses on extracting packet-level features.

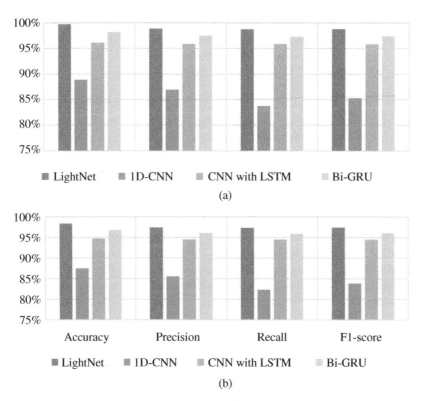

Figure 6.3 Dataset A: comparisons between LightNet and the three baseline models on accuracy, precision, recall, and F1-score. (a) LightNet with the embedding method we illustrated in Section 6.4.2.1. (b) LightNet that only embeds the packet bytes as the original features like the three baseline works.

However, this work inspires us to explore an end-to-end approach for traffic classification. The second benchmark model, CNN with LSTM, utilizes both the packet features and flow features as considered in our model, where CNN extracts the packet-level features and LSTM is used to obtain the flow-level features. Experimental results show that LSTM is not as effective as multihead attention in the extraction of flow features. This is because the multihead attention is attributed to the one-step interaction of all packets and the parallel computing of all subspaces. Owing to the use of multihead attention, a key advantage of our model is that the number of parameters and running time are significantly reduced. Therefore, the multihead attention mechanism is proved to be effective to extract features in high dimensions. Besides, our model also can benefit from the application of ResNet, layer normalization, and learning rate warm-up. The Bi-GRU model performs better than the other two baselines, which utilizes an attention mechanism to assign greater attention to more important features. Similar with the LSTM, the Bi-GRU model can only handle the interaction of two packets at a clip. As a result, it is time-consuming and inefficient to wait for the output from the previous interaction in the RNN model due to the extra time overheads required.

- Efficiency analysis

To improve running efficiency, we adopt some principles, which can be summarized as (i) reuse of thin modules, (ii) parallel computation in multiple heads (i.e. subspaces), and (iii) multiple training optimization techniques, such as ResNet, layer normalization, and learning rate warm-up.

LightNet benefits greatly from the principles mentioned above. The number of parameters of LightNet is 1.8% of 1D-CNN, 2.7% of CNN with LSTM, and 19.8% of the Bi-GRU model. With respect to the time efficiency, training and testing time of every 100 batches are considered as metrics. The training time of LightNet is 44.0% of 1D-CNN, 5.7% of CNN with LSTM, and 33.7% of the Bi-GRU model. It should be noted that LSTM and Bi-GRU can also be conducted to extract flow-level features, but only two adjacent packets can interact at a time in LSTM, which leads to high time consumption.

6.5.4.2 Evaluation on Dataset B

To make the results more credible, we also conduct an experiment on Dataset B as we do on Dataset A, in terms of accuracy, precision, recall, and F1-score. As shown in Figure 6.4, the accuracy, precision, recall, and F1-score of LightNet reach 96.84%, 95.98%, 95.53% and 95.75%, respectively. Improvements of 10.22%, 3.85%, and 1.49% on F1-score compared to the 1D-CNN, CNN with LSTM, and the Bi-GRU models give more evidence that our model performs well for encrypted traffic classification.

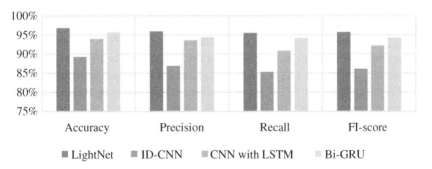

Figure 6.4 Dataset B: comparisons between LightNet and the three baseline models on accuracy, precision, recall, and F1-score.

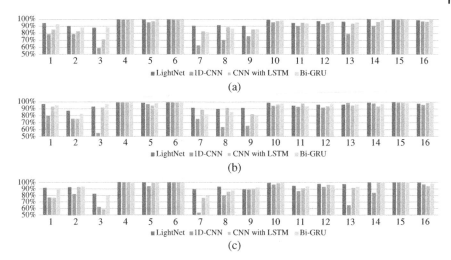

Figure 6.5 Dataset B: comparisons with the three baseline models. The values of 1–16 on the *x* axis represent the classes of "hpd.baidu.com," "wx3.sinaimg.cn," "i1.hdslb.com," "sz.btfs.mail.ftn.qq.com," "sdk1xyajs-data.xycdn.com," "tracker3.wps.cn," "ss0.bdstatic.com," "mp.weixin.qq.com," "ss0.baidu.com," "long.open.weixin.qq.com," "wenku.baidu.com," "hm.baidu.com," "s.qhupdate.com," "browserkernel.baidu.com," "clients1.google.com," "dw-online.ksosoft.com." (a) Precision. (b) Recall. (c) F1-score.

Figure 6.5 contains three subgraphs, which display the precision, recall, and F1-score values of 16 classes in Dataset B. In Figure 6.5(a), the precision values for 10 classes are greater than 95%, and the average precision of LightNet is greater than that of the other three models by 9.12%, 2.33%, and 1.56%, respectively. As shown in Figure 6.5b, for the class "s.qhupdate.com," LightNet achieves a recall of 96.89%, with improvements of 17.81%, 3.10%, and 1.50%, respectively, compared to the other three baselines. In Figure 6.5c, the F1-scores of 5 classes are greater than 99%. However, all models perform poorly on the "i.hdslb.com," because there are only 1806 flows in this class. Through the experiment in this section, it can be concluded that for services from different providers, LightNet can achieve excellent performance.

6.6 Related Work

Our model involves three lines of works: (i) encrypted traffic classification, (ii) flow-based methods, and (iii) packet-based methods, which are introduced in this section. Meanwhile, the differences and improvements that are compared with the previous work will be summarized.

6.6.1   Encrypted Traffic Classification

Traffic classification task is to categorize the encrypted network traffic into appropriate classes. First, the target of traffic classification should be defined clearly. The general goals include QoS provisioning, intrusion detection, malware detection, resource usage planning, and so on. To meet its target, the traffic classification is usually carried out based on (i) protocols (e.g. HTTP, SSL, SMTP, DNS, or QUIC), (ii) traffic types (e.g. video, chat, or browsing), (iii) applications (e.g. Amazon, Apple, Microsoft, or Google), and (iv) websites. For all the above four cases, labeling each flow with the corresponding traffic classes is a necessity. In our work, we identify the application of the flow. Second, a large and representative dataset is required. Although a few public datasets are available for research, there is no agreed common dataset in the field of traffic classification (Rezaei and Liu, 2019).

6.6.2   Packet-Based Methods

The packet-based methods for traffic classification take the bytes of a packet as the input directly. The packet bytes include the information of the packet header and payload data. Table 6.2 shows a summary of the packet-based methods. With respect to the packet header, the information in layers 3 and 4 are useful for nonencrypted traffic (Rezaei and Liu, 2019). Before the deep learning era, fields including port number, protocol, and packet length were carefully chosen by domain experts as representative features. In some recent approaches, entire packets are taken as the input. For payload data, the information above the layer 4 header can be exploited for traffic classification. In work Lotfollahi et al. (2020), after an initial preprocessing phase, packets were fed into the model with stacked autoencoder and CNN to classify network traffic. Liang et al. (2019) proposed a deep reinforcement learning approach to solve the packet classification problem. The method in Liang et al. (2019) used succinct representations to encode state and action space, and efficiently explored candidate decision trees to optimize a global objective. Finamore et al. (2010) proposed a classification approach that leveraged the statistical characterizations of the payload by extracting payload signatures. However, the packet-based methods focus on the detailed information of a few packets and lack attention to global characteristics. In our model, both packet-level and flow-level features are considered, making the model efficient and effective.

6.6.3   Flow-Based Methods

Flow-based methods require the selection of flow features, and these features are then fed into the classifier. Table 6.2 also shows a summary of the flow-based methods. In general, there are two main classes: traditional machine learning-based and deep learning-based.

Table 6.2 A summary of existing traffic classification methods.

Ref. ID	Classifiers	Features
The packet-based method		
Zhao et al. (2019)	Autoencoder and K-means	Packet bytes
Wang (2015)	Autoencoder	Packet payload
Lotfollahi et al. (2020)	Stacked autoencoder (SAE) and CNN	Packet payload
Zhang et al. (2019)	Generative adversarial networks (GAN)	Deep embedding
Liang et al. (2019)	Reinforcement learning (RL)	Packet bytes
Finamore et al. (2010)	Kiss, a novel classification engine	Payload signatures
The flow-based method		
McGregor et al. (2004)	Expectation maximum (EM)	Packet sizes and inter-arrival time
Erman et al. (2007)	K-means	Attribute vectors
Zhu and Zheng (2019)	Support vector machine (SVM)	Packet length and TCP flags
Fu et al. (2016)	Hidden Markov models (HMMs)	Packet length and time delay
Liu et al. (2020)	Gated recurrent unit (GRU)	Sequence of packets
Wang et al. (2017c)	CNN and RNN	Sequence of packets
Yao et al. (2020)	Gaussian mixture models and HMM	Inner-packet time and packet size
Liu and Lung (2011)	Fuzzy C-means	Sequence of packets
Moore and Zuev (2005)	Naive Bayes	Session duration and TCP port
Zou et al. (2018)	CNN and LSTM	Sequence of packet

6.6.3.1 Traditional Machine Learning-Based Methods

Based on complex manual features, existing traditional machine learning-based methods for traffic classification at the flow level have their limitations. Zhu and Zheng (2019) studied the application of support vector machine (SVM) to classify the network traffic by using the packet length and TCP flags, which converted the actual problem into the high-dimensional feature space through the kernel function. Fu et al. (2016) built hidden Markov models (HMMs) to classify the services of mobile messaging Apps by jointly modeling user behavioral patterns, network characteristics, and temporal dependencies. Along this line, the authors in Fu et al. (2016) first segmented Internet traffic from traffic-flows into sessions with several dialogues in a hierarchical way, and two features including packet length and time delay are employed. According to the distribution of time and packet size, the authors in Yao et al. (2020) classified the obfuscated traffic with Gaussian mixture models and HMM, which established the connection between inner-packet time and packet size to improve the accuracy of the flow feature description. However, these classifiers have to observe the whole flow or most of the packets in a flow to obtain these features, which are more appropriate for offline classification. In this chapter, with only a few consecutive packets as the input, the proposed model can meet the real-time requirements in the field of online traffic classification.

6.6.3.2 Deep Learning-Based Methods

Deep learning methods have been widely used in traffic classification. In Liu et al. (2020), the Bi-GRU was used to extract the forward and backward features of the byte sequences in a flow. Authors in Liu et al. (2019) applied Bi-GRU to extract the hidden information in the packet length sequence. The study (Wang et al., 2017c) took a few consecutive packets as the input of 1D-CNN, which was the first work to apply the end-to-end method on the traffic classification and achieved an accuracy of 85.8%. To get spatial and temporal features, both CNN and RNN were used in Wang et al. (2017b). The study (Wang et al., 2017b) first learned the spatial features of network traffic by using deep CNN and then learned temporal features by using the recurrent network. The authors in Zou et al. (2018) proposed a model with 2D-CNN and LSTM networks, which accepts a few consecutive packets as the input. In Zou et al. (2018), CNN was used to extract the packet features for a single packet, and the LSTM network was trained to pick out the flow features based on the inputs of the packet features in a flow. As we can see above, pure CNN lacks the ability to extract interactive information, which leads to the fact that CNN often combines with RNN to extract the flow features. However, the dependencies between units in RNN make it time-consuming to wait for the output of the previous unit. In our proposed method, interactions of all packets are implemented directly by the application of multihead attention.

6.7 Conclusion

Burning requirements on the efficiency of traffic classification are put forward due to the widespread adoption of encrypted traffic. In this chapter, a lightweight model called LightNet was proposed to reduce resource and time consumption. "Maximizing the reuse of thin modules" is our design principle. A thin module has been adopted for the multihead attention and the 1D convolutional network. Attributed to the one-step interaction of all packets and the parallel computation of the multihead attention mechanism, a key advantage of LightNet is that the number of parameters and the training and testing time are significantly reduced. To improve the stability of the model, the designed network is trained with the aid of ResNet, layer normalization, and learning rate warm-up. The proposed model outperformed the state-of-the-art works based on deep learning on two datasets. The results have shown that our model has higher accuracy and running efficiency.

References

Riyad Alshammari and A. Nur Zincir-Heywood. Identification of VOIP encrypted traffic using a machine learning approach. *Journal of King Saud University-Computer and Information Sciences*, 27(1):77–92, 2015.

Jimmy Lei Ba, Jamie Ryan Kiros, and Geoffrey E. Hinton. Layer normalization. *arXiv preprint arXiv:1607.06450*, 2016.

Jin Cheng, Runkang He, Yuepeng E, Yulei Wu, Junling You, and Tong Li. Real-time encrypted traffic classification via lightweight neural networks. In *IEEE Global Communications Conference*, pages 1–6. IEEE, 2020.

Jin Cheng, Yulei Wu, Yuepeng E, Junling You, Tong Li, Hui Li, and Jingguo Ge. MATEC: A lightweight neural network for online encrypted traffic classification. *Computer Networks*, 199:108472, 2021. ISSN 1389-1286. doi: 10.1016/j.comnet .2021.108472. URL https://www.sciencedirect.com/science/article/pii/ S1389128621004217.

Hong-Ning Dai, Raymond Chi-Wing Wong, Hao Wang, Zibin Zheng, and Athanasios V. Vasilakos. Big data analytics for large-scale wireless networks: Challenges and opportunities. *ACM Computing Surveys (CSUR)*, 52(5):1–36, 2019.

Jeffrey Erman, Anirban Mahanti, Martin Arlitt, Ira Cohen, and Carey Williamson. Semi-supervised network traffic classification. In *Proceedings of the 2007 ACM SIGMETRICS International Conference on Measurement and Modeling of Computer Systems*, pages 369–370, 2007.

Alice Este, Francesco Gringoli, and Luca Salgarelli. Support vector machines for TCP traffic classification. *Computer Networks*, 53(14):2476–2490, 2009.

Alessandro Finamore, Marco Mellia, Michela Meo, and Dario Rossi. KISS: Stochastic packet inspection classifier for UDP traffic. *IEEE/ACM Transactions on Networking*, 18(5):1505–1515, 2010.

Yanjie Fu, Hui Xiong, Xinjiang Lu, Jin Yang, and Can Chen. Service usage classification with encrypted internet traffic in mobile messaging apps. *IEEE Transactions on Mobile Computing*, 15(11):2851–2864, 2016.

Xiangnan He and Tat-Seng Chua. Neural factorization machines for sparse predictive analytics. In *Proceedings of the 40th International ACM SIGIR Conference on Research and Development in Information Retrieval*, pages 355–364, 2017.

Kaiming He, Xiangyu Zhang, Shaoqing Ren, and Jian Sun. Deep residual learning for image recognition. In *Proceedings of the IEEE Conference on Computer Vision and Pattern Recognition*, pages 770–778, 2016.

Ali Safari Khatouni and Nur Zincir-Heywood. Integrating machine learning with off-the-shelf traffic flow features for http/https traffic classification. In *2019 IEEE Symposium on Computers and Communications (ISCC)*, pages 1–7. IEEE, 2019.

Jianxun Lian, Xiaohuan Zhou, Fuzheng Zhang, Zhongxia Chen, Xing Xie, and Guangzhong Sun. xDeepFM: Combining explicit and implicit feature interactions for recommender systems. In *Proceedings of the 24th ACM SIGKDD International Conference on Knowledge Discovery & Data Mining*, KDD '18, pages 1754–1763, New York, NY, USA, 2018. Association for Computing Machinery. ISBN 9781450355520. doi: 10.1145/3219819.3220023.

Eric Liang, Hang Zhu, Xin Jin, and Ion Stoica. Neural packet classification. In *Proceedings of the ACM Special Interest Group on Data Communication*, pages 256–269. ACM, 2019.

Duo Liu and Chung-Horng Lung. P2P traffic identification and optimization using fuzzy c-means clustering. In *2011 IEEE International Conference on Fuzzy Systems (FUZZ-IEEE 2011)*, pages 2245–2252. IEEE, 2011.

Chang Liu, Zigang Cao, Gang Xiong, Gaopeng Gou, Siu-Ming Yiu, and Longtao He. MaMPF: Encrypted traffic classification based on multi-attribute Markov probability fingerprints. In *2018 IEEE/ACM 26th International Symposium on Quality of Service (IWQoS)*, pages 1–10, 2018. doi: 10.1109/IWQoS.2018.8624124.

Chang Liu, Longtao He, Gang Xiong, Zigang Cao, and Zhen Li. FS-NET: A flow sequence network for encrypted traffic classification. In *IEEE INFOCOM 2019-IEEE Conference on Computer Communications*, pages 1171–1179. IEEE, 2019.

Xun Liu, Junling You, Yulei Wu, Tong Li, Liangxiong Li, Zheyuan Zhang, and Jingguo Ge. Attention-based bidirectional GRU networks for efficient https traffic classification. *Information Sciences*, 541:297–315, 2020. ISSN 0020-0255. doi: 10.1016/j.ins.2020.05.035. URL https://www.sciencedirect.com/science/article/pii/S002002552030445X.

Mohammad Lotfollahi, Mahdi Jafari Siavoshani, Ramin Shirali Hossein Zade, and Mohammmdsadegh Saberian. Deep packet: A novel approach for encrypted traffic classification using deep learning. *Soft Computing*, 24(3):1999–2012, 2020.

Anthony McGregor, Mark Hall, Perry Lorier, and James Brunskill. Flow clustering using machine learning techniques. In *International Workshop on Passive and Active Network Measurement*, pages 205–214. Springer, 2004.

Juan Meng, Longqi Yang, Yuhuan Zhou, and Zhisong Pan. Encrypted traffic identification based on sparse logistical regression and extreme learning machine. In *Proceedings of ELM-2014 Volume 2*, pages 61–70. Springer, 2015.

Andrew W. Moore and Denis Zuev. Internet traffic classification using Bayesian analysis techniques. In *Proceedings of the 2005 ACM SIGMETRICS International Conference on Measurement and Modeling of Computer Systems*, pages 50–60, 2005.

David Naylor, Alessandro Finamore, Ilias Leontiadis, Yan Grunenberger, Marco Mellia, Maurizio Munafò, Konstantina Papagiannaki, and Peter Steenkiste. The cost of the" s" in https. In *Proceedings of the 10th ACM International on Conference on Emerging Networking Experiments and Technologies*, pages 133–140, 2014.

Weina Niu, Zhongliu Zhuo, Xiaosong Zhang, Xiaojiang Du, Guowu Yang, and Mohsen Guizani. A heuristic statistical testing based approach for encrypted network traffic identification. *IEEE Transactions on Vehicular Technology*, 68(4):3843–3853, 2019.

Steffen Rendle. Factorization machines. In *IEEE International Conference on Data Mining*, pages 0–6. IEEE, 2011.

Shahbaz Rezaei and Xin Liu. How to achieve high classification accuracy with just a few labels: A semi-supervised approach using sampled packets. *arXiv preprint arXiv:1812.09761*, 2018.

Shahbaz Rezaei and Xin Liu. Deep learning for encrypted traffic classification: An overview. *IEEE Communications Magazine*, 57(5):76–81, 2019.

Wazen Shbair, Thibault Cholez, and Jerome Francois. Https websites dataset. 4http://betternet.lhs.loria.fr/datasets/https/, 2016.

Ashish Vaswani, Noam Shazeer, Niki Parmar, Jakob Uszkoreit, Llion Jones, Aidan N. Gomez, Łukasz Kaiser, and Illia Polosukhin. Attention is all you need. In *Advances in Neural Information Processing Systems*, pages 5998–6008, 2017.

Zhanyi Wang. The applications of deep learning on traffic identification. *BlackHat USA*, 24(11):1–10, 2015.

Ruoxi Wang, Bin Fu, Gang Fu, and Mingliang Wang. Deep & cross network for ad click predictions. In *Proceedings of the ADKDD'17*, pages 1–7. ACM, 2017a.

Wei Wang, Yiqiang Sheng, Jinlin Wang, Xuewen Zeng, Xiaozhou Ye, Yongzhong Huang, and Ming Zhu. HAST-IDS: Learning hierarchical spatial-temporal features using deep neural networks to improve intrusion detection. *IEEE Access*, 6:1792–1806, 2017b.

Wei Wang, Ming Zhu, Jinlin Wang, Xuewen Zeng, and Zhongzhen Yang. End-to-end encrypted traffic classification with one-dimensional convolution neural networks. In *2017 IEEE International Conference on Intelligence and Security Informatics (ISI)*, pages 43–48. IEEE, 2017c.

Jingjing Xu, Xu Sun, Zhiyuan Zhang, Guangxiang Zhao, and Junyang Lin. Understanding and improving layer normalization. In *Advances in Neural Information Processing Systems*, pages 4381–4391, 2019.

Zhongjiang Yao, Jingguo Ge, Yulei Wu, Xiaosheng Lin, Runkang He, and Yuxiang Ma. Encrypted traffic classification based on Gaussian mixture models and hidden Markov models. *Journal of Network and Computer Applications* 166, 102711, 2020.

Yongzheng Zhang, Shuyuan Zhao, and Yafei Sang. Towards unknown traffic identification using deep auto-encoder and constrained clustering. In *International Conference on Computational Science*, pages 309–322. Springer, 2019.

Shuyuan Zhao, Yongzheng Zhang, and Yafei Sang. Towards unknown traffic identification via embeddings and deep autoencoders. In *2019 26th International Conference on Telecommunications (ICT)*, pages 85–89. IEEE, 2019.

Youchan Zhu and Yi Zheng. Traffic identification and traffic analysis based on support vector machine. *Neural Computing and Applications* 32, 1–9, 2019.

Zhuang Zou, Jingguo Ge, Hongbo Zheng, Yulei Wu, Chunjing Han, and Zhongjiang Yao. Encrypted traffic classification with a convolutional long short-term memory neural network. In *2018 IEEE 20th International Conference on High Performance Computing and Communications; IEEE 16th International Conference on Smart City; IEEE 4th International Conference on Data Science and Systems (HPCC/SmartCity/DSS)*, pages 329–334. IEEE, 2018.

7

Context-Aware Learning for Robust Anomaly Detection*

7.1 Introduction

With the fast development of the Internet, a wide variety of software systems need to provide uninterrupted services (e.g. social networking and media entertainment) for users. Such systems produce logs for developers or operators to locate and diagnose system anomalies. As the scale of a system expands, a fast-growing number of logs are produced. Manually reviewing and analyzing such abundant logs have become a time-consuming and error-prone work. Many machine learning or deep learning based methods for log-based anomaly detection have been proposed (Guo et al., 2021; Sun et al., 2020; Zuo et al., 2020). However, most of them ignore the following three important problems.

First, with the system upgrade, the produced system logs will also evolve. Developers may change the logging statements in the source code, which in turn changes the output logs. As Kabinna et al. (2018) observed, around 20% ~45% of logging statements in their studied projects changed throughout their lifetime. It was reported that Google's systems have up to thousands of new log printing statements every month (Xu, 2010a). Many previous unseen logs are generated by the ever-changing logging statements. The changes of logs may be insertion, addition, deletion, and replacement of some words in the existing log statements. A possible change is illustrated in Figure 7.1. Most of existing methods of anomaly detection cannot deal with newly presented logs after the training on previous log data.

Second, in most real-world classification tasks, the collected data follow a long-tail distribution, i.e. most data belong to a few classes (Khan et al., 2016), so they belong to imbalanced data. The distribution of imbalanced data makes an anomaly classifier biased toward the majority class (i.e. normal data). This will cause an anomaly classifier to fail to detect anomalies correctly, resulting in a low

---

*This chapter is written based on our previous publication (Sun et al., 2020).

AI and Machine Learning for Network and Security Management, First Edition.
Yulei Wu, Jingguo Ge, and Tong Li.

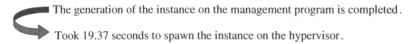

The generation of the instance on the management program is completed.

Took 19.37 seconds to spawn the instance on the hypervisor.

Figure 7.1 The example of evolution of a log.

recall rate. Therefore, imbalanced log data have a significant adverse impact on log anomaly detection.

Third, in the research of log anomaly detection, the problem of high cost on labels acquisition is usually ignored. Generally, after being trained on a large amount of training data, deep learning-based methods can obtain good prediction results. However, it will take tremendous manpower to label all the data, especially when logs can only be correctly labeled by experts (e.g. log data generated from medical applications). Therefore, if the labeled data is not sufficient, how to use part of the labeled data and the rest of the unlabeled data for training has become an urgent problem in the field of log anomaly detection.

Over the past few years, a lot of machine learning-based methods for anomaly detection have been developed (Lou et al., 2010; Xu et al., 2009; He et al., 2018a; Liang et al., 2007; Huang et al., 2017, 2018; Cao et al., 2021). They used a time window to model a log-based sequence. First, they converted a sequence into a log count vector, and then constructed both a supervised and an unsupervised methods to detect anomalies. Lou et al. (2010) proposed a method called IM (i.e. Invariant Mining), which mines in-variants from a log count vector. If a log-based sequence violates the linear relationship, it is considered an anomaly. Xu et al. (2009) put forward an unsupervised method based on Principal Component Analysis (PCA), which constructs normal and abnormal space for log-based sequences to detect anomalies. He et al. (2018a) trained a classifier based on SVM, and Liang et al. (2007) trained a classifier based on logistic regression to detect anomalies. Meng et al. (2018) used PU-Learning to solve the problem caused by insufficient labels. They transformed a traditional classifier into a PU-Learning classifier and used bag-of-words and TF-IDF to compute vector representation for each log. He et al. (2018b) combined system's KPIs with TF-IDF to compute the log representation. Then the vectors were classified by the cascade clustering, which is an iterative process. This process did not stop until all vectors were classified. Finally, the correlation analysis was carried out. The more frequent events related to KPIs occur, the more KPIs fall. That is, the larger the clusters are related to KPIs, the more KPIs fall. In recent years, log anomaly detection methods based on deep learning have developed rapidly. The input of (Zhang et al., 2016; Du et al., 2017; Vinayakumar et al., 2017) are vectors encoded by one-hot. Zhang et al. (2016) trained an long-short term memory (LSTM) classifier through keywords in logs to detect anomalies. Du et al. (2017) used LSTM to predict next log and compared the predicted log and the raw log. If there is a log that is different from the forecast log, it means that an anomaly occurs. Vinayakumar et al. (2017) trained a stacked LSTM to detect anomalies. However, above machine learning or deep learning-based methods do not utilize the semantic information of logs, and they need to change the dimension of vectors and retrain the model when new logs appear. They are not robust enough in practice to previous unseen logs. Bertero et al. (2017) used word2vec and a classic classifier (e.g. SVM or decision tree) to determine whether a log is normal or not. Brown et al. (2018) combined the attention mechanism with word2vec to detect anomalies. However, the methods proposed by Bertero et al. (2017) and Brown et al. (2018) cannot model log-based sequences. Zhang et al. (2019) proposed LogRobust, which combines word embedding and TF-IDF to express a log, and the vector representation contains the contextual information of it. Therefore, LogRobust is robust to previous unseen logs, but it is still struggling to address the two latter issues mentioned above.

For the second issue, resampling and cost-sensitive learning are conventional methods to deal with the imbalanced data. Over-sampling (Chawla et al., 2002; Han et al., 2005; He et al., 2008) and under-sampling (Prusa et al., 2015) are two different ways of resampling. Over-sampling balances the data by synthesizing new samples for a smaller number of categories; while under-sampling balances the data by deleting samples from a larger number of categories. SMOTE (Chawla et al., 2002) synthesizes data between each sample and its neighbors in a feature space. Borderline-SMOTE (Han et al., 2005) is an improved algorithm of SMOTE. Borderline-SMOTE ignore minority samples outside the boundary and use other samples to synthesize new samples. Borderline-SMOTE1 and Borderline-SMOTE2 are two different implementations of Borderline-SMOTE. They divide minority samples into three categories: "safe," "danger" and "noise," and none of them generate new samples for "danger" samples. Borderline-SMOTE ignores the distribution of the minority class when synthesizing new samples. ADASYN (He et al., 2008) is an improved algorithm of Borderline-SMOTE. First, it calculates the number of minority samples that need to be generated according to the expansion ratio set by the user, and then synthesizes new samples. Traditional optimization algorithms believe that the cost of misclassification is the same for each class, and they strive to minimize misclassification. However, in a real scene, since different categories are of different importance, their misclassification costs are also different. Cost-sensitive learning is based on the cost-sensitive theory, which believes that misclassification costs of different categories are different. It pays more attention to the category with high misclassification cost and handles imbalanced data by minimizing the total cost of misclassification.

For the last issue, a feasible solution is the semisupervised learning (SSL), which uses a few labeled data and the rest of unlabeled data to train a model. As the acquisition of unlabeled data does not consume too much manpower, any performance improvement brought by SSL is usually low-cost. Therefore, many semisupervised learning methods were proposed, and they were used in deep learning-based models. A semisupervised learning method can be essentially

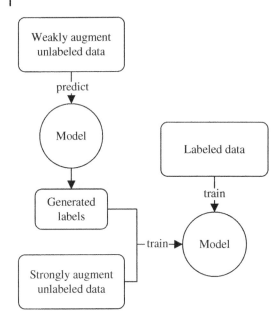

Figure 7.2 The principle of FixMatch.

regarded as generating an artificial label for each of the unlabeled samples, and then using them as part of the input. Pseudolabeling (Lee et al., 2013) regards a model's prediction as a label. Similarly, consistency regularization (Sajjadi et al., 2016; Laine and Aila, 2017) modifies the input data and uses a model to predict, so as to obtain a label generated by the model. FixMatch (Sohn et al., 2020) is a semisupervised learning algorithm proposed by Google Research in 2020. It uses a combination of pseudolabeling and consistency regularization algorithm to generate labels. The principle of FixMatch is illustrated in Figure 7.2. The training data consists of two parts (i.e. labeled data and unlabeled data), and each part includes several batches of data. FixMatch receives weakly augmented version of unlabeled data as the input data and regards model's predictions as generated labels. Then it strongly augments original unlabeled data and uses the enhanced data and generated labels to train a model. Inspired by Sajjadi et al. (2016), FixMatch does not retain generated labels until the predicted value of the model is greater than a certain threshold.

To tackle the crucial issues mentioned above and propose a more robust method, in this chapter, we mainly make the following contributions:

- We propose a context-aware approach called AllRobust for log anomaly detection. Compared to the log vectorization method adopted in LogRobust, our method has stronger capability for capturing the dynamic semantic information embedded in a log event. Word embedding contains semantic information of a word and region embedding contains semantics around the word. They are widely used in natural language processing. AllRobust utilizes both of them for each word in a log event to conduct log vectorization. Such sufficient semantic information makes AllRobust robust to newly presented logs and enables AllRobust to be trained on imbalanced log data. Different from resampling approaches and cost-sensitive learning, AllRobust handles imbalanced log data by optimizing log vectorization representation.

- FixMatch is the most advanced method of semisupervised learning applied in the field of image recognition in the past. In order to conduct training on log data that do not contain sufficient labels, we replace FixMatch's weak augmentation and advanced augmentation methods with easy data augmentation (EDA) (Wei and Zou, 2019) and back-translation accordingly because the original methods are used to augment image data instead of text data. Through semisupervised learning, AllRobust can be trained using a few of labeled data and the rest of unlabeled data.

- AllRobust parses each log into a log event and transforms each log event into a vector representation. To detect anomalies based on a single log, it utilizes the vector representation directly to train a softmax classifier. To detect the anomalies based on a log-based sequence, it adopts attention-based bidirectional long-short term memory (Bi-LSTM) neutron network to compute the vector representation for that sequence, and then utilizes the calculated representation to train a softmax classifier.

The rest of this chapter is organized as follows: In Section 7.2, we introduce log anomaly detection through an example and an architecture diagram. In Section 7.3, we elaborate our robust log anomaly detection method – AllRobust, including log parsing, log vectorization, and anomaly detection. The evaluation of our method is conducted in Section 7.4. In Section 7.5, we explain the advantages of our method compared to traditional methods and then explain the shortcomings of our method. Finally, Section 7.6 concludes this chapter.

7.2 Pronouns

Generally, logs produced by software systems contain several fixed parts (e.g. label, timestamp, component, level, and log content). Figure 7.3 shows some logs generated by a real-world system. The part of log content records run-time states and significant events of a system; therefore, we need to extract the log content for each raw log. Regular expression is a good way to do that, and it is widely used for extracting a fixed part from a piece of text. The part of log content in Figure 7.3 is marked by a red box. The log contents of the first two logs are "generating core.5307" and "generating core.7192," which are the same except for the index

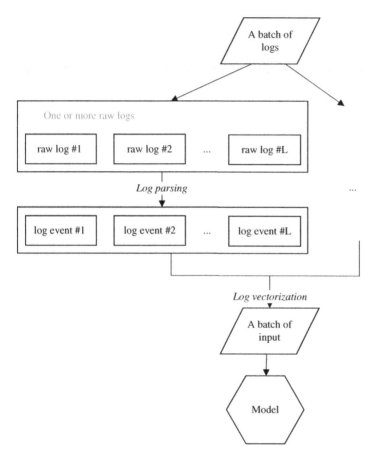

Figure 7.3 An example of logs.

Figure 7.4 The process of log anomaly detection.

of the core. The index of the core can be seen as a parameter, which may hinder automated log analysis. So we replace it with a wildcard "*," and we obtain a log event "generating core *." Similarly, if there are unimportant parameters in other logs, we replace them with wildcards "*." After replacing irrelevant parameters, we get a log event for a raw log.

Machine learning, especially deep learning has been widely used for automatic data analysis, but it only accepts vectors instead of log events as the input; so we need to transform logs into vectors. Existing methods of log anomaly detection model are a single log or a log-based sequence. For the former, we need to compute a vector for a single log event as a part of the input. For the latter, we need to model a log-based sequence and compute a vector for that sequence. The process of log anomaly detection is shown in Figure 7.4. Logs are divided into different batches for transmission and processing. After being trained, a model is able to perform anomaly detection on a single log or a log-based sequence.

7.3 The Proposed Method – AllRobust

7.3.1 Problem Statement

Either machine learning or deep learning-based models, they receive input data in batches, and they can only deal with vectors instead of texts. The following statements describe log anomaly detection for both a single log and a log-based sequence.

- Regarding the anomaly detection for a single log, we need to represent a log event with a vector and regard that vector as part of a batch input. Given a batch of b raw logs, we first need to extract b log messages, which contain run-time states and significant events. After *log parsing*, log messages are transformed into log events $[T_1, T_2, \dots T_b]$. After these log events are processed by *log vectorization*, we obtain $[V_1, V_2, \dots V_b]$, which can be used as a batch input for a model. After training, a model can conduct anomaly detection for a single log.
- Regarding anomaly detection for a log-based sequence, we need to represent N (i.e. the sequence size) log events with a vector and treat that vector as part of a batch input. Given a bath of $N \times b$ raw logs, we first use regular expressions to extract $N \times b$ log contents, which contain run-time states and significant events. After performing *log parsing*, log messages are converted to log events $[T_1, T_2, \dots T_{Nb}]$. In the *log vectorization* stage, we need to represent a log-based sequence of length N with a vector and regard that vector as part of a batch input. After being trained, a model can conduct anomaly detection for a log-based sequence.

7.3.2 Log Parsing

Logs record run-time states and important events of a software system. Therefore, conducting log analysis is important for the maintenance of a software system. A raw log consists of label, timestamp, component, level, log message and so on.

Log content is the main part of a raw log, and we need to extract it from each raw log. Log content contains many irrelevant parameters that hinder automatic log analysis. Therefore, we need to conduct log parsing, where each raw log is converted into a log event. Traditional methods of log parsing usually use regular expressions for matching. These methods are not suitable for modern software systems, and the following are the reasons.

- First, regular expressions are maintained manually, which are labor-intensive.
- Second, logs generated by modern software systems grow fast and evolve constantly. A large-scale service system can produce 50 GB logs per hour (Xu, 2010b).
- An open-source web service usually has hundreds of developers. It is difficult to write suitable regular expressions, because they do not know the intention of the developers who write log statements.

Most of the existing log parsing methods are offline and batch processing. Xu et al. (2009) proposed a method, which automatically produces regular expressions based on the source code, but the source code is often not available in practice. Over the past few years, data-driven log parsing methods (Fu et al., 2009; Makanju et al., 2012) were proposed, and they can get log events directly from original log contents. However, they are offline, and their performance is limited by the memory of a single server. Logs can only be analyzed after log collection, which is very time-consuming.

He et al. (2017) designed an online log parser named Drain, which is able to parse original log contents, in the form of a stream, accurately and efficiently. Figure 7.5

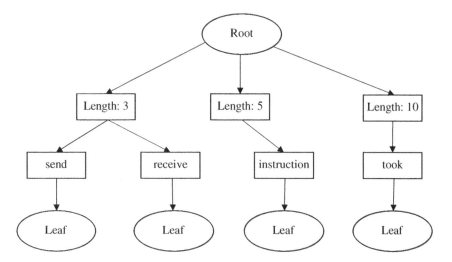

Figure 7.5 A Darin parse tree with a depth of 3.

shows a Drain parse tree with a depth of 3. The root node is at the top layer of the parse tree, and the leaf nodes are at the bottom layer. Other nodes in the tree are internal nodes. The root node and internal nodes encode specially designed rules to guide the search process. A path in the parse tree ends with a leaf node, which stores a list of log groups. A log group has two parts: log event and log ID. Log event is the template that best describes the log contents in this group, which consists of the constant part of a log content. Log ID records the IDs of log contents in this group. Zhu et al. (2019) evaluated 13 log parser using 16 datasets and found that Drain achieves the state-of-the-art performance. The working steps of Drain are as follows:

(1) First, we need to provide a regular expression for extracting each part (e.g. label, timestamp, component, level, and log content) of a raw log.
(2) Second, we need to provide regular expressions for filtering common parameters (e.g. IP address, file path) and special symbols (e.g. comma, semicolon) in a log content.
(3) Third, we need to configure *depth*, *similarity threshold*, and *maxChild*. The fixed *depth* of leaf nodes binds the number of nodes. Drain visits during a search process, which greatly improves its efficiency. The *similarity threshold* is used for log matching. If the similarity value *simValue* of a log content and a log event is greater than *similarity threshold*, the log content and the log event match successfully. The calculation of *simValue* is shown in Eq. (7.1), where $l(i)$ is i-th word in a log content, and $t(i)$ is i-th word in a log event. The length of the log message is L. The function of *eq* is defined by Eq. (7.2), and t_1 and t_2 are two words. Besides, to avoid tree branch explosion, parameter *maxChild* restricts the maximum number of children of a node.
(4) Finally, if a match is successful, Drain will scan the log content and the log event. If the word of the log event is different from the word of the log content at the same location, the word in the log content will be replaced with "*." If the log group cannot be matched, a new log group will be created for the log content, and the log content will be regarded as the log event of the new log group.

$$simValue = \frac{\sum_{i=1}^{n} eq(l(i), t(i))}{L} \tag{7.1}$$

$$eq(t_1, t_2) = \begin{cases} 1, & if\ t_1 = t_2, \\ 0, & otherwise. \end{cases} \tag{7.2}$$

The following describes log parsing through an example. At the beginning, a parse tree has only a root node. We set *similarity threshold* to 0.50. We extract the log content from a raw log whose ID is 1, and we obtain "CE sym 20, at 0x01228120, mask 0x10." After filtering unimportant parameters, we get a log event "CE sym *,

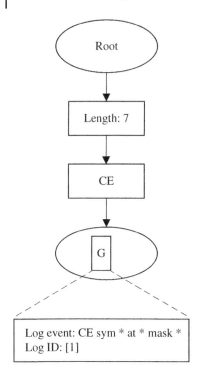

Figure 7.6 The original parse tree.

at *, mask *." The original parse tree is illustrated in Figure 7.6. Then, we extract the log content from a new raw log (its ID is 2), and we get "CE sym 5, at 0x11042a80, mask 0x04." The length of the new log content is 7. We search the existing parse tree, and we arrive at the leaf node. The leaf node contains one log group. In the same position of the new log content and existing log event in the log group, the number of the same words is 4. The calculated *simValue* 0.57 is bigger than *similarity threshold* 0.50; therefore, this match is successful. We add the ID of the new log content to Log ID and the updated parse tree is shown in Figure 7.7.

7.3.3 Log Vectorization

After log parsing, we obtain a log event for a raw log. Given a log event "data address space...............*," there are some noncharacter tokens, which make no sense for extraction of semantic information. We remove all noncharacter tokens to concentrate on dealing with meaningful tokens. There may be some tokens that follow hump nomenclature or Pascal nomenclature, and each of them needs to be split into separated words accordingly. For instance, the token "MidplaneSwitch-Controller" needs to be split into three words: "Midplane," "Switch," and "Controller." After the above treatment, a log event still belongs to text, which cannot

Figure 7.7 The updated parse tree.

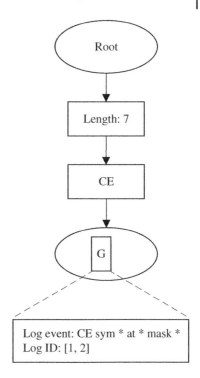

be used to train a model. Therefore, we need to get a vector from a log event or a log-based sequence.

One-hot encoding associates each word in the text with a unique integer index, and then it converts the word into a binary vector of length *n* (i.e. the size of the word set). This vector is sparse and high-dimensional. The value of the index position is 1, and the values of other positions are all 0. One-hot encoding is the most basic method to vectorize words, but it ignores the semantic information contained in a text, and the semantic information is very important for understanding a text. Word embedding is also a method of vectorization. It uses a low-dimensional, distributed vector to represent a word, which carries semantic information. Word embedding-based models can be trained in a language model or in related tasks (e.g. a classification task). Word2Vec-based methods (Mikolov et al., 2013a,b) build a language model of a central word and the words around it to obtain a word embedding matrix. Each column of the matrix corresponds to the word embedding vector of a word. Glove (Pennington et al., 2014) learns a word embedding vector based on the cooccurrence matrix of a word. FastText (Joulin et al., 2017) is a classifier that can quickly classify texts. It can also efficiently perform feature extraction. FastText averages word embedding vectors to represent a document and uses a fully connected linear layer as a classifier. A word embedding vector

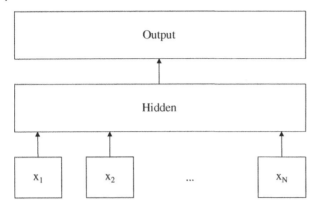

Figure 7.8 The structure of FastText.

can be obtained in a special task. In order to take advantage of the order information of words, it adds some additional hand-selected features. The input of FastText can be a word-based sequence, a sentence or a paragraph of text. FastText extracts features from the context information and converts them into a vector. The vector is passed to the hidden layer through a linear transformation, and the hidden layer is transformed again to output the probability of each category. FastText solves the problem of slow classification caused by too many categories through a multilayer classifier. Category information is stored in a tree, and using a multilayer *Softmax* classifier can greatly accelerate the classification speed. The structure of FastText is illustrated in Figure 7.8.

Johnson and Zhang (2015) used region embedding to extract the contextual information of regions in a text. Their method learns three types of region embedding vectors and uses them as additional input to convolutional neural network (CNN). Compared with the previous methods, it can significantly reduce error rate. Qiao et al. (2018) learned a tensor. Each word in a tensor has a local context unit matrix, and the region embedding corresponding to a word is generated from the embedding vector and the local context unit matrix of a word. The performance of this structure is better than that of the already very good structure, which contains 29 CNN layers. However, there is still room for improvement.

- First of all, once the embedding vector and the local context unit matrix of a word were learned, they are fixed. They can be retrieved by a word index during prediction. However, even in a different context, the resulting word embedding vector and the local context unit matrix are the same. This results in incorrect representation of regional semantic information.
- Second, the ability of this method to express semantic information is still limited. The local context unit matrix only considers a region with a fixed length, ignoring the part outside the region.

- Finally, the number of parameters learned by this method is also very large, resulting in high-spatial complexity.

The region of embedding vector of Adaptive Region Embedding (Xiang et al., 2019) is generated dynamically according to different contexts. Though the region size is fixed, its input is the entire sequence, and only parameters of filters need to be learned. Adaptive Region Embedding first extracts regional semantic information *ACU* (i.e. adaptive context unit) from a text. Then it combines word embedding to generate the final vector representation of a word. Given its great success, we utilize it to transform each log event into a fixed-dimension semantic vector. The generation process of *ACU* is shown in Figure 7.9. First we use the word embedding vectors pretrained by FastText to convert a word into a vector $wv_i \in R^h$. Second, we define a *region(c, i)* centered at position i with radius c, which contains $2c + 1$ (i.e. r) words. *ACU* is obtained by one-dimensional convolution operation *Conv(wv)*. The filter size is $r \times h$, and the number of filters is $r \times h$. We set the padding of the convolution to "same," which results in padding the input such that the output has the same length as the original input. $K_i \in R^{r \times h}$ is one of the elements of *ACU*, which contains the semantics of the region where word t_i is located. Figure 7.10 describes the generation process of e_i. $E_{i-c:i+c} \in R^{r \times h}$ is a set of

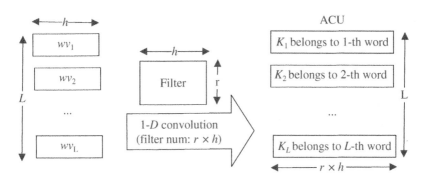

Figure 7.9 The generation process of ACU.

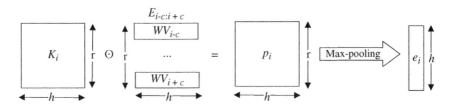

Figure 7.10 The generation process of e_i.

word embedding vectors belonging to the words around word t_i. After conducting multiplication of $E_{i-c:i+c}$ and K_i elementwise, we obtain $p_i \in R^{r \times h}$.

$$p_i = K_i \odot wv_{i+t}, \quad -c \leqslant t \leqslant c \tag{7.3}$$

Therefore, p_i contains not only the semantic information of a word but also the region semantics around that word. We get $e_i \in R^h$ by pooling p_i. The max-pooling operation makes our methods focus on more important semantic information in a region. e_i belongs to a word, which contains sufficient semantic information. Finally, we get the vector representation $V \in R^h$ for a log event by Eq. (7.4).

$$V = \sum_{i=1}^{L} e_i \tag{7.4}$$

7.3.4 Anomaly Detection

The vector representation generated by log vectorization serves as the input of a classifier. There are two typical cases of anomaly detection, one is based on a single log, and the other is based on a log-based sequence. For the former, the vector representation of a log event can serve as the input of the classifier straightforward. For the latter, the vector representations of the log events in a sequence need to be processed by an attention-based Bi-LSTM first. For both cases, a *softmax* layer is adopted to output the classification, including both binary classification (i.e. normal and abnormal classes) and multiclass classification (i.e. normal and multiple anomaly classes). The stochastic gradient descent is utilized for training. The trained AllRobust is able to detect anomalies with imbalanced log data for a single log or a log-based sequence.

The LSTM neural network is mainly used for solving the problem of gradient disappearance and gradient explosion during long sequence training. It is able to capture the contextual information of a sequence because it belongs to a class of artificial neural networks where connections between nodes form a directed graph along a temporal sequence (Zhang et al., 2019). LSTM contains an input layer, a hidden neurons layer, and an output layer. Bi-LSTM splits the hidden neurons layer into two directions: the forward pass and the backward pass for capturing sufficient information of an input log sequence. The structure of attention-based Bi-LSTM is shown in Figure 7.11. Attention mechanism (Brown et al., 2018) is able to assign different weights to different log events in the same log sequence. With the attention mechanism, Bi-LSTM can pay more attention to important log events. The computation of a is shown in 7.5, where W_i^a is the weight of the attention layer at the time step i.

$$a_i = tanh(W_i^a h_i) \tag{7.5}$$

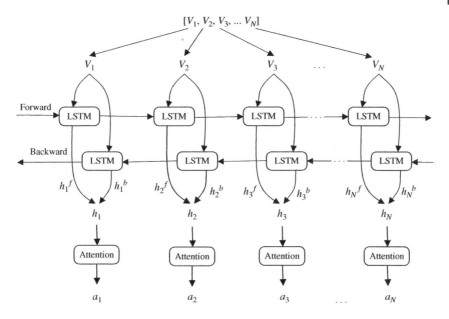

Figure 7.11 The structure of attention-based Bi-LSTM.

Finally, we sum all the hidden states with respect to all the values of a and construct a *softmax* layer to output the classification result, shown in Eq. (7.6), where W is the *softmax* layer weight and N is the total length of the log sequence.

$$pred = softmax\left(W \cdot \left(\sum_{i=0}^{i=N} a_i \cdot h_i \right) \right) \qquad (7.6)$$

7.3.4.1 Implementation of SSL

As described above, deep learning-based methods (e.g. CNN and Bi-LSTM) have been widely used in the field of log anomaly detection. However, they require more labeled data to conduct training. Since the acquisition of labels usually requires a lot of manpower, the performance improvement brought by training on large labeled data will cost a lot. Especially when the labels can only be marked by an expert, the cost will be much greater. Semisupervised learning (SSL) can use a small part of labeled data and the rest of unlabeled data to train a model.

Consistency regularization (Sajjadi et al., 2016; Laine and Aila, 2017) and pseudolabeling (Lee et al., 2013) are typical methods of SSL. Consistency regularization is based on the hypothesis that the model should output similar predictions when they were fed with different perturbed versions of the same samples. The loss function of consistency regularization is shown in Eq. (7.7), where $\alpha(\mu_i)$ is a perturbed version of sample μ_i, and function p_m outputs the prediction of a model. Both α and p_m are stochastic functions, so they output two different values. It uses squared l^2 loss of the difference between two predictions of a model as the cost function. Pseudolabeling (Lee et al., 2013) is based on the idea that we should use a model to obtain artificial labels for unlabeled data. It only keeps the unlabeled data when the prediction of a model is higher than a threshold. The cross-entropy loss function of pseudolabeling is shown in Eq. (7.8), where $\hat{q}_i = argmax(q_i)$ will produce a valid "one-hot" probability distribution, $q_i = p_m(y|u_i)$, and τ are the threshold hyperparameters.

$$\sum_{i=1}^{\mu B} \left\| p_m(y|\alpha(u_i)) - p_m(y|\alpha(u_i)) \right\|_2^2 \tag{7.7}$$

$$\frac{1}{\mu B} \sum_{i=1}^{\mu B} (max(q_i) \geq \tau) H(\hat{q}_i, q_i) \tag{7.8}$$

FixMatch uses a combination of consistency regularization and pseudolabeling to generate labels. In order to comprehensively utilize the labeled data and unlabeled data, FixMatch redefines the loss function. The loss function is the weighted sum of the supervised loss and the unsupervised loss. The supervised loss term is the deviation between a model's prediction and the labels of data. The definition of the supervised loss l_s is shown in Eq. (7.9). x_i is a labeled sample, and α is a weakly augmented version of x_i. p_i is a valid "one-hot" version of the label of x_i. Function p_m is model's prediction distribution, and H is cross-entropy function.

$$l_s = \frac{1}{S} \sum_{i=1}^{S} H(p_i, p_m(y|\alpha(x_i))) \tag{7.9}$$

The unsupervised loss term is the deviation between a model's prediction and the pseudolabels (i.e. the labels generated by the model for unlabeled data) on unlabeled data. The definition of the unsupervised loss l_u is shown in Eq. (7.10), where x_u is an unlabeled sample, and μS is the number of unlabeled data. $A(x_u)$ is an advanced-augmented version of x_u. q_u is a model's prediction distribution on a weakly augmented version of x_u, and the computation process is shown in Eq. (7.11). As shown in Eq. (7.12), $\hat{q}_u$ is a "one-hot" version of q_u. p_m is the cross-entropy of $\hat{q}_u$ and the model's prediction distribution on $A(x_u)$. Not all unlabeled data are used for training. Only when the maximum value of the prediction value q_u is greater than the threshold τ, the pseudolabel is valid, and this sample is retained. For unlabeled data, when a model is trained to a certain extent, the prediction of that model can be used as a pseudo label. At this time, the pseudo label will be very close to the label, and an unlabeled sample also has a label. Calculating the cross entropy between the prediction and the pseudolabel is equivalent to the computation of the cross entropy between the prediction and the label. Eq. (7.13) combines the supervised loss item and the unsupervised loss item, and the result will be the loss obtained during a training batch.

$$l_u = \frac{1}{\mu S} \sum_{i=1}^{\mu S} 1(max(q_u) \geq \tau) H(\hat{q}_u, p_m(y|A(x_u))) \tag{7.10}$$

$$q_u = p_m(y|\alpha(x_u)) \tag{7.11}$$

$$\hat{q}_u = argmax(q_u) \tag{7.12}$$

$$l = l_s + \lambda_u l_u \tag{7.13}$$

7.4 Experiments

In a real production environment, there are always more normal logs than abnormal logs. If a model is directly trained on imbalanced logs, the model's predictions will bias toward the majority class (i.e. the class with more logs). We deal with imbalanced data by optimizing the log vectorization. The log vectorization of All-Robust can capture not only the semantic information of each word but also the semantics of the region where each word is located. We first train AllRobust and baseline methods on imbalanced log data and test their performance. As the software upgrades, the generated logs will evolve. Then we evaluate AllRobust and baseline methods on previous unseen log data. Obtaining labels usually requires considerable labor, and the performance improvement brought by training with larger labeled data may be costly. If labels of training data are insufficient, we apply FixMatch for semisupervised learning, and the training process only requires a few labels.

7.4.1 Datasets

In this part, we introduce three public log datasets: HDFS dataset (Xu et al., 2009), BGL dataset (Oliner and Stearley, 2007), and Thunderbird dataset (Oliner and Stearley, 2007).

7.4.1.1 HDFS Dataset
HDFS dataset marks every block sequence as either "Normal" or "Anomaly." HDFS dataset consists of 11 175 629 logs collected from more than 200 Amazon EC2 nodes in 38.7 hours. There are 575 061 blocks of logs in the dataset, among which 16 838 blocks are labeled as "Anomaly" by Hadoop experts. It can be seen that each log content is related to a block in Figure 7.12. If a block is marked as "Anomaly," the log-based sequence related to the block is abnormal. Logs in

```
081109 204324 34 INFO dfs.FSNamesystem: BLOCK* NameSystem.addStoredBlock: blockMap updated: 10.251.203.80:50010 is added to blk_7888946331804732825 size 67108864
081109 204453 34 INFO dfs.FSNamesystem: BLOCK* NameSystem.addStoredBlock: blockMap updated: 10.250.11.85:50010 is added to blk_2377150260128098806 size 67108864
081109 204525 512 INFO dfs.DataNode$PacketResponder: PacketResponder 2 for block blk_572492839287299681 terminating
081109 204655 556 INFO dfs.DataNode$PacketResponder: Received block blk_3507508140051953248 of size 67108864 from /10.251.42.84
081109 204722 567 INFO dfs.DataNode$PacketResponder: Received block blk_5402003568334525940 of size 67108864 from /10.251.214.112
081109 204815 653 INFO dfs.DataNode$DataXceiver: Receiving block blk_5792489080791696128 src: /10.251.30.6:33145 dest: /10.251.30.6:50010
081109 204842 663 INFO dfs.DataNode$DataXceiver: Receiving block blk_1724757848743533110 src: /10.251.111.130:49851 dest: /10.251.111.130:50010
081109 204908 31 INFO dfs.FSNamesystem: BLOCK* NameSystem.addStoredBlock: blockMap updated: 10.251.110.8:50010 is added to blk_8015913224713045110 size 67108864
081109 204925 673 INFO dfs.DataNode$DataXceiver: Receiving block blk_-5623176793330377570 src: /10.251.75.228:53725 dest: /10.251.75.228:50010
```

Figure 7.12 An example of HDFS logs.

the HDFS system contain six parts (i.e. Date, Time, Pid, Level, Component, and Content).

7.4.1.2 BGL Dataset

BGL dataset is a multiclass dataset. It contains 4 747 963 logs generated by the Blue Gene/L supercomputer in 214.7 days. Figure 7.13 shows some logs of BGL dataset. Each label of BGL dataset is marked for a single log. Logs in BGL supercomputer contain ten parts (i.e. Label, Timestamp, Data, Node, Time, NodeRepeat, Type, Component, Level, and Content). Class is the first part of a log, and there are many types of labels. Table 7.1 shows the label correspondence of BGL dataset.

7.4.1.3 Thunderbird Dataset

Thunderbird dataset is a multiclass dataset. It contains 211 212 192 logs generated by the Thunderbird supercomputer in 244 days, which is deployed at Sandia National Labs (SNL). Figure 7.14 shows some logs of Thunderbird dataset. Each label of Thunderbird dataset is marked for a single log. Logs in Thunderbird supercomputer contain eleven parts (i.e. Label, Timestamp, Data, User, Month, Day, Time, Location, Component, PID, and Content). Class is the first part of a log, and there are many types of labels. Table 7.2 shows the label correspondence of Thunderbird dataset.

```
- 1118351098 2005.06.09 R16-M1-N2-C:J17-U01 2005-06-09-14.04.58.329635 R16-M1-N2-C:J17-U01 RAS KERNEL INFO CE sym 2, at 0x1b85f080, mask 0x02
- 1118354046 2005.06.09 R24-M1-N6-C:J07-U11 2005-06-09-14.54.06.957120 R24-M1-N6-C:J07-U11 RAS KERNEL INFO generating core.254
- 1118354070 2005.06.09 R25-M1-N8-C:J05-U11 2005-06-09-14.54.30.103580 R25-M1-N8-C:J05-U11 RAS KERNEL INFO generating core.1887
- 1118363168 2005.06.09 R16-M1-N2-C:J17-U01 2005-06-09-17.26.08.386218 R16-M1-N2-C:J17-U01 RAS KERNEL INFO CE sym 2, at 0x1b85fe80, mask 0x02
- 1118371043 2005.06.09 R11-M0-N7-C:J16-U11 2005-06-09-19.37.23.866536 R11-M0-N7-C:J16-U11 RAS KERNEL INFO generating core.8280
- 1118371064 2005.06.09 R00-M1-N6-C:J12-U01 2005-06-09-19.37.44.455502 R00-M1-N6-C:J12-U01 RAS KERNEL INFO generating core.12357
KERNDTLB 1118536327 2005.06.11 R30-M0-N9-C:J16-U01 2005-06-11-17.32.07.581048 R30-M0-N9-C:J16-U01 RAS KERNEL FATAL data TLB error interrupt
KERNDTLB 1118536959 2005.06.11 R30-M0-N9-C:J16-U01 2005-06-11-17.42.39.794840 R30-M0-N9-C:J16-U01 RAS KERNEL FATAL data TLB error interrupt
```

Figure 7.13 An example of BGL logs.

```
- 1131566502 2005.11.09 bn999 Nov 9 12:01:42 bn999/bn999 ntpd[14515]: synchronized to 10.100.18.250, stratum 5
- 1131566502 2005.11.09 tbird-sm1 Nov 9 12:01:42 src@tbird-sm1 ib_sm.x[24904]: [ib_sm_sweep.c:1455]: No topology change
- 1131566502 2005.11.09 tbird-sm1 Nov 9 12:01:42 src@tbird-sm1 ib_sm.x[24904]: [ib_sm_sweep.c:1482]: No configuration change required
- 1131566503 2005.11.09 aadmin1 Nov 9 12:01:43 src@aadmin1 dhcpd: DHCPACK on 10.100.4.251 to 00:11:43:e3:ba:c3 via eth1
- 1131566503 2005.11.09 aadmin1 Nov 9 12:01:43 src@aadmin1 dhcpd: DHCPREQUEST for 10.100.4.251 (10.100.0.250) from 00:11:43:e3:ba:c3 via eth1
- 1131566503 2005.11.09 aadmin1 Nov 9 12:01:43 src@aadmin1 xinetd[18274]: START: tftp pid=16563 from=10.100.4.251
- 1131566503 2005.11.09 aadmin2 Nov 9 12:01:43 src@aadmin2 dhcpd: DHCPREQUEST for 10.100.4.251 (10.100.0.250) from 00:11:43:e3:ba:c3 via eth1: unknown lease 10.100.4.251.
- 1131566503 2005.11.09 aadmin3 Nov 9 12:01:43 src@aadmin3 dhcpd: DHCPREQUEST for 10.100.4.251 (10.100.0.250) from 00:11:43:e3:ba:c3 via eth1: unknown lease 10.100.4.251.
- 1131566503 2005.11.09 aadmin4 Nov 9 12:01:43 src@aadmin4 dhcpd: DHCPREQUEST for 10.100.4.251 (10.100.0.250) from 00:11:43:e3:ba:c3 via eth1: unknown lease 10.100.4.251.
- 1131566503 2005.11.09 dn77 Nov 9 12:01:43 dn77/dn77 ntpd[9678]: synchronized to 10.100.30.250, stratum 3
```

Figure 7.14 An example of Thunderbird logs.

Table 7.1 Label correspondence of BGL dataset.

Class	Label	A log message
–	Normal	instruction cache parity error corrected
KERNDTLB	Hardware	data TLB error interrupt
KERNSTOR	Hardware	data storage interrupt
APPSEV	Software	ciod: Error reading … after LOGIN …
KERNMNTF	Software	Lustre mount FAILED :bglio11:block id :location
KERNTERM	Software	rts:kernelterminated for reason 1004rts: …
KERNREC	Software	Error receiving packet on tree network
APPREAD	Software	ciod:failed to read message prefix on controlstream …
KERNRTSP	Software	rtspanic! stopping execution
APPRES	Software	ciod:Error reading … after LOAD …
APPUNAV	Indeterminate	ciod:Error creating node map from file …
31 Others	Indeterminate	machine check interrupt

Table 7.2 Label correspondence of Thunderbird dataset.

Class	Label	A log message
–	Normal	session closed for user root
EXTFS	Hardware	kernel:EXT3-fserror (device sda5) …
SCSI	Hardware	kernel:scsi0(0:0):rejecting I/O to offline device
ECC	Hardware	Server Administrator:Instrumentation Service …
CHK DSK	Hardware	check-disks:[node:time], Fault Statusassert …
PBS CON	Software	pbsmom:Connection refused (111) …
CPU	Software	kernel:Losing some ticks...checking ifCPU …
PBS BFD	Software	pbsmom:Bad file descriptor (9)in tm request …
VAPI	Indeterminate	kernel:[KERNEL IB] …
MPT	Indeterminate	kernel:mptscsih:ioc0:attempting task abort! …
NMI	Indeterminate	kernel:… and confused …

7.4.2 Model Evaluation Indicators

In order to evaluate the effectiveness of our model, we compute accuracy, precision, recall, and F1-score. The calculation methods are as follows:

- Accuracy: the percentage of correctly classified samples.
- Precision: $Precision = \frac{TP}{TP+FP}$.

- Recall: $Recall = \frac{TP}{TP+FN}$.
- F1-Score: $F1\text{-}Score = \frac{2 \times Precision \times Recall}{Precision + Recall}$.

TP represents the number of abnormal logs which are detected. FP represents the number of normal logs misclassified as abnormal. FN indicates the number of abnormal logs that were misclassified as normal. For multiclass anomaly detection, we compute accuracy, macroaverage precision (i.e. precision average for all categories), macroaverage recall (i.e. recall average for all categories), and macroaverage F1-score (i.e. F1-score average for all categories) to evaluate our model.

7.4.3 Supervised Deep Learning-based Log Anomaly Detection on Imbalanced Log Data

7.4.3.1 Data Preprocessing

The same anomaly may occur on multiple nodes, or may occur multiple times on the same node. Therefore, there are a large number of duplicate logs in the BGL dataset and Thunderbird dataset. Too many duplicate logs may cause over-fitting problems. In order to filter duplicate logs, we use the log filtering algorithm proposed in Oliner and Stearley (2007) which has little impact on data distribution. The filtering algorithm is illustrated in algorithm 7.1.

Algorithm 7.1: LOGFILTER(A)

Input: A, a sequence of N unfiltered logs.

Output: a, a collection of logs after filtering.

1   $l = 0$

2   c_i `// the label of log A[i]`

3   X `// A dictionary that maps a label to the latest appearance time of the label`

4 **for** $i \leftarrow 1$ **to** N **do**

5   **if** $t_i - 1 > N$ **then**

6   clear(X)

7     $l \leftarrow t_i$

8   **if** $c_i \in X, t_i - X[c_i] < T$ **then**

9        $X[c_i] \leftarrow t_i$

10   **else**

11       $X[c_i] \leftarrow t_i$

12   add $A[i]$ to a

Table 7.3 Software and hardware environment for supervised learning experiments.

Name	Environment	Version
Operation system	Ubuntu	18.04.2
CPU model	Intel(R) Xeon(R) CPU E5-2609	v3
The number of CPUs	2	—
The number of logical CPUs	12	—
GPU model	NVIDIA GeForce GTX1060	—
GPU memory size	6GB	—
Programming language	Python	3.7.3
Deep learning	Tensorflow	2.3.1

7.4.3.2 Hyperparameters and Environmental Settings

A log-based sequence is a sample unit of HDFS dataset. A single log is a sample unit of BGL dataset and Thunderbird dataset. We use stochastic gradient descent to optimize the model, and we set decay to 0.0001, momentum to 0.9, learning rate to 0.01. We use cross entropy loss as the loss function. The training process stops after 10 epochs. In the log vectorization stage, word embedding will convert each word into a 300-dimensional vector. We set region size to 3, filter size and the number of filters to 900. We set batch size to 10. The experiment is based on Keras and runs on NVIDIA GeForce GTX1060 GPU. The hardware and software environment of the experiment is shown in Table 7.3.

7.4.3.3 Training on Multiclass Imbalanced Log Data

After being filtered, the number of logs in each category of the BGL dataset is shown in Table 7.4. There are 82 "Hardware" samples and 705 "Indeterminate" samples. The number of samples in different categories in BGL dataset are unevenly distributed, and therefore, BGL dataset belongs to multiclass imbalanced log data. Cost-sensitive learning is suitable and has been widely used for solving the issue caused by imbalanced log data. It increases the misclassification cost of the sample points in the minority class. We apply it to LogRobust and the improved method is called Cosen–LogRobust. We evaluate LogRobust,

Table 7.4 The number of logs in each category of the BGL dataset after filtering.

	Normal	Software	Hardware	Indeterminate
Training	440	473	82	705

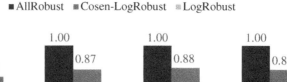

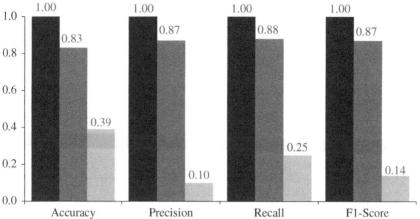

Figure 7.15 Experimental results of LogRobust, Consen–LogRobust, and AllRobust on BGL dataset.

Cosen–LogRobust, and AllRobust, and the experimental results are illustrated in Figure 7.15. The accuracy achieved by LogRobust is 0.39, while that achieved by AllContext is 1.00. AllContext can significantly reduce the adverse impact caused by multiclass imbalanced log data because p_i in the proposed log vectorization phase contains sufficient information. The accuracy, precision, recall, and F1-Score achieved by Cosen–LogRobust are all above 0.80. It shows that cost-sensitive learning effectively reduces the adverse impact caused by imbalanced log data. However, the accuracy achieved by AllContext is still 20% higher than that obtained by Cosen–LogRobust. In addition, the F1-Score achieved by AllContext is 15% higher than that obtained by Cosen–LogRobust. The results demonstrate that AllContext is more effective for anomaly detection than existing typical approaches for learning from multiclass imbalanced log data.

7.4.3.4 Training on Binary Imbalanced Log Data

We select four ratios of the number of "Normal" samples and the number of "Anomaly" samples for HDFS training dataset: 2:1, 3:1, 4:1, and 5:1. We train AllRobust and LogRobust on 1500, 3000, and 8000 samples separately. The results of AllRobust are shown in Figure 7.16. When the ratio of the number of "Normal" samples and the number of "Anomaly" samples increases from 2:1 to 5:1, the accuracy achieved by AllRobust-8000 (i.e. AllRobust trained on 8000 samples) only decreases from 0.99 to 0.94, while the accuracy achieved by LogRobust-8000 (i.e. LogRobust trained on 8000 samples) decreases from 0.89 to 0.74. The

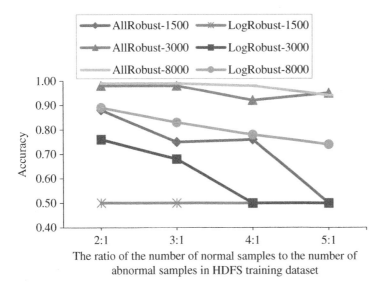

Figure 7.16 The accuracy achieved by models after training on imbalanced HDFS training set.

experimental results show that AllRobust reduces the negative impact caused by binary imbalanced log data and achieves the state-of-the-art performance.

To evaluate our method on previous unseen log data, we first remove all duplicate samples in Thunderbird dataset. Then we transform Thunderbird dataset into a binary dataset according to Table 7.2. All samples in the training dataset do not exist in the testing dataset. In Thunderbird training dataset, the ratio of the number of "Normal" samples and the number of "Anomaly" samples is 17:1. Therefore, the Thunderbird training dataset is imbalanced. As a method of resampling, SMOTE is used to solve the problem caused by imbalanced log data. We apply it to LogRobust, and it is called SMOTE-LogRobust. The experimental results are shown in Figure 7.17. Although the accuracy achieved by AllRobust and LogRobust are similar, the values of precision, recall, and F1-Score achieved by LogRobust are very low. The max pooling operation in log vectorization phase helps our method concentrate on more important semantic information, which facilitates our method to abstract the pattern for each class from previous samples. Compared to LogRobust, the accuracy, precision, recall, and F1-Score achieved by SMOTE-LogRobust are promoted significantly, because the overall performance of SMOTE-LogRobust for imbalanced log data is improved remarkably. Therefore, resampling is effective for improving the performance of LogRobust on imbalanced log data. However, the performance of AllRobust still outperforms SMOTE-LogRobust. We conclude

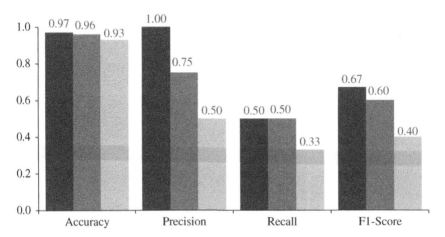

Figure 7.17 Experimental results of LogRobust, SMOTE-LogRobust, and AllRobust on Thunderbird dataset.

that AllRobust is robust to newly presented logs and achieves the state-of-the-art performance in this context.

7.4.4 Semisupervised Deep Learning-based Log Anomaly Detection on Imbalanced Log Data

Deep learning-based methods of log anomaly detection have been widely applied to the field of natural language processing. The success is attributed to their obvious scalability. After training on a large labeled log dataset, they can bring better performance. However, the acquisition of labels usually requires a lot of manpower. The performance improvement brought by the use of larger labeled data training may pay a huge cost. Especially when the labels must be marked by experts, the cost will be even greater. SSL (i.e. semisupervised learning) requires only a few labels to train a model and it is widely used in the training phase.

7.4.4.1 The Methods of Enhancing Log Data

As a state-of-the-art method of SSL, FixMatch combines consistency regularization with pseudolabeling to utilize unlabeled data. However, most of the data enhancement methods (i.e. weak enhancement and advanced enhancement) were used for image data instead of text data. Therefore, we need to adopt two different data enhancement methods for dealing with log data, which belong to text data.

EDA (Wei and Zou, 2019) is a simple enhancement method for text data. It controls the proportion of words in the sentence that are changed by setting an α parameter. We set a small value for the parameter α for EDA to achieve weak enhancement for log data. Given a log, we can perform one of the following operations:

- Synonym replacement: randomly select n nonstop words from the sentence and replace them with their corresponding synonyms. There may be multiple synonyms, and the selection of synonyms is also random.
- Random insertion: randomly select a nonstop word from the sentence, and randomly select one of its synonyms, insert it into a random position in the sentence, and repeat n times.
- Random swap: randomly swap the positions of two words in the sentence, and repeat n times.
- Random deletion: for each word, randomly remove it from the sentence with a certain probability.

Back-translation is a way to enhance text data through translation. Original text is first translated into the text corresponding to an intermediate language, and then the translated text is translated back to text corresponding to the original language. Back-translation enhances data by conducting word replacement and syntactic adjustment for the original text. Existing translation APIs are commonly used for translation. The working principle of back-translation is shown in Figure 7.18. We regard back-translation as a method of advanced augmentation. Some parameters for a translation API is shown in Table 7.5.

7.4.4.2 Anomaly Detection with a Single Log

To detect anomalies for a single log, we need to conduct semisupervised learning for a single log. We first transform BGL dataset into a binary dataset according to Table 7.1. In order to enable our method to better cope with the newly appeared

Table 7.5 Input parameters of a translation API.

Field	Type	Description
q	string	original text
from	string	original language
to	string	target language
appid	string	APP ID
salt	string	a random number
sign	string	signature

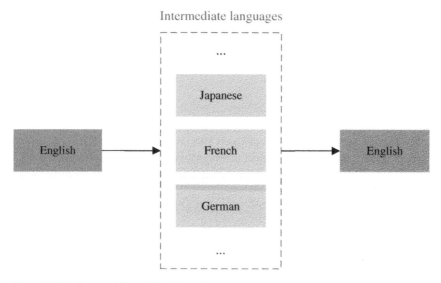

Figure 7.18 The workflow of back-translation.

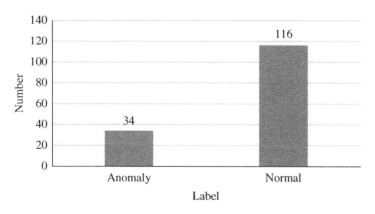

Figure 7.19 The data distribution of BGL-Raw training dataset.

log data, we filter duplicated logs for BGL dataset, and the processed dataset is named BGL-Raw. The data distribution of BGL-Raw training set is illustrated in Figure 7.19. BGL-Raw training dataset only contains 150 logs, and they are not enough to fit a deep neural network. Because EDA is simple and effective, we use it to expand both "Normal" samples and "Anomaly" samples by 10 times. The expanded dataset is called BGL-Imbalance. Because the number of "Normal" samples is 3.4 times that of "Anomaly" samples, BGL-Imbalanced training dataset is

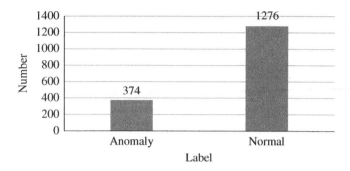

Figure 7.20 The data distribution of BGL-Imbalanced training dataset.

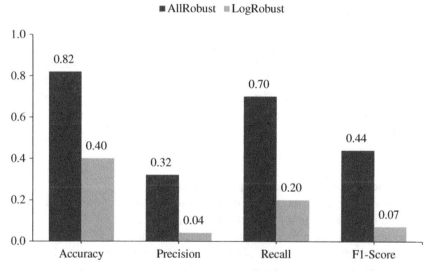

Figure 7.21 The experimental results of models after training with only 6% labels of BGL-Imbalanced training dataset.

imbalanced. The data distribution of BGL-Imbalanced training dataset is shown in Figure 7.20. We train models with 6% labels, and the predicted results are shown in Figure 7.21. The accuracy rate of AllRobust reaches 82%, which is twice than that of LogRobust. The recall of LogRobust is 20%, while the recall rate of All-Robust reaches 70%. The F1-Score of AllRobust is much higher than LogRobust, indicating that its overall performance is better than LogRobust.

In order to verify the impact of using different proportions of labels for semisupervised learning on the model's prediction results, the model was trained with

Table 7.6 The experimental results obtained from models after training with different proportions of BGL-Imbalanced labels.

Model	Accuracy			Precision			Recall			F1-Score		
	6%	24%	100%	6%	24%	100%	6%	24%	100%	6%	24%	100%
LogRobust	0.40	0.43	0.49	0.04	0.06	0.06	0.20	0.30	0.30	0.07	0.10	0.10
AllRobust	0.82	0.95	0.96	0.32	0.73	0.75	0.70	0.80	0.90	0.44	0.76	0.82

6%, 24%, and 100% labels on the BGL-Imbalanced training dataset. The experimental results are shown in Table 7.6. No matter what percentage labels are used, the accuracy achieved by AllRobust is about twice than that of LogRobust. Either using 24% or 100% labels to train LogRobust or AllRobust, there is little difference in accuracy, precision, recall, and F1-Score achieved. When the labels used in training increase from 6% to 24%, the accuracy achieved by AllRobust increases by 13%, and the F1-Score achieved by AllRobust increases by 32%. The above results show that our SSL method is effective for log data. Using only a small number of labels to conduct SSL, the prediction results are close to that achieved by supervised leaning based models.

7.4.4.3 Anomaly Detection with a Log-based Sequence

We first divide the imbalanced ratio between the number of "Normal" samples and the number of "Anomaly" samples into 2:1, 3:1, 4:1, 5:1 for HDFS training dataset. According to the previous experiments, when using 24% labels to train a model, the prediction results are good enough. Therefore, we use 24% labels to train LogRobust, AllRobust, Cosen–LogRobust (i.e. apply cost-sensitive learning algorithm to LogRobust), ADASYN-LogRobust (i.e. apply ADASYN algorithm to LogRobust) and SMOTE2-LogRobust (i.e. apply Borderline-SMOTE2 algorithm to LogRobust). The recall achieved by these models are illustrated in Figure 7.22. The recall achieved by Cosen–LogRobust is lower than that of ADASYN-LogRobust and SMOTE2-LogRobust, because cost-sensitive learning only gives different misclassification weights, while oversampling algorithms will generate new samples to balance training data. Although traditional algorithms to solve the problem of imbalanced logs are effective, the recall they achieved is lower than that of AllRobust. When the ratio increases from 2:1 to 5:1, the recall achieved by AllRobust is 97%, which only decreases by 9%. Therefore, AllRobust is robust to the imbalance ratio of log data.

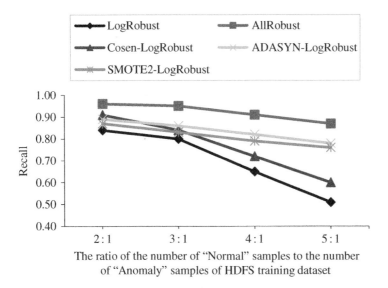

Figure 7.22 The recall achieved after training with 24% labels on HDFS training dataset

7.5 Discussion

Traditional methods of log anomaly detection (Lou et al., 2010; Xu et al., 2009; He et al., 2018a; Liang et al., 2007; Meng et al., 2018; He et al., 2018b; Zhang et al., 2016; Du et al., 2017; Vinayakumar et al., 2017) use a one-hot or a log count vector to represent a single log or a log-based sequence. They ignore the semantic information contained in logs. After training on previous log data, they perform poorly on newly appeared logs. Then, word embedding and attention mechanism-based works (Bertero et al., 2017; Brown et al., 2018; Zhang et al., 2019) were proposed. They focus on extracting semantic information from a log. LogRobust (Zhang et al., 2019) was the state-of-the-art method in the literature. Though those word embedding-based methods are robust to newly presented logs, they are still not robust to handle imbalanced log data. Training on imbalanced log data will make a classifier biased toward the majority class, and it is difficult for a classifier to learn to detect anomalies correctly. Though applying traditional over-sampling or cost-sensitive learning-based algorithms on state-of-the-art LogRobust (Zhang et al., 2019) can deal with this problem, their performance is not as good as our proposed AllRobust method. Different from them, AllRobust combines word embedding and region embedding to represent a log. Such sufficient semantic information makes AllRobust robust to imbalanced data. Deep learning-based methods of log anomaly detection need a lot of labeled log data to train. However, obtaining labels requires considerable manpower and the corresponding cost is high. We then apply FixMatch to our training phase by replacing the two data augmentation methods previously used for image data with EDA and back-translation, which are widely used for text data.

7.6 Conclusion

In this chapter, we first introduced the realistic situation of newly appeared logs in real-world systems. Most of the methods of log anomaly detection perform poorly on newly presented logs after training on previous log data. Training on imbalanced log data is easy to make a classifier biased toward categories with a large number of logs. Then we introduced typical methods to solve this problem, including cost-sensitive learning and resampling (e.g. SMOTE and ADASYN). We propose AllRobust to conduct log anomaly detection, including log parsing, log vectorization, and anomaly detection. After training, AllRobust is able to detect anomalies for both a single log and a log-based sequence. In the log vectorization phase, it utilized word embedding and region embedding to represent a log with a vector, which contains sufficient contextual information. Therefore, AllContext is robust for newly appeared logs because it can understand the context of anomalies. Different from traditional methods, AllRobust relies on such sufficient contextual information to solve the problem caused by imbalanced log data. We compared AllRobust with previous state-of-the-art method LogRobust. The accuracy of the proposed AllRobust is more than twofold of that by LogRobust. To evaluate the robustness for newly appeared logs, we assess AllContext on imbalanced Thunderbird dataset, where all samples in the testing dataset do not exist in the training dataset, and the accuracy achieved by AllRobust reaches 97%. The experiments show that AllRobust is robust to newly appeared log data after being trained on imbalanced log data.

In a real production environment, the acquisition of labels requires a lot of manpower, especially when data can only be labeled correctly by experts. FixMatch algorithm was proposed by Google Research in 2020. It uses pseudolabeling and consistency regular to generate artificial labels. It sets a threshold, and a sample is not retained until the prediction is higher than the threshold. Although effective, the data augmentation methods (i.e. weak augmentation and advanced augmentation) are used for image data instead of log data that belong to text data. We investigated existing text augmentation methods, including EDA and back-translation. We regard EDA as our weak augmentation method by setting a small α and treat back-translation as our advanced augmentation. The results show that AllRobust still performs better than traditional methods. When the ratio of the number of "Normal" samples and that of "Anomaly" samples increase from 2:1 to 5:1, the recall achieved by AllRobust only decrease by 9%. Therefore, AllRobust is also robust to data imbalance ratio.

References

Christophe Bertero, Matthieu Roy, Carla Sauvanaud, and Gilles Trédan. Experience report: Log mining using natural language processing and application to anomaly detection. In *28th IEEE International Symposium on Software Reliability Engineering, ISSRE 2017*, Toulouse, France, October 23–26, 2017, pages 351–360. IEEE Computer Society, 2017. doi: 10.1109/ISSRE.2017.43.

Andy Brown, Aaron Tuor, Brian Hutchinson, and Nicole Nichols. Recurrent neural network attention mechanisms for interpretable system log anomaly detection. In *Proceedings of the 1st Workshop on Machine Learning for Computing Systems*, MLCS'18, New York, NY, USA, 2018. Association for Computing Machinery. ISBN 9781450358651. doi: 10.1145/3217871.3217872.

Hanlin Cao, Haina Tang, Yulei Wu, Fei Wang, and Yongjun Xu. On accurate computation of trajectory similarity via single image super-resolution. In *2021 International Joint Conference on Neural Networks (IJCNN)*, pages 1–9, 2021. doi: 10.1109/IJCNN52387.2021.9533802.

Nitesh V. Chawla, Kevin W. Bowyer, Lawrence O. Hall, and W. Philip Kegelmeyer. SMOTE: Synthetic minority over-sampling technique. *Journal of Artificial Intelligence Research*, 16(1):321–357, 2002. ISSN 1076-9757.

Min Du, Feifei Li, Guineng Zheng, and Vivek Srikumar. DeepLog: Anomaly detection and diagnosis from system logs through deep learning. In *Proceedings of the 2017 ACM SIGSAC Conference on Computer and Communications Security*, CCS '17, pages 1285–1298, New York, NY, USA, 2017. Association for Computing Machinery. ISBN 9781450349468. doi: 10.1145/3133956.3134015.

Qiang Fu, Jian-Guang Lou, Yi Wang, and Jiang Li. Execution anomaly detection in distributed systems through unstructured log analysis. In *Proceedings of the 2009 9th IEEE International Conference on Data Mining*, ICDM '09, pages 149–158, USA, 2009. IEEE Computer Society. ISBN 9780769538952. doi: 10.1109/ICDM.2009.60.

Y. Guo, Y. Wu, Y. Zhu, B. Yang, and C. Han. Anomaly detection using distributed log data: A lightweight federated learning approach. In *2021 International Joint Conference on Neural Networks (IJCNN)*, 2021.

Hui Han, Wen-Yuan Wang, and Bing-Huan Mao. Borderline-SMOTE: A new over-sampling method in imbalanced data sets learning. In De-Shuang Huang, Xiao-Ping Zhang, Guang-Bin Huang, editors, *Advances in Intelligent Computing*, pages 878–887. Springer, Berlin Heidelberg, 2005. ISBN 978-3-540-31902-3.

Haibo He, Yang Bai, E. A. Garcia, and Shutao Li. ADASYN: Adaptive synthetic sampling approach for imbalanced learning. In *2008 IEEE International Joint*

Conference on Neural Networks (IEEE World Congress on Computational Intelligence), pages 1322–1328, 2008. doi: 10.1109/IJCNN.2008.4633969.

P. He, J. Zhu, Z. Zheng, and M. R. Lyu. Drain: An online log parsing approach with fixed depth tree. In *2017 IEEE International Conference on Web Services (ICWS)*, pages 33–40, 2017. doi: 10.1109/ICWS.2017.13.

P. He, J. Zhu, S. He, J. Li, and M. R. Lyu. Towards automated log parsing for large-scale log data analysis. *IEEE Transactions on Dependable and Secure Computing*, 15(6):931–944, 2018a. doi: 10.1109/TDSC.2017.2762673.

Shilin He, Qingwei Lin, Jian-Guang Lou, Hongyu Zhang, Michael R. Lyu, and Dongmei Zhang. Identifying impactful service system problems via log analysis. In *Proceedings of the 2018 26th ACM Joint Meeting on European Software Engineering Conference and Symposium on the Foundations of Software Engineering*, ESEC/FSE 2018, pages 60–70, New York, NY, USA, 2018b. Association for Computing Machinery. ISBN 9781450355735. doi: 10.1145/3236024.3236083.

Chengqiang Huang, Geyong Min, Yulei Wu, Yiming Ying, Ke Pei, and Zuochang Xiang. Time series anomaly detection for trustworthy services in cloud computing systems. *IEEE Transactions on Big Data*, 8, 60–72, 2017. doi: 10.1109/TBDATA.2017 .2711039.

Chengqiang Huang, Yulei Wu, Yuan Zuo, Ke Pei, and Geyong Min. Towards experienced anomaly detector through reinforcement learning. *Proceedings of the AAAI Conference on Artificial Intelligence*, 32(1), 2018. URL https://ojs.aaai.org/ index.php/AAAI/article/view/12130.

Rie Johnson and Tong Zhang. Semi-supervised convolutional neural networks for text categorization via region embedding. In *Advances in Neural Information Processing Systems 28: Annual Conference on Neural Information Processing Systems 2015*, December 7–12, 2015, Montreal, Quebec, Canada, pages 919–927, 2015.

Armand Joulin, Edouard Grave, Piotr Bojanowski, and Tomás Mikolov. Bag of tricks for efficient text classification. In *Proceedings of the 15th Conference of the European Chapter of the Association for Computational Linguistics, EACL 2017*, Valencia, Spain, April 3–7, 2017, Volume 2: Short Papers, pages 427–431. Association for Computational Linguistics, 2017. doi: 10.18653/v1/e17-2068.

Suhas Kabinna, Cor-Paul Bezemer, Weiyi Shang, Mark D. Syer, and Ahmed E. Hassan. Examining the stability of logging statements. *Empirical Software Engineering*, 23(1):290–333, 2018. doi: https://doi.org/10.1007/s10664-017-9518-0.

S. H. Khan, M. Hayat, M. Bennamoun, R. Togneri, and F. A. Sohel. A discriminative representation of convolutional features for indoor scene recognition. *IEEE Transactions on Image Processing*, 25 (7):3372–3383, 2016. doi: 10.1109/TIP.2016.2567076.

Samuli Laine and Timo Aila. Temporal ensembling for semi-supervised learning. In *5th International Conference on Learning Representations, ICLR 2017*, Toulon,

France, April 24–26, 2017, Conference Track Proceedings. OpenReview.net, 2017. URL https://openreview.net/forum?id=BJ6oOfqge.

Dong-Hyun Lee Pseudo-Label: The simple and efficient semi-supervised learning method for deep neural networks. In *Workshop on Challenges in Representation Learning, ICML*, volume 3, 2013.

Y. Liang, Y. Zhang, H. Xiong, and R. Sahoo. Failure prediction in IBM BlueGene/l event logs. In *7th IEEE International Conference on Data Mining (ICDM 2007)*, pages 583–588, 2007. doi: 10.1109/ICDM.2007.46.

Jian-Guang Lou, Qiang Fu, Shengqi Yang, Ye Xu, and Jiang Li. Mining invariants from console logs for system problem detection. In Paul Barham and Timothy Roscoe, editors, *2010 USENIX Annual Technical Conference, Boston, MA, USA, June 23–25, 2010*. USENIX Association, 2010.

A. Makanju, A. N. Zincir-Heywood, and E. E. Milios. A lightweight algorithm for message type extraction in system application logs. *IEEE Transactions on Knowledge and Data Engineering*, 24(11):1921–1936, 2012. doi: 10.1109/TKDE.2011.138.

W. Meng, Y. Liu, S. Zhang, D. Pei, H. Dong, L. Song, and X. Luo. Device-agnostic log anomaly classification with partial labels. In *2018 IEEE/ACM 26th International Symposium on Quality of Service (IWQoS)*, pages 1–6, 2018. doi: 10.1109/IWQoS.2018.8624141.

Tomas Mikolov, Kai Chen, Greg Corrado, and Jeffrey Dean. Efficient estimation of word representations in vector space. *arXiv preprint arXiv:1301.3781*, 2013a.

Tomas Mikolov, Ilya Sutskever, Kai Chen, Greg Corrado, and Jeffrey Dean. Distributed representations of words and phrases and their compositionality. In *Proceedings of the 26th International Conference on Neural Information Processing Systems - Volume 2*, NIPS'13, pages 3111–3119, Red Hook, NY, USA, 2013b. Curran Associates Inc.

A. Oliner and J. Stearley. What supercomputers say: A study of five system logs. In *37th Annual IEEE/IFIP International Conference on Dependable Systems and Networks (DSN'07)*, pages 575–584, 2007. doi: 10.1109/DSN.2007.103.

Jeffrey Pennington, Richard Socher, and Christopher D. Manning. GloVe: Global vectors for word representation. In *Proceedings of the 2014 Conference on Empirical Methods in Natural Language Processing, EMNLP 2014*, October 25–29, 2014, Doha, Qatar, A meeting of SIGDAT, a Special Interest Group of the ACL, pages 1532–1543. ACL, 2014. doi: 10.3115/v1/d14-1162.

J. Prusa, T. M. Khoshgoftaar, D. J. Dittman, and A. Napolitano. Using random undersampling to alleviate class imbalance on tweet sentiment data. In *2015 IEEE International Conference on Information Reuse and Integration*, pages 197–202, 2015. doi: 10.1109/IRI.2015.39.

Chao Qiao, Bo Huang, Guocheng Niu, Daren Li, Daxiang Dong, Wei He, Dianhai Yu, and Hua Wu. A new method of region embedding for text classification. In *6th*

International Conference on Learning Representations, ICLR 2018, Vancouver, BC, Canada, April 30 - May 3, 2018, Conference Track Proceedings. OpenReview.net, 2018. URL https://openreview.net/forum?id=BkSDMA36Z.

Mehdi Sajjadi, Mehran Javanmardi, and Tolga Tasdizen. Regularization with stochastic transformations and perturbations for deep semi-supervised learning. In *Proceedings of the 30th International Conference on Neural Information Processing Systems*, NIPS'16, pages 1171–1179, Red Hook, NY, USA, 2016. Curran Associates Inc. ISBN 9781510838819.

Kihyuk Sohn, David Berthelot, Nicholas Carlini, Zizhao Zhang, Han Zhang, Colin Raffel, Ekin Dogus Cubuk, Alexey Kurakin, and Chun-Liang Li. FixMatch: Simplifying semi-supervised learning with consistency and confidence. In *Advances in Neural Information Processing Systems 33: Annual Conference on Neural Information Processing Systems 2020*, NeurIPS 2020, December 6–12, 2020, virtual, 2020.

Peijie Sun, E Yuepeng, Tong Li, Yulei Wu, Jingguo Ge, Junling You, and Bingzhen Wu. Context-aware learning for anomaly detection with imbalanced log data. In *2020 IEEE 22nd International Conference on High Performance Computing and Communications; IEEE 18th International Conference on Smart City; IEEE 6th International Conference on Data Science and Systems (HPCC/SmartCity/DSS)*, pages 449–456, 2020. doi: 10.1109/HPCC-SmartCity-DSS50907.2020.00055.

R. Vinayakumar, K. P. Soman, and P. Poornachandran. Long short-term memory based operation log anomaly detection. In *2017 International Conference on Advances in Computing, Communications and Informatics (ICACCI)*, pages 236–242, 2017. doi: 10.1109/ICACCI.2017.8125846.

Jason Wei and Kai Zou. EDA: Easy data augmentation techniques for boosting performance on text classification tasks. In *Proceedings of the 2019 Conference on Empirical Methods in Natural Language Processing and the 9th International Joint Conference on Natural Language Processing (EMNLP-IJCNLP)*, pages 6382–6388, Hong Kong, China, November 2019. Association for Computational Linguistics. doi: 10.18653/v1/D19-1670.

Liuyu Xiang, Xiaoming Jin, Lan Yi, and Guiguang Ding. Adaptive region embedding for text classification. In *The 33rd AAAI Conference on Artificial Intelligence, AAAI 2019, The 31st Innovative Applications of Artificial Intelligence Conference, IAAI 2019, The 9th AAAI Symposium on Educational Advances in Artificial Intelligence, EAAI 2019*, Honolulu, Hawaii, USA, January 27 - February 1, 2019, pages 7314–7321. AAAI Press, 2019. doi: 10.1609/aaai.v33i01.33017314.

Wei Xu, Ling Huang, Armando Fox, David Patterson, and Michael I. Jordan. Detecting large-scale system problems by mining console logs. In *Proceedings of the ACM SIGOPS 22nd Symposium on Operating Systems Principles*, SOSP '09, pages 117–132, New York, NY, USA, 2009. Association for Computing Machinery. ISBN 9781605587523. doi: 10.1145/1629575.1629587.

Wei Xu. *System Problem Detection by Mining Console Logs*. PhD thesis, University of California, Berkeley, USA, 2010a. URL http://www.escholarship.org/uc/item/6jx4w194.

Wei Xu. *System Problem Detection by Mining Console Logs*. PhD thesis, University of California, Berkeley, USA, 2010b. URL http://www.escholarship.org/uc/item/6jx4w194.

Ke Zhang, Jianwu Xu, Martin Renqiang Min, Guofei Jiang, Konstantinos Pelechrinis, and Hui Zhang. Automated IT system failure prediction: A deep learning approach. In *2016 IEEE International Conference on Big Data, BigData 2016*, Washington DC, USA, December 5–8, 2016, pages 1291–1300. IEEE Computer Society, 2016. doi: 10.1109/BigData.2016.7840733.

Xu Zhang, Yong Xu, Qingwei Lin, Bo Qiao, Hongyu Zhang, Yingnong Dang, Chunyu Xie, Xinsheng Yang, Qian Cheng, Ze Li, Junjie Chen, Xiaoting He, Randolph Yao, Jian-Guang Lou, Murali Chintalapati, Furao Shen, and Dongmei Zhang. Robust log-based anomaly detection on unstable log data. In *Proceedings of the 2019 27th ACM Joint Meeting on European Software Engineering Conference and Symposium on the Foundations of Software Engineering*, ESEC/FSE 2019, pages 807–817, New York, NY, USA, 2019. Association for Computing Machinery. ISBN 9781450355728. doi: 10.1145/3338906.3338931.

J. Zhu, S. He, J. Liu, P. He, Q. Xie, Z. Zheng, and M. R. Lyu. Tools and benchmarks for automated log parsing. In *2019 IEEE/ACM 41st International Conference on Software Engineering: Software Engineering in Practice (ICSE-SEIP)*, 2019. doi: 10.1109/ICSE-SEIP.2019.00021.

Yuan Zuo, Yulei Wu, Geyong Min, Chengqiang Huang, and Ke Pei. An intelligent anomaly detection scheme for micro-services architectures with temporal and spatial data analysis. *IEEE Transactions on Cognitive Communications and Networking*, 6(2):548–561, 2020. doi: 10.1109/TCCN.2020.2966615.

8

Anomaly Classification with Unknown, Imbalanced and Few Labeled Log Data

8.1 Introduction

With the development of the Internet of Things, 5G, and cloud computing, the scale of the system size is rapidly growing. In this context, anomalies get easier to turn up and will affect the quality of services and the stability of the system. To maintain the system performance, network operators apply various anomaly classification techniques to monitor the system status, identify and locate anomalies, and then enhance the system reliability (Huang et al., 2018, Cao et al., 2021).

Effective anomaly classification methods need to rely on abundant system data. Compared with other numerical data such as system Key Performance Indicator (KPI), e.g. CPU utilization and memory utilization) (Meng et al., 2018), logs can provide more useful descriptive information for anomaly classification. For example, when the CPU utilization rises sharply, the system may be anomalous. However, the KPI value is not sufficient to determine the anomaly. Logs can therefore help find out the specific events that affect the CPU utilization. Besides, logs are natural language sequences, which can not only represent a single point anomaly but also show collective anomalies.

With the development of AI technologies and the promotion of big data platform, many log-based anomaly classification methods were developed based on machine-learning techniques (Guo et al., 2021, Sun et al., 2020, Zuo et al., 2020). Lin et al. (2016) proposed an unsupervised log-based identification method named LogCluster based on the Agglomerative Hierarchical Clustering (AHC) algorithm and applied it to the real-world online service system. Pande and Ahuja (2017) proposed word embeddings for anomaly classification (WEAC) based on the Skip-Gram (SG) and the Continuous Bag of Words (CBOW) model of the word embedding method, which is called word2Vec for anomaly classification. Meng et al. (2018) proposed LogClass, a data-driven system to detect and classify anomalies based on Positive-Unlabeled (PU) Learning and Support Vector Machines (SVM), to tackle the challenges of device-agnostic vocabulary and

AI and Machine Learning for Network and Security Management, First Edition.
Yulei Wu, Jingguo Ge, and Tong Li.

partial labels. Zhang et al. (2019) proposed LogRobust, a log analysis approach, which is robust to the unstable log data based on word embedding and Long Short-Term Memory (LSTM).

However, there are still limitations in the existing log-based anomaly classification methods. In what follows, we elaborate the limitations.

First, the limitation of the feature extraction. Some existing methods need to build a classification model using the known log events (i.e. the templates of log messages) and log sequences (i.e. a series of log events that record specific execution flows) extracted from the training dataset (Zhang et al., 2019). Some other methods need to build a word dictionary in advance, and then construct feature vectors by counting word frequency (Meng et al., 2018). They fail to work with unseen log events and log sequences. However, real-world logs are unstable, and new but similar log events and log sequences often present due to the system upgrade (Zhang et al., 2019).

Second, the limitation of the few-shot problem. Most machine learning-based anomaly classification methods rely on the large-scale, balanced, and labeled training datasets, which is hard to construct in a real-world system. On the one hand, obtaining such data in real-world systems require tremendous efforts for annotation. On the other hand, compared to the logs under normal system operations, the occurrence of anomalous logs is low. Some anomalous logs only occur a few times and are difficult to reproduce. We may face a few-shot problem (Wang et al., 2020), where each class contains only a small number of samples, which makes it difficult to start a training process for machine learning models.

Third, the limitation of the closed world assumption (Fei and Liu, 2016). Most machine-learning-based anomaly classification methods make the closed-world assumption, which focuses on designing accurate classifiers under the assumption in experimental environment. The closed-world assumption in log-based anomaly classification methods include the "closed" of data categories, data scale, and data balance. The "closed" data categories mean that all test classes are assumed to be known at training time. The "closed" data scale refers to the target system that contains sufficient training data. The "closed" data balance means that each data category in the training dataset contains a similar number of samples. However, the log-based anomaly classification is an open-world problem (Xu et al., 2019). An ideal model not only needs to face a small amount of unbalanced data but also needs to incrementally learn the unknown categories without retraining. However, supervised machine-learning models have a fixed structure and parameters. They are sensitive to data and will classify an unknown anomalous data into a wrong known category.

To address the above problems, the method proposed in this chapter called OpenLog has some exploratory work. For the limitation of the feature extraction, we use a multilevel semantic model, mining the semantic, structural, and sequential information of logs. For the limitation of the few-shot problem, we use a multitask training strategy on the auxiliary datasets obtained from other systems to enhance the performance of the classification model so that it has the ability to work on small samples. For the limitation of the closed-world assumption, we try to transform the multiclassification task into the binary-classification task of learning the depth of relationship between samples so that the model can detect and classify new categories.

We call the unbalanced data with increasing categories and few samples as "open" data and verify OpenLog using such data. We compare OpenLog with two advanced anomaly classification methods called LogRobust and LogClass based on three kinds of experiments to prove the superiority of OpenLog.

The remainder of this chapter is organized as follows: in Section 8.2, we will introduce different feature extraction methods in log analysis, few-shot problem, and strategies of few-shot learning by examples to help readers better understand these concepts. In Section 8.3, we will describe the proposed framework of Open-Log, including problem definition, data preprocessing, and the architecture of our method. In Section 8.4, we will describe our experiments in detail and analyze the results. In Section 8.5, we will discuss the shortcomings and further outlook of our proposed method. In Section 8.6, we will summarize this chapter.

8.2 Examples

8.2.1 The Feature Extraction of Log Analysis

As shown in Figures 8.1 and 8.2, logs are semistructured natural language sequences generated by logging statements and are used to describe the state and behavior of a system. A log consists of a log header and a log content. The log header is fixed and has a particular format, including timestamp, level, component, etc. The log content is a flexible text written by the developers,

Raw log

081109 205157 752 INFO dfs.DataNode$PacketRespondser: Received block blk_9212264480425680329 of size 67108864 from /10.251.123.2

Log header	Timestamp	081109 205157 752
	Level	INFO
	Component	dfs.DataNode$PacketRespondser
Log content	Description text	Received block of size from/
	variable	blk_9212264480425680329, 67108864, 10.251.123.2

Figure 8.1 The components of a Log.

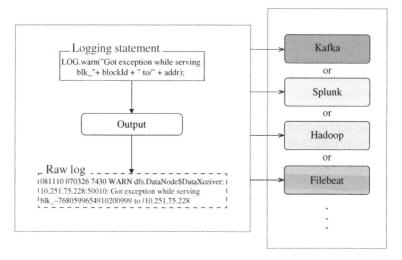

Figure 8.2 Logging and log collection.

including the description text and variables. Logs are usually collected by the big data platforms, such as Kafka[1], Splunk[2], and Hadoop[3], etc.

Different log analysis tasks have different requirements for the components of a log. For example, traditional search-based log analysis methods can focus on the specific system events they are interested in and ignore other unimportant or redundant events by searching the log level in a large-scale data (Gulcu, 2003). Most machine-learning-based log analysis methods need the description text of log content to analyze the system behavior, detect, and predict anomalies (Zhang et al., 2019). Some log analysis methods also can make full use of log information by combining description text and parameters to have a deeper investigation of the system problems (Du et al., 2017). There are also some log analysis methods that can rely on timestamp of logs to detect the sequential or quantitative anomalies of logs (Meng et al., 2019).

To adapt to different log analysis tasks, the feature extraction of logs is very important. In recent years, the common log feature extraction in log analysis can be divided into the statistical feature extraction and the semantic feature extraction.

8.2.1.1 Statistical Feature Extraction

Logs are generated by logging statements written by developers to record important system behaviors and events. The description text in the log is a fixed part,

---

1 https://kafka.apache.org
2 https://www.splunk.com
3 https://hadoop.apache.org

Figure 8.3 The process of creating event count matrices.

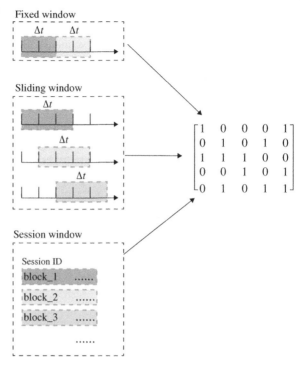

which we call log event or log template. One of the statistical feature extraction methods in log analysis is to create event count matrices (He et al., 2016). As shown in Figure 8.3, first, we need to slice the raw logs into a set of log sequences. There are three slicing strategies, including fixed window, sliding window, and the session window. Then, for each log sequence in a window, an event count vector is generated, which represents the number of occurrences of each event. All feature vectors together can form a feature matrix, that is, an event count matrix.

Another statistical feature extraction method is based on the bag-of-words expression (Wu et al., 2008). Each vector component is assigned a value related to the estimated importance (also known as weight) of words in the logs (Soucy and Mineau, 2005). Among them, the most common weighting expression is Term Frequency–Inverse Document Frequency (TF-IDF). TF indicates how often a word appears in a document. IDF shows how infrequent a word is in all documents. The mathematical expression of TF-IDF is as follows:

$$TF - IDF = tf_{i,j} \times log(\frac{N}{df_i}) \tag{8.1}$$

where $tf_{i,j}$ is the number of occurrences of the word i in document j, df_i is the number of documents containing the word i, and N is the total number of documents.

8.2.1.2 Semantic Feature Extraction

The statistical feature extraction has some limitations. For example, to create an event count matrix, we need to slice log sequence in advance and fix the number of log events; to create a weighted feature matrix, we need to build a dictionary in advance and count the word frequency. This feature extraction method will fail to work with previously unseen log events and log sequences. With the development of Natural Language Processing (NLP), the semantic feature extraction based on word embedding has been widely used. Word embedding is a feature extraction method based on extensive pretraining. The common word embedding methods include word2Vec (Mikolov et al., 2013), GloVe (Pennington et al., 2014), Bert (Vaswani et al., 2017a), just to name a few. Word embedding can provide a vector representation for each word by learning on large-scale corpus. The words with similar semantics are close to each other, while dissimilar words can be more easily differentiated. On this basis, a log is represented by the average/weighted average semantic vector of all words, or the concatenation of all word vectors of the fixed dimension, which will not change with log events and log sequences.

8.2.2 Few-Shot Problem

The target of machine learning models is to minimize the prediction error, which is the gap of the predicted value according the hypothetical function h and the true value. In general, the error can be reduced by training on a large number of examples I and learning a proper h which is shown in Figure 8.4(a), where $\hat{h}$ is a hypothetical function that minimizes the gap of the predicted value and the real value in all data, including the training data, validation data, and the testing data. h^* is a function in hypothetical space that minimizes the gap of the predicted value

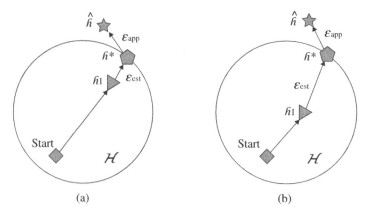

(a)   (b)

Figure 8.4 Comparison of learning with sufficient and few training samples. (a) Large I and (b) Small I.

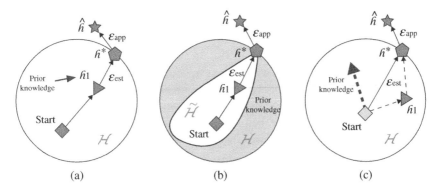

Figure 8.5 Different strategies on how few-shot learning methods can solve the few-shot problem. (a) Data, (b) Model, and (c) Algorithm.

and the real value for all data. h_I is a function in hypothetical space that minimizes the gap of the predicted value and the real value for the training data. Thus, the goal of machine-learning models is to learn h_I on the training data as close to h^* as possible. However, when the machine learning model meets the few-shot problem, the number of available examples I is small. It is then hard to learn an appropriate hypothetical function and get an accepted error as shown in Figure 8.4(b).

To address the few-shot problem caused by a small training samples, the few-shot learning based on prior knowledge is proposed. Few-shot learning usually relieves the few-shot problem from the three aspects shown in Figure 8.5, including data, model, and the algorithm (Wang et al., 2020).

- Data. The data-based strategy uses prior knowledge to augment the training data as shown in Figure 8.5(a). The common methods include data enhancement (Kozerawski and Turk, 2018, Santoro et al., 2016) and data transforming (Pfister et al., 2014, Liu et al., 2018). After enhancing the training data, standard machine learning models and algorithms can then be used with the augmented data.
- Model. The model-based strategy uses prior knowledge to constrain the complexity of hypothetical space as shown in Figure 8.5(b). For example, the gray area is not considered for optimization as they are known to be unlikely to contain the optimal hypothetical function according to prior knowledge. The common methods include multitask learning (Hu et al., 2018, Luo et al., 2017) and embedding learning (Triantafillou et al., 2017). This strategy is used in the proposed OpenLog projected in Section 8.3.
- Algorithm. The algorithm-based strategy uses prior knowledge to search for the parameters set which parameterizes the best hypothetical function as shown in Figure 8.5(c). Prior knowledge alters the search strategy by providing a good initialization or guiding the search steps.

8.3 Methodology

8.3.1 Data Preprocessing

Logs are unstructured data and have different types of components, including *texts* (constant strings), *numerical values* (variable values like IP address and port number), and other *special structures* such as the CamelCase variables (shaped like "isCommittable"). Therefore, before a log analysis, we need to perform data preprocessing to obtain the structured log information.

8.3.1.1 Log Parsing

Log parsing can convert each log message into a specific log template associated with key parameters. In a parsed log template, natural language text denotes the constant token as a log event. OpenLog adopts log parser, Drain (a fixed depth tree based online log parsing method) (He et al., 2017), to conduct log parsing. Drain is an online log parser with a fixed depth of tree, which encodes specially designed rules for parsing as shown in Figure 8.6. The process of log parsing based on the parse tree is as follows:

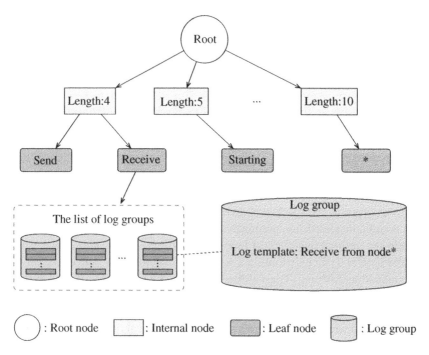

Figure 8.6 Log parsing tree-using Drain with depth of 3.

1. Log segmentation. Through the predefined regular expression, a raw log information is extracted and divided into different components, including timestamp, level, component, etc.
2. Search by length. The first-layer nodes in the parse tree represent log groups whose log messages are of different log message lengths. For example, the length of the raw log "PacketResponder for block blk_123" is 4, and it should be traversed to the internal node "Length: 4."
3. Search by preceding tokens. This step is based on the assumption that tokens in the beginning positions of a log message are more likely to be constants. For example, for log message "Receive from node 4," Drain traverses from the first-layer node "Length: 4" to the second-layer node "Receive," because the token in the first position of the log message is "Receive.".
4. Search by token similarity. Before this step, Drain has traversed to a leaf node, which contains a list of log groups. In this step, Drain selects the most suitable log group from the log group list by token similarity.
5. Update the parse tree. If a new log finds a suitable log group, the corresponding log template will be updated. Drain scans the tokens in the same position of the log message and the log template. If the two tokens are the same, we do not modify the token in that token position. Otherwise, we update the token in that token position by "*" in the log template. If the log does not find a suitable log group, a new log group is created according to the log. The log template of the log group is the log itself.

The online version of Drain is used to parse the raw log messages. That is, it processes log entries instead of log files, so the same log event may have a different parsed result at a different time, which can simulate the evolution and changes of the log to a certain extent due to the system upgrade or processing noise. We treat a parsed log event as a sentence $S = [w_1, w_2, ..., w_N]$ and a log template event as a document $D = [s_1, s_2, ..., s_M]$ in natural language, where $w_i, i \in [1, N]$ is the i-th token (word) in the sentence (log event), and $s_j, j \in [1, M]$ is the j-th sentence (log event) in the document (log event sequence). To facilitate the subsequent analysis, we filter out some tokens in log messages as follows: (1) remove non-character tokens such as numerical and nonnatural language tokens, (2) remove stop words such as "a" and "the", (3) split the CamelCase variable (e.g. split "isCommittable" into "is" and "Committable"), and (4) change all tokens to lowercase.

8.3.1.2 Log Enhancement

We set up three types of experiments to evaluate our method, using unknown class data, imbalanced data, and few-shot data, respectively. In order to ensure the uniqueness of variable factors, we need balanced datasets in the experiments with the unknown class data and few-shot data. Therefore, we enhance our datasets by Easy Data Augmentation (EDA) (Wei and Zou, 2019). For a given log in the training dataset, EDA randomly chooses and performs one of the following operations:

- Synonym replacement: Randomly choose n nonstop words from the sentence and replace each of the words with one of its synonyms chosen at random.
- Random insertion: Randomly select a nonstop word from the sentence, and randomly select one of its synonyms and insert it into a random position in the sentence. Do this n times.
- Random swap: Randomly choose two words in the log and swap their positions. Do this n times.
- Random deletion: Randomly remove each word in the sentence with a probability.

Through the above four operations, a log entry can be enhanced to multiple similar but different log entries. The category with few samples can be enhanced to balance with the category with more samples.

8.3.1.3 Log Vectorization

In order to extract the semantic information of logs and achieve the purpose that log events with a similar meaning have a similar vector representation, we adopt the widely used method, *word embedding* to vectorize the log event to log vector representations that are pretrained via *GloVe*. Each token in the log event is converted into the corresponding d-dimensional semantic vector, where $d = 200$ in our settings. For unknown words, we replace them with a unique token "UNK" and fix its embedding as a zero vector. After vectorization, a log event S is transformed into an embedding matrix $s = [e_1, e_2, ..., e_N]$, where $e_i, i \in [1, N]$ is the i-th word vector in the list, and N is the number of tokens in a log event sentence.

8.3.2 The Architecture of OpenLog

The overall architecture of OpenLog, depicted in Figure 8.7, consists of three modules: *Encoder Module*, *Prototypical Module* and *Relation Module*. There is also an important knowledge base that can dynamically add and delete log data to achieve the purpose of class increments without retraining. We elaborate these components in the following sections.

8.3.2.1 Encoder Module

After log preprocessing, we need to encode the log event sequence sample d_i into a lower-dimensional numerical feature vector, whereby classifiers can be applied. In this way, similar samples are close with each other, while dissimilar samples can be more easily differentiated. The encoder module in OpenLog consists of a

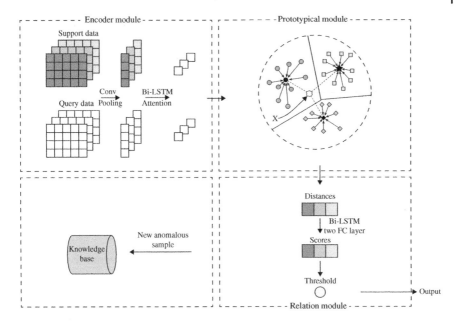

Figure 8.7 The architecture of OpenLog.

word sequence encoder based on Convolutional Neural Network (CNN) and a sentence encoder base on Bidirectional Long Short-Term Memory (Bi-LSTM) with self-attention, as shown in Figure 8.8).

Word-level encoder. After log vectorization which has been mentioned in Section 8.3.1.3, we embed the tokens in a log event into word embedding vectors $s = [e_1, e_2, ..., e_N]$ through a *GloVe* embedding matrix, where $e_i, i \in [1, N]$ is the i-th word vector in the list, and N is the number of tokens in a log event sentence. In the word-level encoder, we will encode the s into the d_w-dimensional embeddings m. CNN (Zeng et al., 2014) is used to encode the embedding inputs and merge the word-level features. It slides a convolution kernel with the windows size k over the inputs to get the d-dimensional hidden embedding H,

$$h_i = CNN\left(e_{i-\frac{m-1}{2}}, ..., e_{i-\frac{m+1}{2}}\right) \tag{8.2}$$

where h_i is the hidden state of the i-th convolution operation. This process can be repeated for d_w times with the kernels to increase the feature coverage of the encoder. Then, we input the hidden annotations into a max-pooling layer as follows:

$$[m]_j = maxH(j, \cdot), 0 \leq j \leq d_w \tag{8.3}$$

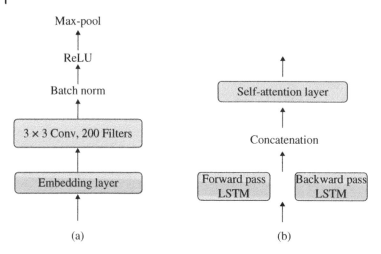

Figure 8.8 The encoder module. (a) Word-level encounter and (b) Sentence-level encounter.

where $H(j, \cdot)$ denotes the j-th row of matrix H. Finally, we obtain the word-level feature vector $\boldsymbol{m}$, the dimension d_w of which is preset and is no longer related to the sentence length. For simplicity, we denote the operations in word-level encoder as the following equation:

$$\boldsymbol{m} = f_\phi^w(\boldsymbol{s}) \tag{8.4}$$

where ϕ is the learnable parameter of the word-level encoder.

Sentence-level encoder. In the anomaly classification, the order of log templates in a log sequence is critical. Therefore, we use a Bi-LSTM to encode the sentence, which is a good choice for sequential data processing. LSTM is a recurrent neural network that is specifically designed for sequential data processing. It has a chain form of repeated neural network modules and is suitable for processing and predicting important events with very long intervals and delays in time series. LSTM has been widely used in natural language processing tasks and is able to capture the contextual information of the word sequence (Meng et al., 2019). Bi-LSTM can capture more sufficient information of sequential data, because it makes full use of the information transmission in the forward pass direction and the backward pass direction (Zhang et al., 2019). Given the word-level feature vector $\boldsymbol{m}$, we encode it to a sentence-level feature vector $\boldsymbol{x}$ using a sentence-level encoder based on Bi-LSTM with self-attention mechanism. h_t^f and h_t^b are hidden state vectors at time t in the two directions of LSTM:

$$h_t^f = \overrightarrow{LSTM}\left(w_t, h_{t-1}\right) \tag{8.5}$$

$$h_t^b = \overleftarrow{LSTM}\left(w_t, h_{t+1}\right) \tag{8.6}$$

We concatenate h_t^f and h_t^b as h_t, where $h_t = concat(h_t^f, h_t^b)$. The size of the hidden state vector of each direction is set to D. The importance of different log templates will affect the results of anomaly classification, so we use the attention mechanism to the Bi-LSTM to assign different weights to different log templates. The input of attention layer is h_t, and the output of the attention layer is a vector of attention weights, denoted by α. The self-attention mechanism uses the attention weights to assign the different attentions to the model and obtains different log templates. The weight α_t is given as follows:

$$\alpha_t = softmax\left(W_{\alpha 2} \cdot tanh\left(W_{\alpha 1} \cdot h_t\right)\right) \tag{8.7}$$

where $W_{\alpha 1} \in R^{d_s \times 2D}$ and $W_{\alpha 2} \in R^{d_s}$ are the weight matrixes and d_s is a hyperparameter. The result x of the sentence-level encoder is the weighted sum of the hidden size at every time t.

$$x = \Sigma_{t=1}^{T}\alpha_t \cdot h_t \tag{8.8}$$

For simplicity, we denote the operations in the sentence-level encoder using the following equation:

$$x = f_\phi^s(m) \tag{8.9}$$

where ϕ is the learnable parameter of the sentence-level encoder.

8.3.2.2 Prototypical Module

We apply the *prototypical network* (Snell et al., 2017) in this module as shown in Figure 8.9, which is an embedding learning method of the few-shot classification. It learns a metric space in which classification can be performed by computing

Figure 8.9 The prototypical module.

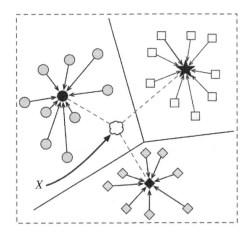

the distances to the prototype representations of each class (Snell et al., 2017). The classification part of prototypical networks is a nonparameter, so we can train a more general encoder model in a multiepisode training manner. Given an encoded feature representation x of a log template sequence, the size of x is d_s. This module will compute a prototype $p_k \in R^{d_s}$ of each class of samples, where k is the k-th class in the support set. Each prototype is the mean vector of the embedded representation belonging to its class. p_k can be expressed as follows:

$$p_k = \frac{1}{|S_k|} \Sigma_{x_i \in S_k} x_i \tag{8.10}$$

where S_k is the sample set of the class k. Then we choose a distance function, which is a squared Euclidean distance $d : R^{d_s} \times R^{d_s} \to [0, +\infty)$, to calculate the distance between two points in the prototypical network,

$$d(x, p_k) = \sqrt{(x_1 - p_{k1})^2 + (x_2 - p_{k2})^2 + \cdots + (x_{d_s} - p_{kd_s})^2}$$
$$= \sqrt{\Sigma_{i=1}^{d_s} (x_i - p_{ki})^2} \tag{8.11}$$

where $d(x, p_k)$ is the squared Euclidean distance between the query point x and the prototype of class k. Prototypical networks then produce a probability distributions over distance based on a softmax function,

$$P_\varphi(y = k|x) = \frac{exp(-d(x, p_k))}{\Sigma_{k'} exp(-d(x, p_{k'}))} \tag{8.12}$$

where $P_\varphi(y = k|x)$ is the probability that point x belongs to the class k.

8.3.2.3 Relation Module

This module is learning to compare the encoded testing sample and the prototype pairs from labeled support set and unlabeled testing set by a deep learning network and outputs the relation score of them. Figure 8.10 is the architecture of the relation module. Given a testing point x_i and a prototype p_k, we apply a combination operation $C(x_i, p_k)$ on them. In this work, we set $C(\cdot, \cdot)$ to an absolute subtraction operation. The result of $C(x_i, p_k)$ is fed into the relation module, which produces a scalar in the range of 0-1 representing the similarity between testing point x_i and the prototype p_k, called the relation score. If there are C classes of anomaly data in the knowledge base, we will get C scores in this module, used to classify x_i as a known class or detect it as an unknown class. The relation network consists of a Bi-LSTM layer and two fully connected networks as follows:

$$s_{x_i, p_k} = \sigma(W_2 \cdot Relu(W_1 \cdot BiLSTM(C(x_i, p_k)) + b_1) + b_2) \tag{8.13}$$

where s_{x_i, p_k} is the relation score between the testing point x_i and the prototype p_k. For the sake of the purpose of illustration and simplicity, we denote the operations

Figure 8.10 The relation module.

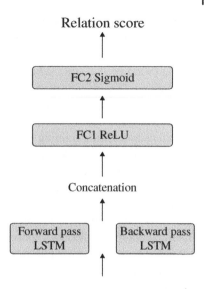

Relation score

in the relation module as the following equation:

$$s_{x_i, p_k} = f_\phi^r \left(x_i, p_k \right) \tag{8.14}$$

where ϕ is the learnable parameter of the relation module. We set the relation score threshold to 0.5 for the sigmoid function, which is a common threshold for a relatedness score (Xu et al., 2019, Pushp and Srivastava, 2017), to indicate the probability of the testing point x_i and the prototype p_k belonging to the same class k. If the score of the sample pairs is less than or equal to 0.5, they are not in the same class. Otherwise, they belong to the same class.

$$y = \begin{cases} 0, & \text{iff}\, f_\phi^r \left(x_i, p_k \right) \leq 0.5, \\ 1, & \text{iff}\, f_\phi^r \left(x_i, p_k \right) > 0.5, \end{cases} \tag{8.15}$$

8.3.3 Training Procedure

Different from the traditional deep learning methods, OpenLog has a special two-stage training procedure. The first stage is the representation learning phase like a pretraining. The model structure in this phase consists of the encoder module and the prototypical module. We apply the episode-based meta-training (Geng et al., 2019). The representation learning phase is an episode-based meta-training, OpenLog aims to train the encoder module through multiple meta-tasks. We select the part of the preprocessed auxiliary datasets as the training dataset T and the validation dataset. In every episode, OpenLog randomly chooses classes and samples in the training dataset T to train the model. For example, it randomly selects C classes from the training dataset, chooses K samples in each class as the sample dataset S, and chooses Q samples in each class as the query dataset Q. It is called a C-Way-K-Shot-Q-Queries meta-training setting (Sung et al., 2018), where the value of C, K, and Q are set manually as parameters. The classification results of the sample pairs in the prototypical module are used to tune the parameters of the encoder module continuously via the backpropagation and parameter optimization, which is the same as the normal deep-learning training procedure. The validation set is used to adjust the hyperparameters and make a preliminary assessment of the model's performance. The second stage is the relation-learning phase. The model structure in this phase consists of the encoder module, prototypical module, and the relation module. We apply a similar but different training strategy in this phase. We aggregate the rest of the auxiliary datasets and the small part of the target dataset as set M. OpenLog randomly chooses a subset of classes from M like the former phase. The difference with the former phase is that, in every episode, we choose some pairs of samples with positive labels and negative labels instead of multiple labels, to indicate that they belong to the same class or different classes. Besides, if there are more samples in each class, we can also use the method mentioned in Xu et al. (2019), to select the top-k different-class nearest samples from M to improve the performance and reduce the complexity of calculation. One of the sample pairs is a query sample, and the other is a prototype calculated from multiple support samples (randomly selected or top-k nearest neighbors). We set the ratio of the sample pairs belonging to the same class and the different classes as 2:1 to avoid overfitting. This phase also needs the help of the validation set to evaluate the generalization of the model.

8.3.4 Objective Function

The representation-learning phase is a multiclassification task. We therefore use the *cross-entropy loss function* to train the model as follows:

$$J_1(\phi) = -logP_\varphi(y = k|x) \tag{8.16}$$

The relation-learning phase is a binary classification task. We thus use *the mean square error* (MSE) loss function to train the model as follows:

$$J_2(\phi) = \Sigma_{i=1}^m \Sigma_{j=1}^n \left(s_{i,j} - 1\left(y_i == y_j\right)\right)^2 \tag{8.17}$$

8.4 Experimental Results and Analysis

We evaluate OpenLog by a variety of experiments, including the anomaly classification experiment using the unknown class data, the anomaly classification experiment using the imbalanced data, and the anomaly classification experiment using the few-shot data. We use two existing important methods as baselines: a deep-learning method LogRobust based on Bi-LSTM and self-attention (Zhang et al., 2019), and a traditional machine learning method based on SVM, called LogClass (Meng et al., 2018). In what follows, we introduce the datasets we used in the experiments and the details of the experiment settings and analyze the results of the experiments.

8.4.1 Experimental Design

8.4.1.1 Baseline

LogRobust. As shown in Figure 8.11(a), LogRobust is a deep learning anomaly detection method to overcome the instability problem of real-world logs. The model used in LogRobust is a Bi-LSTM and self-attention mechanism. The feature extraction in LogRoubust is based on word embedding which can adapt to the evolution of log events. LogRobust can be extended to log anomaly classification tasks.

LogClass. As shown in Figure 8.11(b), LogClass is an anomaly classification method based on PU learning and SVM to overcome the limitations of the device-agnostic vocabulary and partial labels in log analysis. LogClass uses PU learning to separate the abnormal and normal logs, and then it uses SVM for multiclassification. The feature extraction in LogClass is based on bag-of-words and TF-IDF weighting.

8.4.1.2 Evaluation Metrics

We use accuracy, recall, precision, and macro-F1 score as the evaluation metrics to measure the performance of OpenLog in terms of classifying the known anomalies as multiclass classification. In the binary classification, the evaluation metrics depend on the true positives (TP) indicating that the number of positive samples that are predicted correctly, true negatives (TN) denoting the number of negative samples that are predicted correctly, false positives (FP) showing the number of positive samples of incorrect predictions, and false negatives (FN) representing the number of negative samples of incorrect predictions:

$$Accuracy = \frac{TP + TN}{TP + TN + FP + FN} \tag{8.18}$$

$$Precision = \frac{TP}{TP + FP} \tag{8.19}$$

$$Recall = \frac{TP}{TP + FN} \tag{8.20}$$

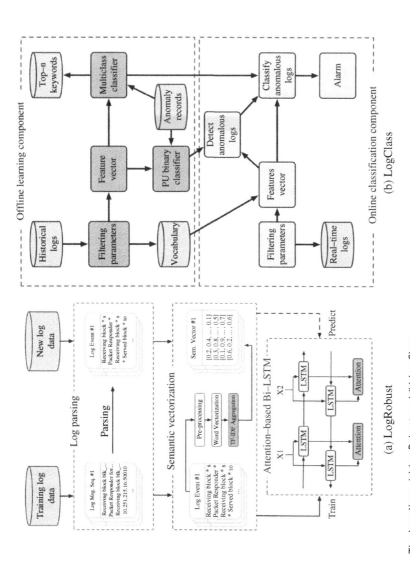

Figure 8.11 The baselines. (a) LogRobust and (b) LogClass.

$$F1 = \frac{2 \times Precision \times Recall}{Precision + Recall} \tag{8.21}$$

In multiclassification, we split the task into multiple binary classifications and perform the statistics of the corresponding TP, FP, TN, and FN in every class. Then, we calculate the accuracy and recall F1 score according to the above formulas. The average of the F1 scores from all classes is called macro-F1 shown as follows:

$$macro - F1 = \frac{1}{n} \sum_{i=1}^{N} F1_i \tag{8.22}$$

where $F1_i$ is the F1 score of the i-th class.

8.4.2 Datasets

We use four public real-world *High-Performance Computer* (HPC) log datasets (Chen et al., 2013) in our experiments, namely *Blue Gene/L, Thunderbird, Liberty* and *Spirit*. The log examples of four datasets are shown in Figure 8.12.

BGL. The BGL dataset is collected from *the Blue Gene/L systems* after its deployment at *Lawrence Livermore National Lab* (LALL). It consists of 128K processors. The BGL datasets contain 4,747,963 logs, including 348,460 anomaly logs, three coarse-grained anomaly classes as "Software anomaly," "Hardware anomaly," and "Indeterminate anomaly," as well as 41 fine-grained classes.

Thunderbird. The thunderbird dataset is generated by *the Thunderbird supercomputer* in 244 days, which is deployed at *Sandia National Labs* (SNL). It contains 211212192 logs, including 3,248,239 anomaly logs, three coarse-grained

BGL

Normal	-1117838571 2005.06.03 R02-M1-N0-C:J12-U11 2005-06-03-15.42.51.885834 R02-M1-N0-C:J12-U11 RAS KERNEL INFO instruction cache parity error corrected
Anomaly	APPREAD 1117869872 2005.06.04 R23-M1-N8-I J18-U11 2005-06-04-00.24.32.398284 R23-M1-N8-I:J18-U11 RAS APP FATAL ciod: failed to read message prefix on control stream (CioStream socket to 172.16.96.116:33399

Thunderbird

Normal	- 1131567327 2005.11.09 dn639 Nov 9 12:15:27 dn639/dn639 ntpd[905]: synchronized to 10.100.30.250, stratum 3
anomaly	EXT_FS 1152635207 2006.07.11 cn467 Jul 11 09:26:47 cn467/cn467 kernel EXT3-fs error (device sda5) in start_transaction: Journal has aborted

Liberty

Normal	- 1103000465 2004.12.13 ladmin1 Dec 13 21:01:05 ladmin1/ladmin1 CROND[4690]: (root) CMD (run-parts/etc/cron.hourly)
anomaly	N_NFS 1116006425 2005.05.13 ladmin1 May 13 10:47:05 ladmin1/ladmin1 netfs: Mounting NFS filesystems: failed

Spirit

Normal	-,1104566435,rrd update var lib ganglia rrds compute nodes sn temp proc rrd conversion of to float not complete tail
anomaly	N_PBS_CHK,task check cannot tm reply to sadmin task

Figure 8.12 The examples of BGL, Thunderbird, Liberty, and Spirit logs.

anomaly classes as "Software anomaly," "Hardware anomaly," and "Indeterminate anomaly," as well as 10 fine-grained classes.

Liberty. The Liberty dataset is generated by *Liberty* in 315 days, which is deployed at *Sandia National Labs* (SNL). It contains 265,569,231 logs, including 2,452 anomaly logs, three coarse-grained anomaly classes as "Software anomaly," "Hardware anomaly," and "Indeterminate anomaly," as well as 18 fine-grained classes. The proportion of anomaly logs in the Liberty dataset is small. This dataset can simulate real-world scenarios with few anomalies.

Spirit. The Spirit dataset is generated by *Spirit(ICC2)* in 558 days, which is deployed at *Sandia National Labs* (SNL). It contains 272,298,969 logs, including 172,816,564 anomaly logs, three coarse-grained anomaly classes as "Software anomaly," "Hardware anomaly," and "Indeterminate anomaly," as well as 8 fine-grained classes.

8.4.2.1 Data Processing

Since the four datasets are all HPC log data, they share some common characteristics, so they can be used as the auxiliary datasets to each other. We use the following strategy to organize the experimental data. The BGL dataset contains rich anomaly classes (41 categories), where it is suitable for organizing them into different meta-tasks in meta-training; therefore, we use BGL as the basic auxiliary datasets. Then, we use the Thunderbird, Liberty, and Spirit datasets as target datasets for comparative experiments. For example, when the Thunderbird dataset is used as the target dataset, we merge the BGL, Liberty, and Spirit dataset into a large training dataset with 61 anomaly classes, and randomly choose 60% of the training dataset as the encoder training set, and the rest of the training data and the different proportions of the target datasets (Thunderbird) as the relation training set. For the different experiments, we have different data processing and construct different training/testing datasets. We also filter the duplicate logs because the datasets contain many redundant log templates. Table 8.1 summarizes the information of the filtered datasets.

In the anomaly classification experiment using the unknown class data, we use the EDA method described in Section 8.3.1.2 to enhance the dataset, so that each class in the dataset contains 2000 samples. Then, we use the 25%, 50%, 75%, and 100% of class size in the target dataset as the training classes, respectively, and 80% samples of the training class dataset as the training dataset, and 20% of the samples in the target dataset as the testing data, which contains model-unseen anomaly samples. In this experimental setup, we evaluate the performance of different methods in the presence of the unknown class data. In the anomaly classification experiment using the imbalanced data, we use the imbalanced data as shown in Figure 8.13 and use the 100% of class size in the target dataset. We can find that some classes of data account for more than 30% of all data, since some classes of data account for less than 0.1% of all data. In some classes, for example, for the "R_EXT_CCISS" of Spirit dataset in Figure 8.13(c), the number of samples is even less than 10. In this experimental setup, we evaluate the performance of different methods in the presence of the imbalanced data. In the anomaly classification experiment using the few-shot data, we conduct an experiment dataset based on the setting of few-shot learning. There is only a very small amount of training data (5, 10, 15, 20 samples) in each class. In this experimental setup, we evaluate the performance of different methods in the presence of the few-shot data.

8.4.3 Experiments on the Unknown Class Data

In order to break the closed-world assumption of data categories and evaluate the performance of anomaly classification methods in "open" environment, new anomaly classes will continue to be present. We split the training data and the testing data and set the 5%, 25%, 75%, and 100% of all classes in the target dataset as unseen classes. The experimental results are shown in Figure 8.14. The feature extraction of LogClass is based on the bag-of-words and TF-IDF weighting. LogClass needs to build a global index-based vocabulary dictionary and statistics word frequency of every vocabulary in the dictionary. However, the new class is likely to bring new log events containing new vocabulary. Many key words are likely to be placed as the same unknown index. As the experimental results show, many important features that are useful for anomaly classification are lost through the feature extraction method in LogClass. When the ratio of class size in the training data is under 100%, LogClass has a lower-performance score on the three datasets. The feature extraction of LogRobust is based on word embedding, and therefore, it is not easy to be affected by the changes of logs. But neither logRobust nor logClass has the ability to detect unknown class anomalous samples, and they will classify the samples of unknown class as the wrong seen class. OpenLog focuses on the comparison between log representation learned

Table 8.1 The details of datasets.

Datasets	Total	Anomaly class size	Anomalies	Filtered data
BGL	4 713 493	41	348 460	93
Thunderbird	211 212 192	10	3 248 239	360
Liberty	265 569 231	18	2452	746
Spirit	272 298 969	8	172 816 564	250

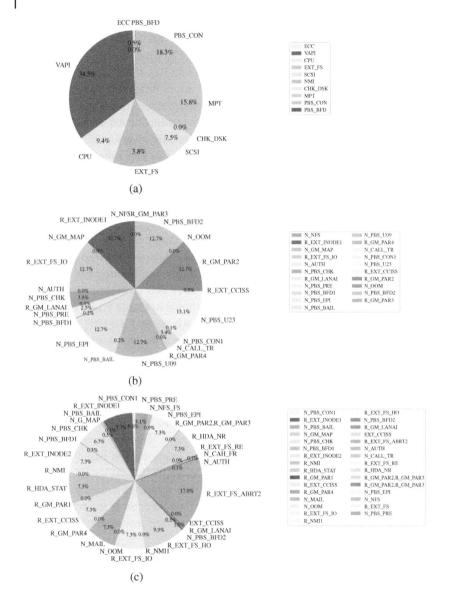

Figure 8.13 The samples proportion of raw imbalanced log in Thunderbird, Liberty, and Spirit datasets. (a) BGL, (b) Liberty, and (c) Spirit.

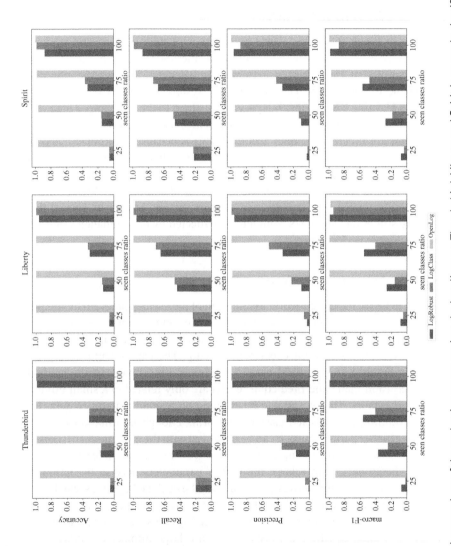

Figure 8.14 A comparison of the evaluation scores against the baselines on Thunderbird, Liberty, and Spirit in anomaly classification on the unknown class data.

from the auxiliary datasets, instead of the parameter model mapping based on a large amount of data. Therefore, OpenLog achieves better scores and is almost unaffected by unseen classes.

8.4.4 Experiments on the Imbalanced Data

In order to break the closed-world assumption of data balance and evaluate the performance of anomaly classification methods in open environment where samples of each class is extremely imbalanced. We use the raw data ratio of the three datasets. The experimental results are shown in Figure 8.15. The deep-learning based LogRobust is very sensitive to the imbalanced data. The experimental results show that LogRobust gets the recall, precision, and macro-F1 scores that are much lower than accuracy. This is because LogRobust has good classification ability for some classes containing sufficient training data but is incompetent for other classes containing few samples. The SVM-based logClass is not easily affected by the imbalance of training data because SVM's decision plane is only related to a few decisive support vectors. Due to its special data sampling strategy, OpenLog is completely unaffected by data imbalance and can maintain stable performance.

8.4.5 Experiments on the Few-shot Data

In order to break the closed-world assumption of data scale and evaluate the performance of anomaly classification methods in "open" environment, where the target system contains a few training samples. There are only 5, 10, 15, 20 samples in each class in our experimental setup. The experimental results are shown in Figure 8.16. The SVM-based LogClass is a machine-learning method, and its decision plane and prediction results are only related to a small number of support vectors. That is suitable for training on a small amount of data. But the few training data in each class cannot bring enough information for SVM to achieve higher performance. It can be improved with the enrichment of training data from 5 samples to 20 samples in each class. However, a deep learning-based method, LogRobust, with a large number of parameters need to be optimized depending on the training on a large amount of labeled data. LogRobust can hardly work on the few-shot data, where it can only get very low-performance scores. Based on the sufficient auxiliary datasets, OpenLog can keep stable performance on few-shot data. OpenLog is fully trained on a large number of different but similar meta-tasks sampled from the auxiliary datasets and is not limited by the lack of training data in the target dataset. Even when each class contains only five samples, OpenLog can also achieve the average accuracy and macro-F1 score higher than 90%.

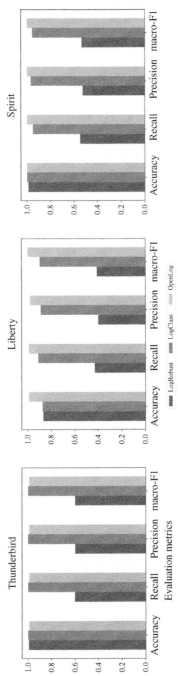

Figure 8.15 A comparison of the evaluation scores against the baselines on Thunderbird, Liberty, and Spirit in anomaly classification on the imbalanced data.

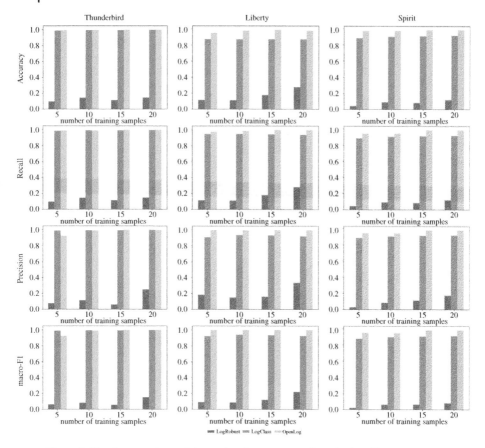

Figure 8.16 A comparison of the evaluation scores against the baselines on Thunderbird, Liberty, and Spirit in anomaly classification on the few-shot data.

8.5 Discussion

In this chapter, we proposed an anomaly classification method based on meta-learning and few-shot learning and proved the advantages and effectiveness of the proposed method. However, there are some aspects that need to be improved in the future.

1. The idea of meta-learning and few-shot learning can provide exploration and development direction for some of the bottlenecks in the existing log analysis methods. However, due to the characteristic of meta-learning and few-shot learning, most of methods belong to the supervised learning, which can solve

the problem of anomaly classification, fault diagnosis, etc., but it is more difficult for other unsupervised log analysis tasks, for example, correlation analysis and failure prediction.

2. The prototypical module of the proposed method is based on metric learning, that is, by comparing the relationship between the samples, to achieve the purpose of classification and detection of unknown class samples. This strategy is convenient, effective, and flexible, but the cost of time and calculation will increase with the increase in data size.

3. The experiments in this chapter are based on limited public datasets, limited by the format and complexity of the datasets. If more experiments are carried out on real industrial datasets, the algorithm can be further extended and improved.

The components of the proposed OpenLog architecture can be replaced with any neural network structures. For example, the encoder can be selected according to the organization of the log. We can use a separate CNN or recurrent neural network (RNN), or other complex mature models in NLP, such as TextCNN (Kim, 2014) and Transformer (Vaswani et al., 2017b).

8.6 Conclusion

Large-scale systems are generating a large amount of log data every day. Intelligent log analysis methods based on machine learning are constantly being proposed to ensure the stability and reliability of large-scale systems. In this chapter, we addressed three problems and restrictions encountered by most of the existing methods: (1) The problem of the feature extraction; (2) The problem of the few-shot problem; (3) The problem of the closed-world assumption. In this chapter, we briefly introduced the feature extraction in log analysis and the few-shot problem by examples. Then, we proposed a general anomaly classification method based on meta-learning and few-shot learning to address these issues. For the problem of the feature extraction, this proposed method used two layers of deep learning semantic coding in the encoder module to simplify the complex feature engineering and adapt to the changing log events. For the few-shot problem, the proposed method used meta-learning strategy to train the models on sufficient auxiliary datasets to enhance the model performance and reduce its dependence on the labeled samples of the target system. For the problem of the closed-world assumption, the method transformed the multiclassification task of the fixed model into the binary-classification task of learning the depth relationship between samples and can classify new anomalies incrementally without retraining. Extensive experimental results showed that OpenLog achieves better results than the existing important methods in terms of the classification with the unknown anomaly class data, imbalanced data, and few-shot data.

References

Hanlin Cao, Haina Tang, Yulei Wu, Fei Wang, and Yongjun Xu. On accurate computation of trajectory similarity via single image super-resolution. In *2021 International Joint Conference on Neural Networks (IJCNN)*, pages 1–9, 2021. doi: 10.1109/IJCNN52387.2021.9533802.

Xin Chen, Charng-Da Lu, and Karthik Pattabiraman. Predicting job completion times using system logs in supercomputing clusters. In *43rd Annual IEEE/IFIP Conference on Dependable Systems and Networks Workshop, DSN Workshops*, pages 1–8, Budapest, Hungary, 2013. IEEE Computer Society. URL http://dblp.uni-trier.de/db/conf/dsn/dsn2013w.html#ChenLP13.

Min Du, Feifei Li, Guineng Zheng, and Vivek Srikumar. DeepLog: Anomaly detection and diagnosis from system logs through deep learning. In Bhavani M. Thuraisingham, David Evans, Tal Malkin, and Dongyan Xu, editors, *Proceedings of the 2017 ACM SIGSAC Conference on Computer and Communications Security, CCS 2017*, Dallas, TX, USA, October 30 - November 03, 2017, pages 1285–1298. ACM, 2017. doi: 10.1145/3133956.3134015.

Geli Fei and Bing Liu. Breaking the closed world assumption in text classification. In Kevin Knight, Ani Nenkova, and Owen Rambow, editors, *NAACL HLT 2016, The 2016 Conference of the North American Chapter of the Association for Computational Linguistics: Human Language Technologies*, San Diego California, USA, June 12–17, 2016, pages 506–514. The Association for Computational Linguistics, 2016. doi: 10.18653/v1/n16-1061.

Ruiying Geng, Binhua Li, Yongbin Li, Yuxiao Ye, Ping Jian, and Jian Sun. Few-shot text classification with induction network. *CoRR*, abs/1902.10482, 2019. URL http://arxiv.org/abs/1902.10482.

C. Gulcu. The complete Log4j manual. 2003.

Y. Guo, Y. Wu, Y. Zhu, B. Yang, and C. Han. Anomaly detection using distributed log data: A lightweight federated learning approach. In *2021 International Joint Conference on Neural Networks (IJCNN)*, 2021.

Shilin He, Jieming Zhu, Pinjia He, and Michael R. Lyu. Experience report: System log analysis for anomaly detection. In *27th IEEE International Symposium on Software Reliability Engineering, ISSRE 2016*, Ottawa, ON, Canada, October 23–27, 2016, pages 207–218. IEEE Computer Society, 2016. doi: 10.1109/ISSRE.2016.21.

P. He, J. Zhu, Z. Zheng, and M. R. Lyu. Drain: An online log parsing approach with fixed depth tree. In *2017 IEEE International Conference on Web Services (ICWS)*, pages 33–40, 2017. doi: 10.1109/ICWS.2017.13.

Zikun Hu, Xiang Li, Cunchao Tu, Zhiyuan Liu, and Maosong Sun. Few-shot charge prediction with discriminative legal attributes. In Emily M. Bender, Leon Derczynski, and Pierre Isabelle, editors, *Proceedings of the 27th International Conference on Computational Linguistics, COLING 2018*, Santa Fe, New Mexico, USA, August 20–26, 2018, pages 487–498. Association for Computational Linguistics, 2018. URL https://www.aclweb.org/anthology/C18-1041/.

Chengqiang Huang, Yulei Wu, Yuan Zuo, Ke Pei, and Geyong Min. Towards experienced anomaly detector through reinforcement learning. *Proceedings of the AAAI Conference on Artificial Intelligence*, 32(1), 2018. URL https://ojs.aaai.org/index.php/AAAI/article/view/12130.

Yoon Kim. Convolutional neural networks for sentence classification. In *Proceedings of the 2014 Conference on Empirical Methods in Natural Language Processing (EMNLP)*, pages 1746–1751, Doha, Qatar, 2014. Association for Computational Linguistics. URL https://www.aclweb.org/anthology/D14-1181", doi = "10.3115/v1/D14-1181.

Jedrzej Kozerawski and Matthew A. Turk. CLEAR: Cumulative learning for one-shot one-class image recognition. In *2018 IEEE Conference on Computer Vision and Pattern Recognition, CVPR 2018*, Salt Lake City, UT, USA, June 18–22, 2018, pages 3446–3455. IEEE Computer Society, 2018. doi: 10.1109/CVPR.2018.00363. URL http://openaccess.thecvf.com/content_cvpr_2018/html/Kozerawski_CLEAR_Cumulative_LEARning_CVPR_2018_paper.html.

Qingwei Lin, Hongyu Zhang, Jian-Guang Lou, Yu Zhang, and Xuewei Chen. Log clustering based problem identification for online service systems. In Laura K. Dillon, Willem Visser, and Laurie A. Williams, editors, *Proceedings of the 38th International Conference on Software Engineering, ICSE 2016*, Austin, TX, USA, May 14–22, 2016 - Companion Volume, pages 102–111. ACM, 2016. doi: 10.1145/2889160.2889232.

Bo Liu, Xudong Wang, Mandar Dixit, Roland Kwitt, and Nuno Vasconcelos. Feature space transfer for data augmentation. In *2018 IEEE Conference on Computer Vision and Pattern Recognition, CVPR 2018*, Salt Lake City, UT, USA, June 18–22, 2018, pages 9090–9098. IEEE Computer Society, 2018. doi: 10.1109/CVPR.2018.00947. URL http://openaccess.thecvf.com/content_cvpr_2018/html/Liu_Feature_Space: Transfer_CVPR_2018_paper.html.

Zelun Luo, Yuliang Zou, Judy Hoffman, and Fei-Fei Li. Label efficient learning of transferable representations acrosss domains and tasks. In Isabelle Guyon, Ulrike von Luxburg, Samy Bengio, Hanna M. Wallach, Rob Fergus, S. V. N. Vishwanathan, and Roman Garnett, editors, *Advances in Neural Information Processing Systems 30: Annual Conference on Neural Information Processing Systems 2017*, December 4–9, 2017, Long Beach, CA, USA, pages 165–177, 2017. URL https://proceedings.neurips.cc/paper/2017/hash/a8baa56554f96369ab93e4f3bb068c22-Abstract.html.

Weibin Meng, Ying Liu, Shenglin Zhang, Dan Pei, Hui Dong, Lei Song, and Xulong Luo. Device-agnostic log anomaly classification with partial labels. In *26th IEEE/ACM International Symposium on Quality of Service, IWQoS 2018, Banff, AB, Canada*, June 4–6, 2018, pages 1–6. IEEE, 2018. doi: 10.1109/IWQoS.2018.8624141.

Weibin Meng, Ying Liu, Yichen Zhu, Shenglin Zhang, Dan Pei, Yuqing Liu, Yihao Chen, Ruizhi Zhang, Shimin Tao, Pei Sun, and Rong Zhou. LogAnomaly: Unsupervised detection of sequential and quantitative anomalies in unstructured logs. In Sarit Kraus, editor, *Proceedings of the 28th International Joint Conference on Artificial Intelligence, IJCAI 2019*, Macao, China, August 10–16, 2019, pages 4739–4745. ijcai.org, 2019. doi: 10.24963/ijcai.2019/658.

Tomás Mikolov, Kai Chen, Greg Corrado, and Jeffrey Dean. Efficient estimation of word representations in vector space. In Yoshua Bengio and Yann LeCun, editors, *1st International Conference on Learning Representations, ICLR 2013*, Scottsdale, Arizona, USA, May 2–4, 2013, Workshop Track Proceedings, 2013. URL http://arxiv.org/abs/1301.3781.

Amit Pande and Vishal Ahuja. WEAC: Word embeddings for anomaly classification from event logs. In Jian-Yun Nie, Zoran Obradovic, Toyotaro Suzumura, Rumi Ghosh, Raghunath Nambiar, Chonggang Wang, Hui Zang, Ricardo Baeza-Yates, Xiaohua Hu, Jeremy Kepner, Alfredo Cuzzocrea, Jian Tang, and Masashi Toyoda, editors, *2017 IEEE International Conference on Big Data, BigData 2017*, Boston, MA, USA, December 11–14, 2017, pages 1095–1100. IEEE Computer Society, 2017. doi: 10.1109/BigData.2017.8258034.

Jeffrey Pennington, Richard Socher, and Christopher D. Manning. GloVe: Global vectors for word representation. In Alessandro Moschitti, Bo Pang, and Walter Daelemans, editors, *Proceedings of the 2014 Conference on Empirical Methods in Natural Language Processing, EMNLP 2014*, October 25–29, 2014, Doha, Qatar, A meeting of SIGDAT, a Special Interest Group of the ACL, pages 1532–1543. ACL, 2014. doi: 10.3115/v1/d14-1162.

Tomas Pfister, James Charles, and Andrew Zisserman. Domain-adaptive discriminative one-shot learning of gestures. In David J. Fleet, Tomás Pajdla, Bernt Schiele, and Tinne Tuytelaars, editors, *Computer Vision - ECCV 2014 - 13th European Conference*, Zurich, Switzerland, September 6–12, 2014, Proceedings, Part VI, volume 8694 of *Lecture Notes in Computer Science*, pages 814–829. Springer, 2014. doi: 10.1007/978-3-319-10599-4_52.

Pushpankar Kumar Pushp and Muktabh Mayank Srivastava. Train once, test anywhere: Zero-shot learning for text classification. *CoRR*, abs/1712.05972, 2017. URL http://arxiv.org/abs/1712.05972.

Adam Santoro, Sergey Bartunov, Matthew Botvinick, Daan Wierstra, and Timothy P. Lillicrap. Meta-learning with memory-augmented neural networks. In Maria-Florina Balcan and Kilian Q. Weinberger, editors, *Proceedings of the 33nd International Conference on Machine Learning, ICML 2016*, New York City, NY, USA, June 19–24, 2016, volume 48 of *JMLR Workshop and Conference Proceedings*, pages 1842–1850. JMLR.org, 2016. URL http://proceedings.mlr.press/v48/santoro16.html.

Jake Snell, Kevin Swersky, and Richard S. Zemel. Prototypical networks for few-shot learning. In *Advances in Neural Information Processing Systems 30: Annual Conference on Neural Information Processing Systems*, pages 4077–4087, Long Beach, CA, USA, 2017. Curran Associates, Inc. URL http://papers.nips.cc/paper/6996-prototypical-networks-for-few-shot-learning.

Pascal Soucy and Guy W. Mineau. Beyond TFIDF weighting for text categorization in the vector space model. In Leslie Pack Kaelbling and Alessandro Saffiotti, editors, *IJCAI-05, Proceedings of the 19th International Joint Conference on Artificial Intelligence*, Edinburgh, Scotland, UK, July 30 - August 5, 2005, pages 1130–1135. Professional Book Center, 2005. URL http://ijcai.org/Proceedings/05/Papers/0304.pdf.

Peijie Sun, E Yuepeng, Tong Li, Yulei Wu, Jingguo Ge, Junling You, and Bingzhen Wu. Context-aware learning for anomaly detection with imbalanced log data. In *2020 IEEE 22nd International Conference on High Performance Computing and Communications; IEEE 18th International Conference on Smart City; IEEE 6th International Conference on Data Science and Systems (HPCC/SmartCity/DSS)*, pages 449–456, 2020. doi: 10.1109/HPCC-SmartCity-DSS50907.2020.00055.

Flood Sung, Yongxin Yang, Li Zhang, Tao Xiang, Philip H. S. Torr, and Timothy M. Hospedales. Learning to compare: Relation network for few-shot learning. In *2018 IEEE Conference on Computer Vision and Pattern Recognition, CVPR 2018*, Salt Lake City, UT, USA, June 18–22, 2018, pages 1199–1208. IEEE Computer Society, 2018. doi: 10.1109/CVPR.2018.00131. URL http://openaccess.thecvf.com/content_cvpr_2018/html/Sung_Learning_to_Compare_CVPR_2018_paper.html.

Eleni Triantafillou, Richard S. Zemel, and Raquel Urtasun. Few-shot learning through an information retrieval lens. In Isabelle Guyon, Ulrike von Luxburg, Samy Bengio, Hanna M. Wallach, Rob Fergus, S. V. N. Vishwanathan, and Roman Garnett, editors, *Advances in Neural Information Processing Systems 30: Annual Conference on Neural Information Processing Systems 2017*, December 4–9, 2017, Long Beach, CA, USA, pages 2255–2265, 2017. URL https://proceedings.neurips.cc/paper/2017/hash/01e9565cecc4e989123f9620c1d09c09-Abstract.html.

Ashish Vaswani, Noam Shazeer, Niki Parmar, Jakob Uszkoreit, Llion Jones, Aidan N. Gomez, Lukasz Kaiser, and Illia Polosukhin. Attention is all you need. In Isabelle Guyon, Ulrike von Luxburg, Samy Bengio, Hanna M. Wallach, Rob Fergus, S. V. N. Vishwanathan, and Roman Garnett, editors, *Advances in Neural Information Processing Systems 30: Annual Conference on Neural Information Processing Systems 2017*, December 4–9, 2017, Long Beach, CA, USA, pages 5998–6008, 2017a. URL https://proceedings.neurips.cc/paper/2017/hash/3f5ee243547dee91fbd053c1c4a845aa-Abstract.html.

Ashish Vaswani, Noam Shazeer, Niki Parmar, Jakob Uszkoreit, Llion Jones, Aidan N. Gomez, Lukasz Kaiser, and Illia Polosukhin. Attention is all you need. In *Advances in Neural Information Processing Systems 30: Annual Conference on Neural Information Processing Systems*, pages 5998–6008, Long Beach, CA, USA, 2017b. Curran Associates, Inc. URL http://papers.nips.cc/paper/7181-attention-is-all-you-need.

Yaqing Wang, Quanming Yao, James T. Kwok, and Lionel M. Ni. Generalizing from a few examples: A survey on few-shot learning. *ACM Computing Surveys*, 53(3):63:1–63:34, 2020. doi: 10.1145/3386252.

Jason Wei and Kai Zou. EDA: Easy data augmentation techniques for boosting performance on text classification tasks. In *Proceedings of the 2019 Conference on Empirical Methods in Natural Language Processing and the 9th International Joint Conference on Natural Language Processing (EMNLP-IJCNLP)*, pages 6382–6388, Hong Kong, China, November 2019. Association for Computational Linguistics. doi: 10.18653/v1/D19-1670.

Ho Chung Wu, Robert Wing Pong Luk, Kam-Fai Wong, and Kui-Lam Kwok. Interpreting TF-IDF term weights as making relevance decisions. *ACM Transactions on Information and System*, 26(3):13:1–13:37, 2008. doi: 10.1145/1361684.1361686.

Hu Xu, Bing Liu, Lei Shu, and Philip S. Yu. Open-world learning and application to product classification. In Ling Liu, Ryen W. White, Amin Mantrach, Fabrizio Silvestri, Julian J. McAuley, Ricardo Baeza-Yates, and Leila Zia, editors, *The World Wide Web Conference, WWW 2019*, San Francisco, CA, USA, May 13–17, 2019, pages 3413–3419. ACM, 2019. doi: 10.1145/3308558.3313644.

Daojian Zeng, Kang Liu, Siwei Lai, Guangyou Zhou, and Jun Zhao. Relation classification via convolutional deep neural network. In *COLING 2014, 25th International Conference on Computational Linguistics, Proceedings of the Conference: Technical Papers*, pages 2335–2344, Dublin, Ireland, 2014. ACL. URL https://www.aclweb.org/anthology/C14-1220.

Xu Zhang, Yong Xu, Qingwei Lin, Bo Qiao, Hongyu Zhang, Yingnong Dang, Chunyu Xie, Xinsheng Yang, Qian Cheng, Ze Li, Junjie Chen, Xiaoting He, Randolph Yao, Jian-Guang Lou, Murali Chintalapati, Furao Shen, and Dongmei Zhang. Robust log-based anomaly detection on unstable log data. In Marlon Dumas, Dietmar Pfahl, Sven Apel, and Alessandra Russo, editors, *Proceedings of the ACM Joint Meeting on European Software Engineering Conference and Symposium on the Foundations of Software Engineering, ESEC/SIGSOFT FSE 2019*, Tallinn, Estonia, August 26–30, 2019, pages 807–817. ACM, 2019. doi: 10.1145/3338906.3338931.

Yuan Zuo, Yulei Wu, Geyong Min, Chengqiang Huang, and Ke Pei. An intelligent anomaly detection scheme for micro-services architectures with temporal and spatial data analysis. *IEEE Transactions on Cognitive Communications and Networking*, 6(2):548–561, 2020. doi: 10.1109/TCCN.2020.2966615.

9

Zero Trust Networks

9.1 Introduction to Zero-Trust Networks

9.1.1 Background

The traditional enterprise security model is based on perimeter security, which means that users and devices in the enterprise intranet are assumed to be secure (Ward and Beyer, 2014; Sengupta and Lakshminarayanan, 2021). However, with the fast development of information technology, the following trends are gradually blurring the boundaries of enterprise networks:

- Mobile office has become the future trend. With the increasing popularity of intelligent terminals, more employees carry personal mobile devices (Hatakeyama et al., 2021) (including mobile phones, tablets, etc.). In addition, these mobile devices are usually not under the control of the company and may be not trusted. According to Feng and Li (2016), these untrusted devices may be subject to threats from application services, terminal software or hardware resource management, and data storage.
- Massive use of cloud. The development of cloud computing brings revolution to the current business model. Cloud workloads are often fragmented across several different geolocations and environments, making it difficult to define perimeter (Bharadwaj et al., 2018; DeCusatis et al., 2017; Singh and Chatterjee, 2016).
- Widespread use of virtual personal network (VPN). With the increasing demands for employees to remotely access the company's intranet, VPNs have been widely used and deployed by various enterprises. As a result, it becomes increasingly difficult to assure the security of such systems. Allowing them to connect to a VPN potentially undermines perimeter security and may expose the network to outside attacks (Schulz and Sadeghi, 2009).

AI and Machine Learning for Network and Security Management, First Edition.
Yulei Wu, Jingguo Ge, and Tong Li.
© 2023 The Institute of Electrical and Electronics Engineers, Inc. Published 2023 by John Wiley & Sons, Inc.

In summary, we can find that key assumptions of the traditional perimeter-based defense model are no longer valid: everything in perimeter is no longer trusted. In addition, with the rapid growth of the traffic inside the data center, namely East-West traffic, the security issue inside the enterprise has become more severe, because of the lack of internal network security protection (Zaheer et al., 2019). In order to adapt to the current new Internet trends, researchers have tried to dispense with a privileged corporate network and propose the concept of zero-trust networks (Ward and Beyer, 2014).

9.1.2 Zero-Trust Networks

Different from traditional network defense models, zero-trust networks allow no default trust for any entities (e.g. devices, applications, packets, and users), regardless of its type or whether it is related to the corporate network (Puthal et al., 2017). Based on the assumption that "all network traffic are not trusted," the zero-trust network "never trust, always verify, and enforce least privilege" to privileged access. As shown in Figure 9.1, any user/device is untrusted before verified.

The core idea of zero-trust networks is to establish a dynamic access control system centered on identity authentication between the access subject and the object (Yao et al., 2020). No matter which Internet access method a visitor uses at any location, identity authentication and authorization are required. Therefore, all access requests need examination, continuous trust evaluation of the access subject, and dynamic adjustment of permissions based on the degree of trustworthiness (Yao et al., 2020).

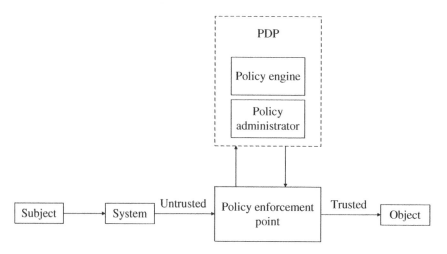

Figure 9.1 The core logical components of zero-trust networks.

According to Rose et al. (2020), the logical components of zero trust networks are shown in Figure 9.1. Hence, zero trust networks need to implement the following functions:

- Policy enforcement point (PEP). The PEP is responsible for enabling, monitoring, and eventually terminating connections between a subject and an enterprise resource. It may be broken into two different components: the client side (e.g. agent on user's laptop) and the resource side (e.g. gateway component in front resources that control access). Alternatively, it is a single component acting as a gatekeeper (e.g. access proxy) for communication paths.
- Policy engine (PE). This component is responsible for the ultimate decision to grant access to a resource for a given subject. The PE uses enterprise policy as well as data from external sources (e.g. CDM systems) as input to the trust algorithm to grant, deny, or revoke access to the resource. The PE is paired with the policy administrator's component. The PE makes and logs the decision, and the policy administrator executes the decision.
- Policy administrator. This component is responsible for establishing and/or shutting down the communication between a subject and a resource. It would generate any authentication token or credential used by a client. It is closely tied to the PE and relies on its decision to allow or deny a session. The PA communicates with the PEP when creating the communication path.

9.2 Zero-Trust Network Solutions

Existing studies mainly complete the construction of a zero-trust network based on Access Proxy, software-defined perimeter (SDP), and micro-segmentation methods (Yao et al., 2020).

9.2.1 Zero-Trust Networks Based on Access Proxy

After suffering a highly complex advanced persistent threat (APT) attack in 2009, Google began to redesign a new security model that dispenses with a privileged corporate network. Instead, Google proposed BeyondCorp (Ward and Beyer, 2014; Beyer et al., 2016; Saltonstall et al., 2016), a zero-trust network based on Access Proxy to fully authenticate, fully authorize, and fully encrypt all access to enterprise resources. The major components of BeyondCorp are shown in Figure 9.2.

A brief introduction of the components is shown as follows (Ward and Beyer, 2014):

- Access Proxy. Google extends the Google Front Ends (GFE) which are a fleet of HTTP/HTTPS reverse proxies, to provide other features, including self-service

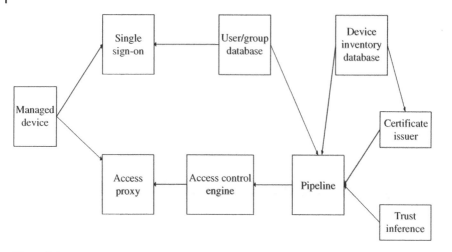

Figure 9.2 The components and access flows of BeyondCorp.

provisioning, authentication, authorization, and centralized logging. The resulting extended GFE is called Access Proxy (AP) (Spear et al., 2016). All enterprise applications at Google are exposed to external and internal clients via an Internet-facing access proxy that enforces encryption between the client and the application. In addition, an **Access Control Engine** within the access proxy provides service-level authorization to enterprise applications on a prerequest basis. After the access control checks complete, this proxy delegates requests as appropriate to the back-end application.

- Managed Devices. To securely identifying the device, BeyondCorp uses the concept of a "managed device," which is a device that is procured and actively managed by the enterprise. Only managed devices can access corporate applications. In order to accomplish device identification, device certificate, which is stored on the hardware or software Trusted Platform Module or a qualified certificate store, is used. What's more, Google keeps track of changes made to the device and store this information in **Device Inventory Database** so that they can monitor the security of devices and certificates in real time. Because Google has multiple inventory database, a meta-inventory database is used to amalgamate and normalize device information from these multiple sources. With this meta-inventory in place, Google has knowledge of all devices that need to access enterprise.
- Single Sign-on. Single Sign-on (SSO) system is a centralized user authentication portal that validates primary and second-factor credentials for users requesting access to the enterprise resources. After validating against the **User Database and Group Database**, which is used to track and manage all users, the SSO

system generates short-lived tokens that can be used as part of the authorization process for specific resources.

- Pipeline. In order to dynamically infer the level of trust to assign to a device or user, the pipeline extracts information to use for access decisions. Among other factors, this information includes certificate whitelists, trust levels of devices and users, and inventory details about the device and the user. Finally, this information is provided to **Access Control Engine** so that appropriate access decisions can be made.

As we can see in Figure 9.2, BeyondCorp only exposes Access Proxy and SSO components to the external access, so its attack surface is very limited. In addition, the location where the client initiates the connection is no longer a necessary factor for authentication and authorization, which means that all access requests need to be authenticated and authorized by a logically centralized access proxy. After authentication and authorization, the access proxy will act as an intermediary to forward the data between the user and services.

However, as we described before, BeyondCorp only natively supports applications based on the HTTP/HTTPS protocol and can only manage and authorize managed devices, which limits scalability and compatibility with third-party software.

9.2.2 Zero Trust Networks Based on SDP

The concept of SDP is built on the notion of providing application/service owner(s) with the power to deploy perimeter (i.e. dynamic gateway) functionality as needed to protect their servers (Kumar et al., 2019; Singh et al., 2020). This is done by adopting logical components in place of any physical appliances (Moubayed et al., 2019). The SDP is composed of three main components listed as follows:

- SDP controller. The SDP controller is the central element in the SDP framework (Cloud Security Alliance, 2022). It is responsible for all the control messages exchanged by functioning as a trust broker between the initiating SDP host (see below) and the backend security controls. After determining the services that each initiating host is authorized to, the controller helps configure both the SDP initiating host and the accepting host in real time to create the mutual TLS tunnel.
- SDP client/Initiating Host(IH). SDP IHs are SDP-enabled clients that submit a request to connect to a server or an application. This request is submitted to the SDP controller which will authenticate the IH by requesting information about hardware or software within the IH. Once authentication is completed using the previously issued certificate, a mutual TLS tunnel is created which connects the IH to the server or application for which it has authorization.

- SDP Accepting Hosts (AH): The SDP AH is the device instructed to accept authorized services or applications, i.e. AH typically includes **Gateway** and servers to be protected. It is originally set up to reject all incoming packets and requests from all hosts except for the SDP controller. After the SDP controller provides the gateway with the verified and authenticated IH's IP address and certificates, the **Gateway** will allow the connection requests to go through and the client-server data transfer can take place.

The access flow of SDP is shown in Figure 9.3. Different from the Zero-Trust Network based on access proxy, SDP separates the control and the data plane for different hosts that are communicating using a controller and a gateway, which means the controller will not participate in the communication between the user and the protected service after the authentication is completed. In addition, different from BeyondCorp, SDP not only supports applications based on the HTTP/HTTPS protocol but also supports applications based on the other TCP/UDP protocols.

9.2.3 Zero-Trust Networks Based on Micro-Segmentation

Microsegmentation, also called security isolation based on subdivision groups, divides data centers into groups according to certain principles, and then deploys traffic control strategies based on the grouping. Micro-segmentation, which is based on placing individual or groups of resources on its own network segment

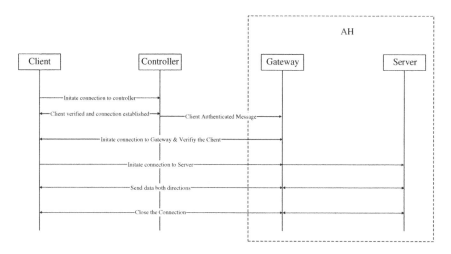

Figure 9.3 The access flow of SDP.

protected by a gateway security component, can overcome the disadvantages of traditional service isolation technologies (such as virtual local area network [VLAN] and access control list ACL) that are complicated to configure and maintain and cannot isolate services in subnets. In practice, HuaWei CloudEngine 12800 series switches (Huawei Technologies Co., Ltd., 2020) can complete micro-segmentation in a VXLAN network. There are two main concepts in the micro-segmentation network:

- End Point Group (EPG): Refers to the grouping of endpoints (servers) according to certain principles.
- Group Based Police (GBP): Refers to the group-based flow control strategy, which specifies the flow control strategy within/between EPG. Users can specify their own GBP strategy for different EPG groups.

The source VTEP transmits micro-segmentation information to the destination VTEP through the G flag bit and the Group Policy ID field in the VXLAN packet header. As shown in Figure 9.4, the flag G is 0 by default. When this bit is 1, it means that the EPG group number to which the source server belongs is carried in the Group Policy ID field in the VXLAN packet header.

The following uses Server1 to access Server2 as an example to introduce the working mechanism of micro-segmentation when Layer 3 packets are locally forwarded in the VXLAN network as shown in Figure 9.5.

- Step1. After VTEP1 receives the message sent from Server1 to Server2, it obtains the source IP address from the message (192.168.10.1) and the destination IP address (192.168.20.2).
- Step2. VTEP1 searches the TCAM table entry based on the source IP address (192.168.10.1) according to the longest match principle, and obtains the EPG group number (EPG1) which Server1 belongs to.
- Step3. VTEP1 looks up the routing table information according to the destination IP address (192.168.20.2) and finds that the destination Server2 is also

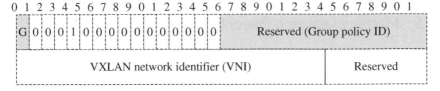

Figure 9.4 Micro-segmentation information in the VXLAN packet header.

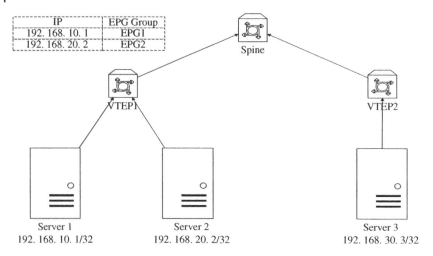

Figure 9.5 The VXLAN network example.

connected under VTEP1, so the message only needs to be forwarded locally. Therefore, VTEP1 searches the TCAM table entry according to the longest match principle using the destination IP address (192.168.20.2), and obtains the EPG group number (EPG2) to which the destination Server2 belongs.

- Step4. VTEP1 looks up the TCAM table entry according to the group number (EPG1) to which Server1 belongs at the source and the group number (EPG2) to which Server2 belongs at the destination, obtains the GBP policy between the two groups, and performs packet processing according to the GBP policy flow control.

We can find that, every packet will be forwarded according to access polices. Different from BeyondCorp and SDP, the micro-segmentation mechanism mainly focuses on East–West traffic and the implementation of micro-segmentation pays more attention to the bottom layer of the network, i.e. IP layer and MAC layer of the network.

9.3 Machine Learning Powered Zero Trust Networks

As shown in Figure 9.1, the main difference between zero-trust networks and traditional networks is that zero-trust networks treat all traffic untrusted, which means every access request over the network needs to be captured and authorized. Thanks to different zero-trust network solutions (i.e. access proxy-based, SDP based, micro-segmentation based), all traffic can be reviewed by the component of zero-trust architectures. The next question is how to authorize users/devices

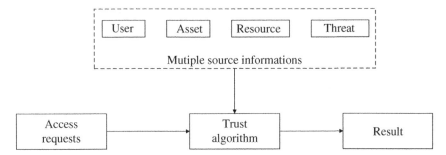

Figure 9.6 The trust algorithm process in zero-trust networks.

accurately and efficiently, i.e. designing a trust algorithm suitable for zero-trust networks.

The process of a trust algorithm (TA) is shown in Figure 9.6. Taking the input from multiple sources, the trust algorithm ultimately grants or denies requested accesses. The main components in Figure 9.6 are described as follows:

- Access requests. This is the actual request from the subject. The resource requested is the primary information used, but information about the requester is also used. This can include OS version, application used, and patch level. Depending on these factors and the asset security posture, access to assets might be restricted or denied.
- Multiple source information. In order to ensure the security of networks, the TA should take as much information as possible into consideration. For example, the identification and attributes of users (i.e. the request subject), the observable status of asset (i.e. the request device), the access requirements of resources, and the alerts of threat intelligence can be obtained and fused by TA in order to evaluate more comprehensively whether an access request can be authorized.
- Trust Algorithm. Taking multiple source information and access requests as input, TA makes the final decision and passes the access decision to PA for execution. According to whether the output of TA is binary-based decisions or the confidence level, the TA can be classified into criteria- versus score-based algorithms. A score-based TA computes a confidence level and if the confidence level is greater than the configured threshold, access is granted. In addition, according to whether the TA takes the user/application history into consideration or not, the TA can be classified into Singular versus contextual algorithms. Although a singular algorithm can allow faster evaluation than a contextual algorithm, there is a risk that an attack can be undetected if it stays within a user's allowed role.

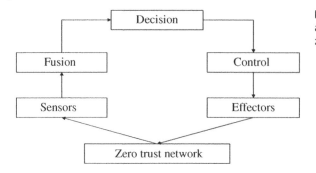

Figure 9.7 The authorization system in zero-trust networks.

In this section, we abstract the authorization system in the zero-trust networks into three decoupled layers: information fusion layer, access decision-making layer, and control layer, as shown in Figure 9.7. The brief descriptions of those components are provided as follows:

- Sensors are the information providers deployed in the zero trust network, such as Snort, Snmp, Netflow anaylzer, and so on. They can collect and process user and asset information, service operation status, and threat intelligence in parallel.
- Fusion is a technology that merges data from multiple sensors to obtain more consistent, informative, and accurate information than the overall original raw data that are mostly uncertain, imprecise, inconsistent, conflicting, and alike (Meng et al., 2019). As the technique with strong abilities to compute and classify data, machine learning is highly expected to improve the performance of data fusion algorithms.
- Decision-making is the process to make access policy, which contains a set of access rules to determine whether a request is permitted to access a resource or not.
- Control is the process of generating operation commands for network devices so that the access rules can be executed. In this layer, different commands should be generated according to the Effector type.
- Effectors. It is the device, such as firewall, access proxy, and gateway, that executes the commands to deny the unauthorized access.

In the rest of this section, we will mainly introduce the application of machine learning in "the brain of the authorization system": information fusion and decision-making layers.

9.3.1 Information Fusion

According to Meng et al. (2019), the most important elements of data fusion are listed as follows:

- Data Sources: Single or multiple data sources from different positions and at different points of time are involved in data fusion.
- One needs an operation of combination of data and refinement of information, which can be described as "transforming."
- Purpose: Gaining improved information with less error possibility in detection or prediction and superior reliability as the goal of fusion. Example purposes of actual applications are decision-making, entity identification, situation estimation, and so on.

According to the patterns of input data (i.e. data sources), the information fusion algorithm can be classified into three levels: signal level, feature level, and decision level. In the signal level, raw data captured from sensors are the input into fusion models to be combined directly, and sometimes those models are also called "low-level fusion" and "raw data fusion." In the feature level, sensors data are often preprocessed into certain necessary features, and then, these extracted features take part in the fusion process. Feature-level fusion is also known as "medium-level fusion." The decision-level data fusion refers to dealing with some decisions that are refined from sensor data, which represent some decisions of doing a task.

In the decision level, many schemes have been developed in the field of network security. In order to fully detect the network security events by multisensors such as IDS, firewall, antivirus software, and Human judge, Xiao et al. (2006) used the RBF neural network to predict the network security status from the output decision of the security devices. However, this is an initial work, and the authors do not consider the situation when the data conflict, so the effectiveness of the plan is unreliable. In Xl et al. (2019), Dempster–Shafer evidence theory is used to fuse the determinations of security devices. In order to eliminate the inconsistent evidences (i.e. the inconsistent determinations of different sensors), a distance-based indicator is used to evaluate the conflict degree of two evidences, and the algorithm will only fuse the consistent evidence. In addition, in order to deal with homogeneous network environment where the heterogeneous detectors have different importance for the final fusion result, Particle Swarm Optimization (PSO) is used to assign weights to different data sources during the process of information fusion. It is worth mentioning that the authors complete weight training in an unsupervised way, which can greatly reduce labor costs.

Feature-level and signal-level fusions can get more comprehensive data instead of relying solely on independent decision-making from data sources. In Zhang et al. (2021), after manually extracting m basic feature sets from the original data, authors used the method of permutation and combination to fuse n group characteristics, resulting in C_m^n comprehensive data sets. However, it cannot generate features automatically, and fault features need to be designed by experts manually,

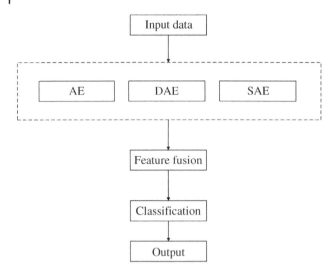

Figure 9.8 Feature fusion framework proposed by Han et al. (2020).

which means a lot of preanalysis and comparison processes are required. In order to overcome those disadvantage, Han et al. (2020) proposed a framework, as shown in Figure 9.8, that complete auto feature extraction and feature fusion. Taking raw data as input, authors used Autoencode (AE), Denoising Autoencoder (DAE), and Sparse Autoencoder (SAE) to encode the input and generate three basic feature sets. Then, feature fusion methods are used to generate comparison feature sets. However, authors did not consider the case of multisource data as input. Guo et al. (2021) proposed a framework, as shown in Figure 9.9, which can combine both semantic and behavioral patterns to solve spammer detection problems. In the feature fusion stage, authors introduced two trainable weights, W_1, W_2, to fuse the feature extracted by bidirectional autoencoder (Bi-AE) and graph convolutional networks (GCN).

After fusing the data, feature, and decision captured by sensors, the Decision-Making algorithm will work on the fusion result to generate access control policy.

9.3.2 Decision Making

Decision-making is the process to make access policies, which contain a set of access rules to determine whether a request is permitted to access a resource or not. At present, access control policy has been extensively studied, especially attribute-based access control (ABAC), which can generate fine-grained, expressive access control policies. However, most of prior works assume the access control policies are defined by the network administrators based on

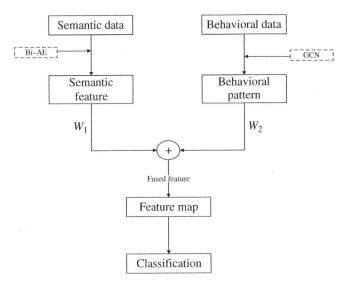

Figure 9.9 Feature Fusion Framework Proposed by Guo et al. (2021).

their knowledge about the network, failing to consider dynamic environment of the network.

In order to no longer rely on human prior knowledge to set access control strategies, researchers try to use machine-learning techniques to analyze various information. Li et al. (2019) proposed a policy generate scheme based on the outcome of anomaly-based IDS. After extracting the traffic features, authors generated samples that are "close" to the given input (i.e. the extracted feature). Then, they used a regression model to approximate the local decision boundary of anomaly-based IDS, as shown in Guo et al. (2018), to determine the scores that indicate how significantly each individual feature contributes to the prediction against the given input. The features are then sorted based on their importance. Finally, top-k features are selected to aid access control policies.

Although the scheme proposed by Guo et al. (2018) can generate the network access control policies with the help of IDS, it does not enable full automation and needs to manually extract features. In order to automatically learn access control rules, Alkhresheh et al. (2020) proposed the LAD framework, in which association rule mining algorithms (such as a-priori and FP-growth) are used to find which attributes often occur together to allow access to a resource.

However, in a highly dynamic nature of network environment, the access privileges of users often change, so the policy needs to be adjusted online. Alkhresheh et al. (2020) used two subcomponents to adjust the policies: (1) access behavior classifier; and (2) access policy adjuster. The first subcomponent taking the access request as input to determine whether the behavior of users is abnormal or not. Then, in second subcomponent, authors calculated the contribution of attribute RA to the abnormal behavior, namely C_{RA}. If C_{RA} is greater than the adjustment threshold, the rules which contain RA will be adjusted.

9.4 Conclusion

In this chapter, we first briefly introduced the background and design principles of Zero-Trust Networks, namely, "never trust, always verify." Then, we presented three different implementation cases of Zero-Trust Networks in detail, i.e. Beyond-Corp, SDP, and HuaWei CloudEngine 12800. Finally, we briefly discussed how machine learning can improve the efficiency of the information fusion layer and the decision-making layer in the zero-trust network.

References

Ashraf Alkhresheh, Khalid Elgazzar, and Hossam S. Hassanein. DACIoT: Dynamic access control framework for IoT deployments. *IEEE Internet of Things Journal*, 7(12):11401–11419, 2020. doi: 10.1109/JIOT.2020.3002709.

Betsy Beyer, Luca Cittadini, Batz Spear, and Max Saltonstall. BeyondCorp part III: The access proxy. *;login:: the magazine of USENIX and SAGE*, 41, pges 28–33, 2016.

D. R. Bharadwaj, A. Bhattacharya, and M. Chakkaravarthy. Cloud threat defense a threat protection and security compliance solution. In *2018 IEEE International Conference on Cloud Computing in Emerging Markets (CCEM)*, 2018.

Cloud Security Alliance. Software defined perimeter specification v2. 2022 https://cloudsecurityalliance.org/artifacts/software-defined-perimeter-zero-trust-specification-v2/.

Casimer DeCusatis, Piradon Liengtiraphan, and Anthony Sager. Zero trust cloud networks using transport access control and high availability optical bypass switching. *Advances in Science, Technology and Engineering Systems Journal*, 2:30–35, 2017. doi: 10.25046/aj020305.

Q. Feng and X. Li. *Research and Implementation Key Technology of Security Mobile Office*. Springer International Publishing, 2016.

Wenbo Guo, Dongliang Mu, Jun Xu, Purui Su, Gang Wang, and Xinyu Xing. LEMNA: Explaining deep learning based security applications. In *Proceedings of the 2018 ACM SIGSAC Conference on Computer and Communications Security*, CCS '18, page 364–379, New York, NY, USA, 2018. Association for Computing Machinery. ISBN 9781450356930. doi: 10.1145/3243734.3243792.

Zhiwei Guo, Yu Shen, Ali Kashif Bashir, Muhammad Imran, Neeraj Kumar, Di Zhang, and Keping Yu. Robust spammer detection using collaborative neural network in internet-of-things applications. *IEEE Internet of Things Journal*, 8(12):9549–9558, 2021. doi: 10.1109/JIOT.2020.3003802.

Y. Han, Y. Ma, J. Wang, and J. Wang. Research on ensemble model of anomaly detection based on autoencoder. In *2020 IEEE 20th International Conference on Software Quality, Reliability and Security (QRS)*, 2020.

Koudai Hatakeyama, Daisuke Kotani, and Yasuo Okabe. Zero trust federation: Sharing context under user control towards zero trust in identity federation. pages 514–519, 2021. doi: 10.1109/PerComWorkshops51409.2021.9431116.

Huawei Technologies Co., Ltd. Micro-segmentation technology white paper. 2020.

Palash Kumar, Abdallah Moubayed, Ahmed Refaey, Abdallah Shami, and Juanita Koilpillai. Performance analysis of SDP for secure internal enterprises. pages 1–6 2019. doi: 10.1109/WCNC.2019.8885784.

Hongda Li, Feng Wei, and Hongxin Hu. Enabling dynamic network access control with anomaly-based IDS and SDN. In *Proceedings of the ACM International Workshop on Security in Software Defined Networks and Network Function Virtualization*, SDN-NFVSec '19, pages 13–16, New York, NY, USA, 2019. Association for Computing Machinery. ISBN 9781450361798. doi: 10.1145/3309194.3309199.

T. Meng, X. Jing, Z. Yan, and W. Pedrycz. A survey on machine learning for data fusion. *Information Fusion*, 57:115–129, 2019.

Abdallah Moubayed, Ahmed Refaey, and Abdallah Shami. Software-defined perimeter (SDP): State of the art secure solution for modern networks. *IEEE Network*, 33(5):226–233, 2019.

Deepak Puthal, Saraju P. Mohanty, Priyadarsi Nanda, and Uma Choppali. Building security perimeters to protect network systems against cyber threats [future directions]. *IEEE Consumer Electronics Magazine*, 6(4):24–27, 2017. doi: 10.1109/MCE.2017.2714744.

S. Rose, O. Borchert, S. Mitchell, and S. Connelly. Zero trust architecture. 2020.

Max Saltonstall, Barclay Osborn, Justin McWilliams, and Betsy Beyer. BeyondCorp: Design to deployment at Google. *Login*, 41:28–34, 2016.

S. Schulz and A. R. Sadeghi. Secure VPNs for trusted computing environments. 2009.

Binanda Sengupta and Anantharaman Lakshminarayanan. DistriTrust: Distributed and low-latency access validation in zero-trust architecture. *Journal of Information Security and Applications*, 63:103023, 2021. ISSN 2214-2126. doi: 10.1016/j.jisa.2021.103023. URL https://www.sciencedirect.com/science/article/pii/S2214212621001976.

Ashish Singh and Kakali Chatterjee. Cloud security issues and challenges: A survey. *Journal of Network and Computer Applications*, 79, 2016. doi: 10.1016/j.jnca.2016.11.027.

Jaspreet Singh, Ahmed Refaey, and Abdallah Shami. Multilevel security framework for NFV based on software defined perimeter (SDP). *IEEE Network*, PP:1–6, 2020. doi: 10.1109/MNET.011.1900563.

B. Spear, B. Beyer, L. Cittadini, and M. Saltonstall. BeyondCorp: The access proxy. *;login:: the magazine of USENIX and SAGE*, 40:pages 6–11, 2016.

R. Ward and B. Beyer. BeyondCorp: A new approach to enterprise security. *;login:: the magazine of USENIX and SAGE*, 39:pges 6–11, 2014.

Debao Xiao, Ying Zhou, and Meijuan Wei. Neural network-based multi-sensor fusion for security management. In *2006 1ST IEEE Conference on Industrial Electronics and Applications*, pages 1–5, 2006. doi: 10.1109/ICIEA.2006.257103.

A. Xl, A. Jybc, D. Wl, E. Dy, C. Ywb, and W. F. Yu. Network security situation: From awareness to awareness-control. *Journal of Network and Computer Applications*, 139:15–30, 2019.

Qigui Yao, Qi Wang, Xiaojian Zhang, and Jiaxuan Fei. Dynamic access control and authorization system based on zero-trust architecture. In *2020 International Conference on Control, Robotics and Intelligent System*, CCRIS 2020, pages 123–127, New York, NY, USA, 2020. Association for Computing Machinery. ISBN 9781450388054. doi: 10.1145/3437802.3437824.

Zirak Zaheer, Hyunseok Chang, Sarit Mukherjee, and Jacobus Merwe. eZTrust: Network-independent zero-trust perimeterization for microservices. pages 49–61, 2019. ISBN 978-1-4503-6710-3. doi: 10.1145/3314148.3314349.

H. Zhang, J. L. Li, X. M. Liu, and C. Dong. Multi-dimensional feature fusion and stacking ensemble mechanism for network intrusion detection. *Future Generation Computer Systems*, 122:130–143, 2021.

10

Intelligent Network Management and Operation Systems

10.1 Introduction

The development of traditional IT operation and maintenance (O&M) systems tends to mature. However, due to the fast development of the Internet and the sharp increase in the volume of data and the business complexity, traditional IT operation and maintenance methods are gradually getting difficult to cope with the complex and dynamic situations faced by today's Internet. In recent years, machine-learning techniques have experienced rapid development. Intelligent operation and maintenance apply advanced machine learning techniques to automate operation and maintenance so as to help achieve a more efficient and reliable operation and maintenance system.

The rest of this chapter is organized as follows: Section 10.2 reviews the development process of operation and maintenance system from traditional operation and maintenance systems to intelligent operation and maintenance systems. Section 10.3 introduces a variety of open-source security related tools and classifies them from different functions. Section 10.4 introduces the existing open-source systems and cutting-edge algorithms of AIOps. Section 10.5 proposes an architecture of network security monitoring and management system according to the methods of machine learning techniques developed in previous chapters (Sections 10.2 10.3 10.4) and the various open-source security operation and management software. Finally, Section 10.6 concludes this chapter.

10.2 Traditional Operation and Maintenance Systems

10.2.1 Development of Operation and Maintenance Systems

IT operation and maintenance refer to the comprehensive management of IT software and hardware operating environments, IT business systems, and IT operation and maintenance personnel by using relevant methods, means, technologies,

AI and Machine Learning for Network and Security Management, First Edition.
Yulei Wu, Jingguo Ge, and Tong Li.

and systems. With the consolidation of enterprise IT informatization, enterprises are increasingly dependent on IT systems. System operators are finding it harder to predict the occurrence of errors. The more complex a system is, the more difficult it is to maintain. To minimize the resulting damage, operators try to fix system errors as quickly as possible. The Internet has changed a lot in recent decades, and each technological change represents a higher level of user demands. With the rapid development of the telecommunication industry, the business of fixed telephone, data transmission, Internet and broadband is growing rapidly, and many burning issues owing to this are also troubling telecom operators. How to ensure efficient and effective operation and maintenance of many software and hardware equipment in telecom operation enterprises is very important. It is in this situation that the operation and maintenance management of information system in telecommunication industry has attracted the attention of a group of far-sighted software enterprises.

With the popularization of the Internet and the rapid development of information technologies, the means of operation and maintenance have undergone earth-shaking changes. According to the degree of manual intervention, operation and maintenance development can be broadly divided into five stages, elaborated as follows.

10.2.1.1 Manual Operation and Maintenance

Decades ago, the SCALE of the IT system was small, and the operation and maintenance problems were basically carried out manually. During this period, problems were relatively simple, and most of them were concentrated at the hardware, network, and the system levels. Personnel with certain operating system or network maintenance experiences can solve the problem, and they usually rely on their experiences and the available technologies to manually troubleshoot problems. The system operation and maintenance tools and operation guide were not widely available. As systems become more complex, with more components and more user flows, companies had to hire more operators to deal with the increasing number of events. System operation and maintenance costs became increasingly high.

10.2.1.2 Tool-Based Operation and Maintenance

A large number of repetitive and tedious operations exist in the manual operation and maintenance stage. Scripts were then used to execute these operations in batches instead of repeating similar commands every time. Operators began to use various operation tools and different scripts emerged to handle different types of operation problems. But each team has its own tools, which need to be adjusted each time the operational requirements change. This is mainly due to the insufficient specification of the operation environment, resulting in weak programmable processing ability. In this scenario, some scripting tools and scripting languages began to appear, and some standard documentation of the tools begins to be produced. In the early stage, operators were mainly using various shells. Later, well-known dynamic languages such as Perl, Ruby, and Python were also widely used in the implementation of script tools, especially the automated implementation of relatively complicated logic and scenes.

10.2.1.3 Platform Operation and Maintenance

When some complex operations were encapsulated using scripts, the efficiency was improved. However, with the more complex business scenarios, increasing volume of users and devices, and diversified deployed services, simply relying on scripts execution is completely inadequate. Operation and maintenance personnel need to face the implementation of more complicated scenarios. There needs to be a process to connect multiple script functions and verify and judge the script execution results. At the same time, there were standard operation specifications and procedures for the upgrade and change of products in the telecom field. At this stage, there are higher requirements for the efficiency and misoperation rate of operation and maintenance. The operation and maintenance platform began to be introduced, through standards and processes, and then was used to free manpower and improve operation efficiency. The platform also abstracts the service change action and forms a unified standard for operation methods, service catalog environment, and service operation modes.

10.2.1.4 DevOps

With the development of operation and maintenance processes, operation and maintenance personnel are responsible for more and more works. In addition to system operation and maintenance (SYS), they are also responsible for application operation and maintenance (SRE), operation and maintenance research and development (DEV), database operation and maintenance (DBA), as well as operation and maintenance security (SEC). The communication between operation and maintenance personnel and developers is increasing, and the work of operation personnel is also advanced to the product design stage, assisting research and development personnel to adapt services to be integrated into automated operations and maintenance systems. With the increasing degree of online society, major enterprises have begun to realize that system operation and maintenance plays a decisive role in the efficiency, stability, and cost of enterprises, and their demands and requirements for operation and maintenance are becoming increasingly high. Enterprises hope to automatically complete the linkage with the surrounding operation and maintenance systems, such as monitoring systems, log systems, backup systems, to name a few, to reduce the repetitive works, reduce the cost of knowledge transfer, make operation and maintenance delivery more efficient, safer, and make product operations more stable.

10.2.1.5 AIOps

With the breakthrough of machine learning techniques and the improvement of GPU and CPU computing capabilities, massive data have brought about the AI revolution. AIOps applies AI to the field of operation and maintenance. Based on the existing operation and maintenance data (e.g. logs, monitoring information, application information), AIOps further solves the problems that cannot be solved by operation and maintenance tools and platforms used in the previous stages through advanced machine learning techniques, improves the predictive ability and stability of the system, reduces IT costs, and improves the product competitiveness of enterprises. On the basis of automatic operation and maintenance, AIOps adds a brain based on machine learning. The command and monitoring systems collect the data required by the brain for decision-making, make analysis and decision, and direct the automatic scripts to execute the decision of the brain, so as to achieve the overall goal of the operation and maintenance system. AIOps does not rely on manually specified rules, but advocates that machine learning algorithms should automatically learn from massive operation and maintenance data, and continuously refine and summarize rules.

10.2.2 Open-Source Operation and Maintenance Systems

This section investigates some open-source operational systems, as shown in Table 10.1. In general, a complete operation and maintenance system includes:

- Sampling. Periodically obtains the relevant data of some monitored indicators.
- Storage. Stores the collected data in a specified storage system.
- Display. After data collection, in order to make the data more intuitively displayed in front of users, the collected data can be processed and displayed in visual panels.
- Alarm. When the monitored indicators are abnormal, the monitoring system can automatically send out alarm information, and even can automatically complete the repair after the alarm.

The operational system monitors the system continuously and feeds back the status of the system in real time to provide necessary information for finding, locating, and rectifying problems and faults. This ensures the reliability and security of services and ensures stable and continuous running of services. The core of operation and maintenance systems is to find, locate, solve, and summarize problems. When a fault occurs in the system, the system or operation and maintenance personnel can detect and alarm the fault based on the collected status information. The operation and maintenance personnel can analyze and locate faults. After locating the source and cause of a fault, the operational personnel rectifies faults based on the fault priority, summarizes the fault causes, adjusts the system, or formulates corresponding policies to prevent the fault from recurring.

Table 10.1 Open-source operation and maintenance system.

Name	Language	Collect	Store	Show	Alert	Link
Cacti	PHP	×	×	√	×	https://github.com/Cacti/cacti
Nagios	C	Plugin	Plugin	×	Plugin	https://github.com/NagiosEnterprises
Zabbix	C,PHP	√	×	√	√	https://github.com/zabbix/zabbix
Icinga 2	C++	Plugin	√	√	√	https://github.com/Icinga
Ganglia	C	√	×	√	×	https://github.com/ganglia
Open-falcon	Go, Python	√	×	√	√	https://github.com/open-falcon
Prometheus	Go	√	√	√	√	https://github.com/prometheus/
Graphite	Python	×	√	√	×	https://github.com/graphite-project
Wgcloud	Java	√	×	√	×	https://github.com/tianshiyeben/wgcloud
Munin	Perl	√	×	√	×	https://github.com/munin-monitoring/munin
grafana	TypeScript, Go	×	×	√	√	https://github.com/grafana/grafana

10.2.2.1 Nagios

Nagios (Nagios, 2022) is an open-source computer system and network monitoring tool that can effectively monitor the status of Windows, Linux, and Unix hosts, switches, routers, and other network devices, printers, etc. When the system or service status is abnormal, it sends an e-mail or SMS alarm to inform the website operation and maintenance personnel in the first instance, and sends a normal e-mail or SMS notification after the status recovers. Nagios is structurally divided into two parts: core and plug-in. The core of Nagios provides very little monitoring functionality, and the rest is integrated into the system through plug-ins. The overall framework of Nagios is shown in Figure 10.1 below. Nagios consists of the following parts:

- NRPE (Nagios Remote Plugin Executor) remote execution plugins perform on the remote host as transparent as possible. The plugin is made up of two parts NRPE and check_nrpe. NRPE runs as a background process on a remote host and handles command execution requests from the check_nrpe plug-in on the Nagios host. Upon receiving the plug-in request from the authorized host, it executes the command line associated with the command name it received and sends the program output and returns code back to the check_nrpe plug-in.

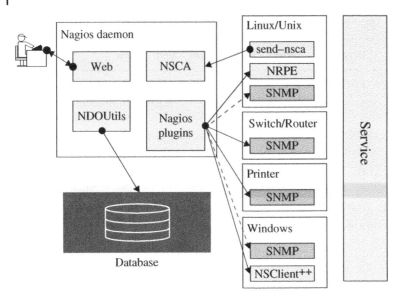

Figure 10.1 The Nagios structure.

Check_nrpe is a plug-in that runs on the Nagios host to communicate with NRPE processes on remote hosts. The plug-in requests execution of the plug-in on a remote host and waits for the NRPE process to execute the plug-in and return results. The plug-in then uses the output and the returned code from the plug-in execution on the remote host for its own output and returned code.

- NCPA (Nagios cross-platform agent) is a Nagios cross-platform agent – a single-monitoring agent installed on all major operating systems. NCPA allows active checking through check_NCPA.py and passive checking through NRDP. NCPA comes with a built-in Web GUI, documentation, websocket graphics, and is ssl-protected by default.
- NRDP (Nagios remote data processor) for use with Nagios is a simple passive result collector based on PHP. It is designed as a flexible data transfer mechanism and processor with a simple and powerful architecture that can be easily extended and customized to meet the needs of individual users. By default, NRDP has functionality that allows remote agents, applications, and Nagios instances to submit commands, and host and service checks, to the Nagios server. This enables Nagios administrators to use NRDP to configure distributed monitoring, passive checking, and remote control of their Nagios instances in a fast and efficient manner. The functionality of NRDP can be extended by developing other NRDP plug-ins.
- NSCA (Nagios service check acceptor) is composed of the NSCA program and the send_nsca. The NSCA program runs as a daemon on the central server where

Nagios is running. It listens for host and service checking results from the remote machine (sent using the send_NSCA program described below). Once the data is received from the remote client, the daemon will basically attempt to validate the data received from the client. This is done by decrypting the data using the cipher stored in the nsca.cfg file. If the decrypted data looks okay (that is, it was originally encrypted by the send_NSCA program using the same password), the daemon will create an entry in the Nagios external command file that tells Nagios to process the host and service checking results. Send_NSCA is the client program used to send service checking information from the remote machine to the NSCA daemon on the central machine running Nagios. The reads service checks the information from the standard input in TAB-separated format.

- NSTI (The Nagios SNMP trap interface) is designed to be an intelligent user interface and an organized database that meets all your SNMP requirements.

Due to the development over the time, more and more devices need to be monitored in operation and maintenance. Nagios active monitoring mode has become the bottleneck due to the client expansion. Therefore, Nagios stopped maintaining active monitoring plug-in in version 4.0 and enabled passive monitoring mode by default. In the passive monitoring mode, the server only receives information collected from the agent, which greatly saves resources occupied by the server, transfers more tasks of consuming resources to the agent, and greatly increases the number of hosts monitored by the server. The overall functions of Nagios are mainly provided by the plug-in mode. The core framework is kept simple and has good scalability. Users only need to install different plug-ins according to different needs to achieve specific functions. However, with the refinement of operation and maintenance, the operation of Nagios plug-in mode is relatively complicated. Operational and maintenance personnel need to install a large number of plug-ins because many functions are required. Meanwhile, Nagios configuration information can only be modified in the form of configuration files, which is not convenient for operation and extension. Nagios does not support visualization, so users need to install other tools to provide this functionality. The default is to use "Cacti+Nagios" to implement a complete monitoring system.

10.2.2.2 Zabbix

Zabbix (ZABBIX, 2022) is an enterprise-class distributed open-source monitoring solution capable of monitoring the health and integrity of numerous network parameters and servers. Zabbix uses a flexible alarm mechanism that allows users to configure mail-based alarms for almost any event, providing excellent reporting and data visualization based on stored data. Zabbix is mainly composed of the following functional components: server, database, Web, proxy, and agent. The overall framework of Zabbix is shown in Figure 10.2.

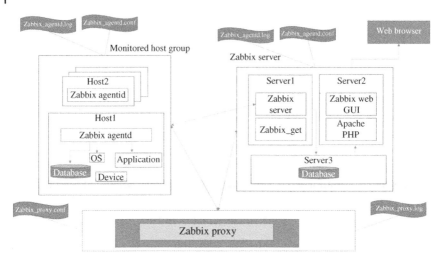

Figure 10.2 The Zabbix structure.

- Zabbix server is the core component of Zabbix software, to which agent reports availability, system integrity information, and statistics. The Server is also the core repository for all configuration information, statistics, and operational information.
- All configuration information, as well as data collected by Zabbix, are stored in a database.
- The Web interface allows users to easily access Zabbix from anywhere and on any platform. This interface is part of Zabbix server and usually (but not necessarily) runs on the same physical machine as Zabbix server.
- Zabbix proxies can replace Zabbix servers to collect performance and availability data. Zabbix proxy deployment in Zabbix is optional. However, proxy deployment can share the load of a single Zabbix server.
- Zabbix agents are deployed on monitored targets and are used to actively monitor local resources and applications and send the collected data to the Zabbix server.

As an enterprise-class distributed open-source monitoring solution, Zabbix supports distribution, high availability, flexible alarm mechanisms, and has relatively complete functions. However, Zabbix itself integrates many functions, but the API introduction is rough, and the database entries are complex, so the subsequent secondary development is not straightforward. At the same time, the system itself is large and has many functions, so the demand for simple lightweight versions is high. Zabbix configuration is not completely textual, and some configurations require interface operations, which is difficult to automate.

10.2.2.3 Prometheus

Prometheus (Prometheus, 2022) is a Cloud Native Computing Foundation project, which is a system and service monitoring system. It collects metrics from configured targets at a given time interval, evaluates regular expressions, displays results, and triggers alerts when a specified condition is observed.

Compared to traditional Zabbix and Nagios, the objects monitored by Prometheus have changed. Zabbix is monitoring software that was created in 1998. At that time, most servers were identified only by their IP address or host, so Zabbix's feature was that all data must "belong" to one host. With the emergence of cloud computing, elastic computing, container technologies, SaaS, and other IT forms, operation and maintenance systems such as Zabbix can no longer cover the required monitoring, or they can only be monitored in a compatible way. Prometheus, however, does not target hosts or IP addresses; it targets metrics only and provides a fixed data format that allows access to systems in the correct format, providing greater coverage and flexibility.

The overall framework of Prometheus is shown in Figure 10.3. It is mainly composed of the following parts, namely server, exporter, push gateway, alert manager, and webui.

- Server. Server is the core part of Prometheus, which is responsible for obtaining, storing, and querying monitoring data. The server can statically configure monitoring targets and also provide service discovery. Server itself is a sequential database and provides PromQL query language for stored data to query and analyze data.

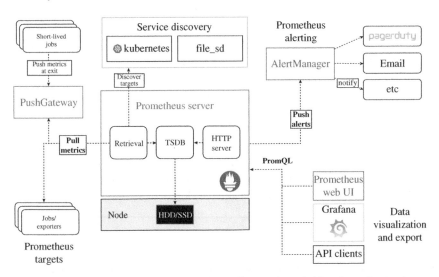

Figure 10.3 The Prometheus structure (https://prometheus.io/docs/introduction/overview/). Source: Prometheus/CC BY 4.0.

- Exporter. Exporter exports monitoring data collection endpoints to Prometheus Server through HTTP, and exports monitoring information back to Prometheus in a format supported by Prometheus. Collection is classified into direct collection and indirect collection. As a built-in function of monitoring targets, direct collection supports Promtheus in its implementation, and directly exposes related data to Prometheus. An indirectly collected exporter is a monitoring target and does not support Prometheus. Therefore, an agent must be compatible with the monitoring target, and an exporter can collect indicators and expose them to Prometheus.

- AlertManager. Prometheus Server supports the creation of alarm rules based on the PromQL. If the rules defined by the PromQL are met, an alarm is generated. After receiving alerts from the Prometheus server, the AlertManager removes duplicate data, groups the alarms, routes the alarms to the receiving mode, and generates an alarm.

- PushGateway. PushGateway is used for short jobs. Because such jobs were short-lived, they may have disappeared before Prometheus came to pull. To do so, jobs could push their metrics directly to the Prometheus intermediate gateway. This approach is primarily used for metrics at the service level, while node exporter is required for metrics at the machine level.

- Webui. Prometheus provides users with a simple graphical user interface for configuring the system or retrieving data.

Prometheus provides multidimensional data models and flexible query methods. It can add monitoring information to multiple tags, use these tags in arbitrary combination of dimensions, and process the data through the PromQL query language, making it easy to process and use the data. Prometheus supports the monitoring of various types of objects, which is a good way to monitor popular cloud infrastructure such as containers. It supports data collection in pull and push modes, flexibly responding to multiple monitoring scenarios. Prometheus also supports service discovery, partition sampling and federated deployment of data, and large-scale cluster monitoring. Prometheus does a good job of collecting and processing data, but it does not provide persistent long-term storage, anomaly detection, automatic horizontal scaling, or user management, and has a crude display panel that requires visual tools such as Grafana. Although Prometheus itself is mature, it lacks some common operational functions and support for these functions requires additional configuration and development by operations personnel.

10.2.3 Summary

This section summarizes traditional operation and maintenance systems and briefly introduces three common operation and maintenance tools. Prometheus is an emerging solution compared to Zabbix and Nagios to solve container monitoring problems that other current operation systems cannot easily solve. It can be seen that the traditional operation and maintenance system has become increasingly mature and complete after nearly 20 years of development. But with the fast development of the Internet, more and more new concepts are put forward, and the monitoring system needs to evolve with the development of business. The current era is in the stage of operation and maintenance automation. Although there are many mature automatic operation and maintenance systems, the system is still in constant iteration and optimization.

We can see the fast development of cloud platforms based on virtualization technologies, and the recent development of fusion cloud or hybrid cloud to integrate cloud resources, to provide a bigger platform to support big data, AI intelligence, system operation, and management. This is a big trend of the next few years' business development. The operation and maintenance system also needs to follow the business objectives of such changes. At the same time, the data are transitioning from the traditional relational data to the time-series data. The intelligence operations are being added into the traditional operational system. The data are becoming the core of the operational system, so the development of data storage and handling is becoming more and more important. Efficient standard query language, such as data processing methods are growing and developing.

10.3 Security Operation and Maintenance

10.3.1 Introduction

With the continuous development of business scales, the more mature the Internet company is, the more detailed the division of operation and maintenance jobs is. At present, many large Internet companies only have system operation and maintenance in their initial stage. With the requirements of service scale and service quality, they gradually subdivide their work. Today's operation and maintenance work is mainly divided into the following four parts: system, application, database operation, and security operation and maintenance. In operation and maintenance, the security of services and systems is an important part for operation and maintenance personnel. With the development of IT technology and business, as well as the emergence of all kinds of security vulnerabilities, operation and maintenance and security are increasingly integrated, people pay more attention to security operation and maintenance, and a new cross-field called "security operation and maintenance" has emerged. Operation and maintenance security is responsible for security hardening of networks, systems and services, conducting routine security scanning and penetration tests, developing security tools and systems, and handling security incidents.

Security operation and maintenance are not only the guarantee of enterprise networks and information security but also the cornerstone of enterprise survival and rapid development. In recent years, security problems have become increasingly prominent, such as struts2 remote code execution vulnerability, OpenSSL heart bleeding, bash shell breaking vulnerability, and other problems, which have caused inestimable losses in Internet enterprises. Different from web security, mobile security, or service security, operation and maintenance security problems tend to be serious. On the one hand, the security loopholes in operation and maintenance are very serious. Operation and maintenance services are located at the bottom layer, involving servers, network equipment, basic applications, etc. Once security problems occur, the security of servers will be directly affected. On the other hand, an operation and maintenance vulnerability usually reflects a problem in an enterprise's security norms and processes or the execution of these norms and processes. In this case, many servers may have such security problems, or the service may also have other operation and maintenance security problems. Enterprise investment in security operation and maintenance has increased rapidly, and various security operation and maintenance problems have attracted widespread attention. Until today, security operation and maintenance have become the top priority of enterprise security construction.

10.3.2 Open-Source Security Tools

This section examines a variety of open-source security tools, grouped by functionality into the following categories.

10.3.2.1 Access Control

Access control refers to the means by which the system limits the ability of users to use data resources based on their identities and predefined policy groups to which they belong (Butun and Österberg, 2021). The main purpose of access control is to restrict the access of the accessing subject to an object, so as to ensure the effective use and management of data resources within the legal scope. For security operation and maintenance, there are many ways to implement access control. Network security domain isolation is one of the most important and basic means of network security defense, and it is also the first basic problem to be considered in the construction of enterprise data centers and information systems. A network security domain is a system consisting of computers, servers, databases, and service systems with the same security level and similar service types and functions. Loose security policies can be implemented in a security domain and access permissions can be centrally managed at domain boundaries. In case of intrusion, exceptions can be limited within the domain as far as possible to reduce the overall damage of the system. In the domain boundary, a range of devices including security gateway, firewall, and fortress machine can be used to monitor and control the access information. Once a unified gateway is established, each security zone can mask access to sensitive ports externally and limit inbound traffic internally, which is effective in risk mitigation and attack blocking. Several open-source security tools that can be applied to access control such as gateways, firewalls, and fortresses are presented in Table 10.2.

10.3.2.2 Security Audit and Intrusion Detection

Security audit and intrusion detection collects and analyzes system information to check whether the system has been attacked or is being attacked. Security audit refers to the systematic and independent inspection and verification of relevant activities or behaviors in the computer network environment by professional auditors according to relevant laws and regulations, the entrustment of property owners and the authorization of management authorities, and the corresponding evaluation. Security audit is mainly to identify, record, store, and analyze information related to security-related activities in the system, check which security-related activities occur in the network, and who (which user) is responsible for this activity. Intrusion detection is a reasonable supplement to firewall. It helps the system deal with network attacks, expands the security management ability of system administrators (including security audit, monitoring, attack identification, and response), and improves the integrity of information security infrastructure (Denning, 1986). It collects information from a number of key points in a computer network system and analyzes it to see if there are security policy violations and signs of attacks. Intrusion detection is considered as the second security gate after the firewall, which can monitor the network without affecting the performance of the network, thus providing real-time protection against internal attacks, external attacks, and misoperations. Security audit focuses on postaudit. It detects whether insecure behaviors have occurred in the system and analyzes and traces the source. Intrusion detection focuses on real-time analysis or advance analysis to detect whether security anomalies are occurring in the system, identify and restrict the activities of the object in advance, and prevent the occurrence or spread of attacks. Open-source tools are summarized in Table 10.3.

10.3.2.3 Penetration Testing

Penetration test is a method to evaluate the security of computer network systems by simulating the attack method of malicious hackers. This process involves the active analysis of any weaknesses, technical flaws, or vulnerabilities in the system from where an attacker might be and from which the vulnerability can be actively exploited. Penetration test refers to that the penetration personnel tests a specific network in different locations (such as from the internal network, from the external network) by various means, in order to find and mine the loopholes

Table 10.2 Open-source tools related to access control.

Name	Language	Link	Description
ModSecurity	C++	https://github.com/SpiderLabs/ModSecurity	ModSecurity is an open source, cross platform web application firewall (WAF) engine for Apache, IIS, and Nginx that is developed by Trustwave's SpiderLabs
ngx_lua_waf	Lua	https://github.com/loveshell/ngx_lua_waf	ngx_lua_waf is a web application firewall based on lua-nginx-module (openresty)
JXWAF	Lua	https://github.com/jx-sec/jxwaf	JXWAF is an open-source web application firewall
x-waf	Lua	https://github.com/xsec-lab/x-waf	X-WAF is a cloud WAF system suitable for small and medium-sized enterprises, so that small and medium-sized enterprises can easily have their own free cloud WAF
pfSense	PHP	https://github.com/pfsense/pfsense	The pfSense project is a free network firewall distribution, based on the FreeBSD operating system with a custom kernel and including third-party free software packages for additional functionality
OpenRASP	C++	https://github.com/baidu/openrasp	Unlike perimeter control solutions such as WAF, OpenRASP directly integrates its protection engine into the application server by instrumentation
JumpServer	Python	https://github.com/jumpserver/jumpserver	JumpServer is the world's first open-source bastion machine, and it is a 4A-compliant professional operation and maintenance security audit system
Teleport	Go	https://github.com/gravitational/teleport	Certificate authority and access plane for SSH, Kubernetes, web applications, and databases
CrazyEye	C	https://github.com/triaquae/CrazyEye	CrazyEye is a simple and easy-to-use IT audit bastion machine developed based on Python
GateOne	js	https://github.com/liftoff/GateOne	Gate One is an HTML5 web-based terminal emulator and SSH client
jxotp	Python	https://github.com/jx-sec/jxotp	Enterprise SSH login two-factor authentication system

Table 10.3 Security audit and intrusion detection-related tools.

Name	Language	Link	Description
Suricata	C	https://github.com/OISF/suricata	Suricata is a network IDS, IPS and NSM engine
OSSEC	C	https://github.com/ossec/ossec-hids	OSSEC is an Open-Source, Host-based Intrusion Detection System that performs log analysis, file integrity checking, policy monitoring, rootkit detection, real-time alerting, and active response
wazuh	C	https://github.com/wazuh/wazuh	Wazuh is a free and open-source platform used for threat prevention, detection, and response
snort3	C++	https://github.com/snort3/snort3	Snort3 is the next-generation Snort IPS (Intrusion Prevention System)
firestorm	Elixir, Phoenix	https://github.com/firestormforum/firestorm	An open-source forum engine, with an Elixir+Phoenix backend and an Elm frontend
YU LONG HIDS	Go	https://github.com/ysrc/yulong-hids-archived	A host intrusion detection system open sourced by YSRC
Elkeid (AgentSmith-HIDS)	Go	https://github.com/bytedance/Elkeid	Elkeid is a Cloud-Native Host-Based Intrusion Detection solution project to provide next-generation Threat Detection and Behavior Audition with modern architecture
Sobek-Hids	Python	https://code.google.com/archive/p/sobek-hids/source	A Python-based HostIDS system
Security Onion	Shell	https://github.com/Security-Onion-Solutions/securityonion/	Security Onion 2 – Linux distro for threat hunting, enterprise security monitoring, and log management
OSSIM	C++	https://github.com/ossimlabs/ossim	Core OSSIM (Open Source Software Image Map) package including C++ code for OSSIM library, command-line applications, tests, and build systems
Apache Metron	Java	https://github.com/apache/metron	Metron integrates a variety of open-source big data technologies in order to offer a centralized tool for security monitoring and analysis. Metron provides capabilities for log aggregation, full packet capture indexing, storage, advanced behavioral analytics and data enrichment, while applying the most current threat intelligence information to security telemetry within a single platform

(continued)

Table 10.3 (Continued)

Name	Language	Link	Description
w3a_SOC	PHP	https://github.com/smarttang/w3a_SOC	A platform that integrates web log auditing and network monitoring
OpenSOC	Java	https://github.com/OpenSOC/opensoc	OpenSOC integrates a variety of open-source big data technologies in order to offer a centralized tool for security monitoring and analysis
Prelude	Emacs	https://github.com/bbatsov/prelude	Prelude is an Emacs distribution that aims to enhance the default Emacs experience. Prelude alters a lot of the default settings, bundles a plethora of additional packages, and adds its own core library to the mix
Nmap	Lua, C	https://github.com/nmap/nmap	Nmap is released under a custom license, which is based on (but not compatible with) GPLv2
Lynis	Shell	https://github.com/CISOfy/lynis	Security auditing tool for Linux, macOS, and UNIX-based systems. Assists with compliance testing (HIPAA/ISO27001/PCI DSS) and system hardening
Mozilla	Python	https://github.com/mozilla/MozDef	MozDef: Mozilla Enterprise Defense Platform
GRR Rapid Response	python	https://github.com/google/grr	GRR is a python client (agent) that is installed on target systems, and python server infrastructure that can manage and talk to clients
Splunk	Python	https://github.com/splunk/docker-splunk	Splunk Enterprise is a platform for operational intelligence. Our software lets you collect, analyze, and act upon the untapped value of big data that your technology infrastructure, security systems, and business applications generate
MIDAS	Python	https://github.com/etsy/MIDAS/tree/pre_archive	MIDAS is a framework for developing a Mac Intrusion Detection Analysis System, based on work and collaborative discussions between the Etsy and Facebook security teams
WSSAT	C#	https://github.com/YalcinYolalan/WSSAT	WSSAT is an open-source web service security scanning tool which provides a dynamic environment to add, update, or delete vulnerabilities by just editing its configuration files

Table 10.3 (Continued)

Name	Language	Link	Description
BTA	Python	https://github.com/airbus-seclab/bta	BTA is an open-source Active Directory security audit framework
Chiron	Python	https://github.com/aatlasis/Chiron	An IPv6 Security Assessment framework with advanced IPv6 Extension Headers manipulation capabilities
LogonTracer	Python, Js (Yamanishi and Takeuchi, 2002)	https://github.com/JPCERTCC/LogonTracer	Investigate malicious Windows logon by visualizing and analyzing Windows event logs.
Rastrea2r	Python	https://github.com/rastrea2r/rastrea2r	Collecting & Hunting for IOCs with gusto and style
Zeek	C++,zeek	https://github.com/zeek/zeek	Zeek is a powerful network analysis framework that is much different from the typical IDS you may know
p0f	C	https://github.com/p0f/p0f	p0f is a tool that utilizes an array of sophisticated, purely passive traffic fingerprinting mechanisms to identify the players behind any incidental TCP/IP communications (often as little as a single normal SYN) without interfering in any way
Arkime	JS,C	https://github.com/arkime/arkime	Arkime (formerly Moloch) is an open source, large scale, full packet capturing, indexing, and database system

in the system, and then output the penetration test report and submit it to the network owner. According to the penetration test report provided by the infiltrator, the network owner can clearly know the security risks and problems existing in the system. Various open-source tools for penetration testing are listed in Table 10.4.

10.3.2.4 Vulnerability Scanning

Vulnerability scanning is a security detection (penetration attack) based on vulnerability database to detect the security vulnerabilities of specified remote or local computer systems by scanning (Viega et al., 2000). Vulnerability scanning technology is an important network security technology. It can cooperate with firewall and intrusion detection systems to improve network security effectively. By scanning the network, network administrators can learn the security settings

Table 10.4 Penetration testing-related tools.

Name	Language	Link	Description
DockerSecurity Playground	JavaScript	https://github.com/giper45/DockerSecurity Playground	A microservices-based framework for the study of network security and penetration test techniques
RouterSploit	Python	https://github.com/threat9/routersploit	The RouterSploit framework is an open-source exploitation framework dedicated to embedded devices
Astra	Python	https://github.com/flipkart-incubator/Astra	REST API penetration testing is complex due to continuous changes in existing APIs and newly added APIs
OWTF	Python, js	https://github.com/owtf/owtf	Offensive web testing framework (OWTF) is a framework which tries to unite great tools and make pen testing more efficient
BeEF	Js,ruby	https://github.com/beefproject/beef	BeEF is short for the browser exploitation framework. It is a penetration-testing tool that focuses on the web browser
DELTA	Java	https://github.com/seungsoo-lee/DELTA	DELTA is a penetration-testing framework that regenerates known attack scenarios for diverse test cases
ShuoGuang	Java	https://github.com/iSafeBlue/TrackRay	Suguang is an open-source penetration testing framework. The framework itself implements vulnerability scanning functions and integrates well-known security tools

and application services of the network, discover security vulnerabilities in a timely manner, and objectively evaluate network risks. Network administrators can correct network security vulnerabilities and wrong settings in the system according to the scan results and take precautions against hacker attacks. If firewall and network monitoring systems are using passive defense means, then security scanning is an active defense measure, which can effectively avoid hacker attacks and prevent them from happening before they happen. Table 10.5 provides a variety of security tools related to vulnerability scanning.

Table 10.5 Vulnerability detection related tools.

Name	Language	Link	Description
XunFeng	Python, Less	https://github.com/ysrc/xunfeng	Xunfeng is a fast emergency response and cruise scanning system for corporate intranets
Nikto	Perl	https://github.com/sullo/nikto	Nikto is an open source (GPL) web server scanner
OWASP JoomScan	Perl	https://github.com/OWASP/joomscan	OWASP Joomla! Vulnerability Scanner (JoomScan) is an open-source project, developed with the aim of automating the task of vulnerability detection and reliability assurance in Joomla CMS deployments
Archery	Python	https://github.com/archerysec/archerysec	Archery is an open-source vulnerability assessment and management tool which helps developers and pen testers to perform scans and manage vulnerabilities
EKTotal	PHP	https://github.com/nao-sec/ektotal	EKTotal is an integrated analysis tool that can automatically analyze the traffic of drive-by download attacks
Insight	js	https://github.com/creditease-sec/insight	Insight is a vulnerability management platform used by the CreditEase Security Department to conduct online full lifecycle management of security vulnerabilities in the company's internal systems
Metasploit	Ruby	https://github.com/rapid7/metasploit-framework	Metasploit is an open-source security vulnerability detection tool
OpenVAS	C	https://github.com/greenbone/openvas-scanner	This is an open vulnerability assessment scanner (OpenVAS) of the greenbone vulnerability management (GVM) solution
OWASP ZAP	Java	https://github.com/zaproxy/zaproxy	The OWASP zed attack proxy (ZAP) is one of the world's most popular free security tools and is actively maintained by a dedicated international team of volunteers

10.3.2.5 CI/CD Security

CI/CD is a way to frequently deliver applications to customers by introducing automation during the application development phase. The core concepts of CI/CD are continuous integration, continuous delivery, and continuous deployment (Poth et al., 2018). As a solution for development and operations teams, CI/CD addresses the questions that arise when integrating new code. Specifically, CI/CD enables continuous automation and monitoring throughout the entire application lifecycle, from the integration and testing phases to delivery and deployment. However, CI/CD has its own security implications. The traditional CI/CD pipeline uses a lot of tools, so it is inevitable that there will be some vulnerabilities, which become the gateway for cyber-attacks. There are also potential bugs in the code, due to omissions by developers. The code should be developed according to certain specifications to prevent the disclosure of sensitive information and sensitive files. The enterprise needs to audit pipes and code regularly to maintain a high level of security at all times. These efforts can improve CI/CD security by reducing the likelihood of network attacks. In order to ensure code security and prevent sensitive information leakage, Table 10.6 lists several open-source security tools.

10.3.2.6 Deception

Honeypot (Honeypot, 2022) technology is essentially a deception technology to the attacker. By arranging some hosts, network services or information as bait, the attacker is induced to attack them so that the attack behavior can be captured and analyzed, the tools and methods used by the attacker can be understood, and the attack intention and motivation can be inferred (Zhang and Thing, 2021). It enables the defense side to clearly understand the security threats they face and enhances the security defense capability of the actual system through technical and management methods. The honeypot is like an intelligence-gathering system. It seems to be a deliberate target, luring hackers to attack. So once an attacker gets in, we can capture its behavior and keep up with the latest attacks and vulnerabilities on the server. It can also eavesdrop on hackers' contacts, gather the tools they use and gain access to their social networks. Table 10.7 provides several open-source honeypot tools.

10.3.2.7 Data Security

Information security or data security has two opposite meanings: One is the security of the data itself, which mainly refers to adopt the modern cryptographic algorithms to active protection of data, such as data confidentiality, data integrity, strong two-way authentication. The second is the security of the data protection, which is mainly to use modern information storage means for active protection of data, such as through the disk array, data backup, and disaster different means

Table 10.6 CI/CD related tools.

Name	Language	Link	Description
Infer	Ocaml	https://github.com/facebook/infer	A static analyzer for Java, C, C++, and Objective-C
Brakeman	Ruby	https://github.com/presidentbeef/brakeman	A static analysis security vulnerability scanner for Ruby on Rails applications
Dependency-Check	Java	https://github.com/jeremylong/DependencyCheck	OWASP dependency-check is a software composition analysis utility that detects publicly disclosed vulnerabilities in application dependencies
rhizobia_J	Java	https://github.com/momosecurity/rhizobia_J	Java security coding standard and JAVA security SDK
rhizobia_P	PHP	https://github.com/momosecurity/rhizobia_P	PHP security coding standard and JAVA security SDK
RIPS	PHP	https://github.com/ripsscanner/rips	A static source code analyzer for vulnerabilities in PHP scripts
Bandit	Python	https://github.com/PyCQA/bandit	Bandit is a tool designed to find common security issues in Python code
Cobra	Python	https://github.com/WhaleShark-Team/cobra	Source Code Security Audit
Banruo	Python	https://github.com/yingshang/banruo	Automated code audit system based on fotify
VCG	vb	https://github.com/nccgroup/VCG	CG is an automated code security review tool that handles C/C++, Java, C#, VB and PL/SQL
OWASP find security bugs	Java	https://github.com/find-sec-bugs/find-sec-bugs	The SpotBugs plugin for security audits of Java web applications and Android applications
Hades	Python	https://github.com/zsdlove/Hades	Static code auditing system
Puma-scan	C#	https://github.com/pumasecurity/puma-scan	Puma Scan is a software security Visual Studio extension that provides real-time, continuous source code analysis as development teams write code

Table 10.7 Honeypot-related tools.

Name	Language	Link	Description
Opencanary	Python	https://github.com/thinkst/opencanary	Modular and decentralized honeypot
T-Pot	C	https://github.com/telekom-security/tpotce	The all in one honeypot platform
HFish	Go	https://github.com/hacklcx/HFish	It is a cross platform honeypot platform developed based on golang, which has been meticulously built for enterprise security
Honeyd	C	https://github.com/DataSoft/Honeyd	Honeyd is a small daemon that creates virtual hosts on a network
MHN	Python	https://github.com/pwnlandia/mhn	MHN is a centralized server for management and data collection of honeypots
Glastopf	Python	https://github.com/mushorg/glastopf	Glastopf is a Python web application honeypot founded by Lukas Rist
Cowrie	Python	https://github.com/cowrie/cowrie	Cowrie is a medium-to-high interaction SSH and Telnet honeypot designed to log brute force attacks and the shell interaction performed by the attacker
Kippo	Python	https://github.com/desaster/kippo	Kippo is a medium interaction SSH honeypot designed to log brute force attacks and, most importantly, the entire shell interaction performed by the attacker
Dionaea	Python	https://github.com/DinoTools/dionaea	Dionaea is meant to be a nepenthes successor, embedding python as scripting language, using libemu to detect shellcodes, supporting IPv6 and TLS
Conpot	Python	https://github.com/mushorg/conpot	Conpot is an ICS honeypot with the goal to collect intelligence about the motives and methods of adversaries targeting industrial control systems
Wordpot	Python	https://github.com/gbrindisi/wordpot	Wordpot is a Wordpress honeypot which detects probes for plugins, themes, TimThumb, and other common files used to fingerprint a wordpress installation
Elastichoney	Go	https://github.com/jordan-wright/elastichoney	Elastichoney is a simple elasticsearch honeypot designed to catch attackers exploiting RCE vulnerabilities in elasticsearch
Beeswarm	Python	https://github.com/honeynet/beeswarm	Beeswarm is a honeypot project which provides easy configuration, deployment, and management of honeypots
Shockpot	Python	https://github.com/pwnlandia/shockpot	Shockpot is a web app honeypot designed to find attackers attempting to exploit the Bash remote code vulnerability, CVE-2014-6271

Table 10.8 Data security-related tools.

Name	Language	Link	Description
tor	C	https://github.com/torproject/tor	Tor protects the privacy on the Internet by hiding the connection between the Internet address and the services a user uses
TrueCrypt	C,C++	https://github.com/FreeApophis/TrueCrypt	Disk encryption system TrueCrypt allows for layered content encryption using two layers of access control
Gitrob	Go	https://github.com/michenriksen/gitrob	Gitrob is a tool to help find potentially sensitive files pushed to public repositories on Github
DeepViolet	java	https://github.com/spoofzu/DeepViolet	DeepViolet is a TLS/SSL scanning API written in Java

to ensure data security. Data security is an active inclusion measure. The security of data itself must be based on reliable encryption algorithms and security systems, mainly including symmetric algorithms and public key cryptography. Generally, operation and maintenance security covers access control, authentication and authorization, backup, encryption, transmission, and storage. Table 10.8 introduces several open-source data security-related tools.

10.3.3 Summary

This section investigates and introduces a variety of open-source security-related tools and classifies them from different functions. However, security tools are not limited to just a few categories, and new defenses are always created as new attacks emerge. At the level of information, confidentiality, integrity, and availability of information should be guaranteed. At the application level, operation and maintenance personnel need to ensure the security of the system, information, and personnel. Operation and maintenance security operations are generally divided into four steps: protection, detection, response, and recovery. Generally speaking, the defender is always in a passive defensive position. Between the same level of attack and defense, the defense side can set up a defense surface, but the attacker only needs to break through one attack point. To defend against the same level of attack, the cost of defense is huge, and between different levels of attack and defense, they are independent of each other.

In addition, with the continuous improvement of security defense systems, security equipment, and system tools continue to increase and enterprise security management gradually shows some problems. For example, there is a lack of interoperability between different devices to effectively collaborate; different security systems are independent from each other. They mainly defend against a certain type of security attacks or a kind type of security attacks. Managers lack a defense view of the whole system. The security operations center (SOC, (SOC, 2022)) integrates a single-defense system into a system so that operation and maintenance personnel can monitor the overall security status of the enterprise network through the SOC. In the future, efforts should be made toward the management and coordination of security tools, real-time defense, detection of potential attacks, and real-time update of vulnerabilities. At the same time, security operation and maintenance should also follow the development of the business. Services are becoming containerized, cloud-based, and distributed. With the introduction of new technologies, security problems arise. Security systems are a gradual process of accumulation and repair, and as new technologies and frameworks emerge, new security-related tools are often required.

10.4 AIOps

10.4.1 Introduction

AIOps refers to intelligent operation and maintenance. Its goal is to further solve the problems that cannot be solved by operation and maintenance methods mentioned in Sections 10.2 and 10.3 by means of advanced machine learning techniques, improve the predictive ability and stability of the system, reduce IT costs, and enhance the product competitiveness of enterprises (Dang et al., 2019). AIOps does not rely on manually specified rules, but it advocates that machine learning algorithms should be able to automatically learn from massive operation and maintenance data (including logs, monitoring information, application information, etc.), and continuously refine and summarize rules. On the basis of automatic operation and maintenance, AIOps adds a brain based on machine learning. The command and monitoring system collects the data required by the brain for decision-making, makes analysis and decision, and directs the automatic scripts to execute the decision of the brain, so as to achieve the overall goal of the operation and maintenance system.

Today, many organizations are transitioning from a traditional infrastructure of stand-alone static physical systems to an in-house, dynamic combination of hosted clouds, private clouds, and public cloud environments that run on virtualized or software-defined resources that are constantly expanding and reconfiguring. The data generated by applications and systems in these environments continue to grow. In fact, Gartner estimates that, on average, enterprise IT infrastructures generate two to three times more IT operational data per year. Traditional domain-based IT management solutions cannot meet the requirements of handling such a surge of data. They cannot intelligently classify important events using the available data. They cannot correlate data in different but interdependent environments. Moreover, they cannot provide the real-time insights and predictive analytics that IT operations teams need to respond quickly enough to meet user and customer service-level expectations. The addition of AIOps provides visibility into performance data and dependencies across all environments, analyzes data to extract significant events related to slowdowns or outages, and automatically alerts IT staffs about problems, root causes, and recommended solutions. To put it simply, AIOps hopes to further solve problems that cannot be solved by previous automatic operation and maintenance tools through advanced machine learning techniques.

10.4.2 Open-Source AIOps and Algorithms

In the AIOps whitepaper (DCA, 2018), there are three common application scenarios for AI:

- In terms of quality assurance, ensuring the stable operation of the live network is subdivided into basic scenarios such as abnormal detection, fault diagnosis, fault prediction, and fault self-healing.
- In terms of cost management, it is subdivided into indicators monitoring, abnormal detection, resource optimization, capacity planning, performance optimization, and other basic scenarios.
- In terms of efficiency, it is subdivided into intelligent prediction, intelligent change, intelligent question and answer, intelligent decision-making, and other basic scenarios.

10.4.2.1 Research Progress of Anomaly Detection

Aiming at the application of AIOps in security, this section mainly sorts out the open-source systems and algorithms related to anomaly detection. The open-source AIOps systems are presented in Table 10.9. The open-source algorithms and toolkits related to the domain are shown in Table 10.10. Meanwhile, in order to achieve the scenario of cost management, efficiency improvement, and quality assurance, AIOps products or platforms should contain the following elements according to Gartner's definition:

- Data sources. They are a large and diverse IT infrastructure.
- Big data platform. It is used to process historical and real-time data.
- Calculation and analysis. It generates new data from existing IT data, such as data cleaning, noise removal.
- Algorithms. They are used for calculation and analysis to produce the results required for IT operations scenarios. This generally refers to unsupervised learning, which can generate new algorithms based on the results of algorithmic analysis.

Table 10.9 Open-source AIOps.

Name	Language	Link	Description
Metis	Python	https://github.com/Tencent/Metis	Metis is a series of application practices in the field of AIOps, which mainly solves the problems of intelligent operation and maintenance in terms of quality, efficiency, and cost
UAVstack	Java	https://github.com/uavorg/uavstack	UAVStack is an intelligent service technology stack. It is a solution for integration of R & D, operation and maintenance
Semisup-learn	Python	https://github.com/tmadl/semisup-learn	Semisupervised learning frameworks for python, which allow fitting scikit-learn classifiers to partially labeled data
Anomalyzer	Go	https://github.com/lytics/anomalyzer	Probabilistic anomaly detection for time series data
Skyline	Python	https://github.com/earthgecko/skyline	Skyline is a real-time anomaly detection system, built to enable passive monitoring of hundreds of thousands of metrics, without the need to configure a model/threshold for each one, which might be needed by Nagios
Surus	Java	https://github.com/netflix/surus	A collection of tools for analysis in Pig and Hive
Nupic	Python	https://github.com/numenta/nupic	The Numenta Platform for Intelligent Computing (NuPIC) is a machine intelligence platform that implements the HTM learning algorithms
Adaptive-alerting	Java	https://github.com/ExpediaDotCom/adaptive-alerting	Anomaly detection for streaming time series, featuring automated model selection
Prometheus-anomaly-detector	Python	https://github.com/AICoE/prometheus-anomaly-detector	This repository contains the prototype for a prometheus anomaly detector (PAD) which can be deployed on OpenShift

Table 10.10 Open-source AIOps algorithms and packages.

Name	Language	Link	Description
Donut	Python	https://github.com/NetManAIOps/donut	Donut is an anomaly detection algorithm for seasonal KPIs
Bagel	Python	https://github.com/NetManAIOps/Bagel	The implementation of "Robust and Unsupervised KPI Anomaly Detection Based on Conditional Variational Autoencoder Models are in model.py
Time2Graph	Python	https://github.com/petecheng/Time2Graph	This project implements the Time2Graph model, which focuses on time series modeling with dynamic shapelets
OmniAnomaly	Python	https://github.com/NetManAIOps/OmniAnomaly	OmniAnomaly is a stochastic recurrent neural network model which glues gated recurrent unit (GRU) and variational auto-encoder (VAE). Its core idea is to learn the normal patterns of multivariate time series and uses the reconstruction probability to do anomaly judgment
MAD-GANs	Python	https://github.com/LiDan456/MAD-GANs	Applied generative adversarial networks (GANs) to do anomaly detection for time series data
AIOpstools	Python	https://github.com/jixinpu/aiopstools	AIOpstools is an open toolkit in the AIOps field
TSFRESH	Python	https://github.com/blue-yonder/tsfresh	This repository contains the TSFRESH python package
adtk	Python	https://github.com/arundo/adtk	A Python toolkit for rule-based/unsupervised anomaly detection in time series data
Anomaly-Detection	R	https://github.com/twitter/anomalydetection	AnomalyDetection is an open-source R package to detect anomalies which is robust, from a statistical standpoint, in the presence of seasonality and an underlying trend
EGADS	Java	https://github.com/yahoo/egads	A Java package to automatically detect anomalies in large-scale time-series data
GluonTS	Python	https://github.com/awslabs/gluon-ts/	GluonTS is a Python toolkit for probabilistic time series modeling, built around Apache MXNet (incubating)

10.4.2.2 Metis

Metis (METiS, 2022), named after the Greek goddess of wisdom Metis, is a collection of applied practices in the field of AIOps. It mainly solves intelligent operation and maintenance problems in quality, efficiency, and cost. The current version of open-source time series anomaly detection software solves the anomaly detection problem of time series data from the perspective of machine learning. The idea of time series anomaly detection software is to jointly detect time series data based on statistical decision, unsupervised, and supervised learning. Statistical decision and unsupervised algorithm were used for the first-level decision to output suspected anomalies, followed by supervised model decision to obtain the final detection results. The detection model is generated by training of a large number of samples and can be updated by continuous training of samples. The architecture of time series anomaly detection kit is shown in Figure 10.4, which can be divided into five layers.

- Data layer (DB). It stores detection anomaly information, sample information, and task information.
- SERVICE layer. It is divided into two modules. Data-driver module DAO encapsulates the common data operation interface with the DB layer. The business module service implements the specific business logic of the API layer.
- LEARNWARE layer. It is divided into three modules.
  Detect. It provides the time series anomaly detection interface.
  Features. Three types of time series (statistical feature, fitting feature, classification feature) are provided for feature extraction of time series data, which is used in the supervised learning and training.

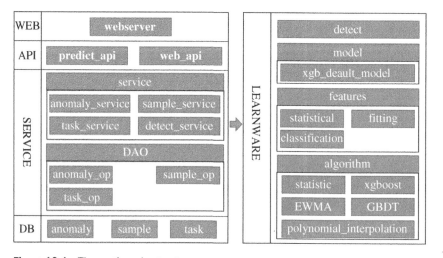

Figure 10.4 The metis code structure.

Algorithm. It provides several common machine-learning algorithm packages (statistical discrimination algorithm, exponential moving average algorithm, polynomial algorithm, GBDT and XGBoost algorithm, etc.) for joint arbitration detection of sequential data.

- Interface layer (API). It provides API capability, time series anomaly detection interface, and WEB management operation interface.
- WEB layer (WEB). The WEB service is provided by the system. Through the service interface, users can perform operations such as exception query, marking, sample database management, and model training.

In metis, the application position of the learner is shown in Figure 10.5. The learning component can be connected to anomaly detection API. It provides rate value detection and quantity value detection API interfaces to detect time series and can also be connected to the learning component support system for time series anomaly detection of learning components.

- Feature extraction. It provides the extraction function of three types of features (statistical feature, fitting feature, and classification feature), with the feature dimension more than 90. It supports adding custom features.

Time series anomaly detection kit

Comparison between the traditional threshold monitoring method and the scope of detection components. Learning components act on data detection, intelligent detection is realized through learning component interface, and iterative evolution of model is realized through learning component support system.

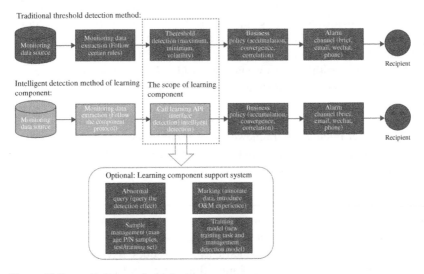

Figure 10.5 metis time series detector.

- Abnormal query. Time series detected by API (only abnormal) are stored in the library, providing management functions, paging query, retrieval, scaling, etc.
- Marking. It provides marking function, marking/unmarking for positive and negative samples, after marking samples will be automatically transferred to the sample library.
- Sample management. It provides sample management functions, such as retrieval, graphical representation, editing, deletion, import, and so on.
- Model management. It provides model management functions and supports custom model training.

10.4.2.3 UAVStack

UAVStack (UAVStack, 2022) is an intelligent service stack, which is a solution for the integration of development and operation. It includes mission robotics (CODE HIT), full-dimensional monitoring (code UAV.monitor), application performance management (code UAV.APM), service governance (code UAV.ServiceGovern), microservice computing (code UAV.MSCP), user experience management (code UAV.UEM), etc. The core content of UAVStack consists of the following parts.

- Health Management Service (HealthManager, HM for short). HM is a comprehensive service center integrating real-time data processing, portrait data processing, real-time warning data processing, log data processing, and other services. It is responsible for computing and processing various data in the UAVStack and supporting related services. The Structure of HM is shown in Figure 10.6.
- MonitorAgent (MA for short). MA is an agent that is used for decoupling and runs independently outside the application. MA is used to periodically capture information in the MOF, automatically discover information in Tomcat, MSCP, and JavaEE, and obtain more derived monitoring information. The data in MA then arrives at HealthManager via Rocketmq. MA obtains values from two parts: One is the points that MonitorFramework buried in J2EE projects; the other is the system.
- Middleware-enhanced MonitorFramework (MOF probe). It integrates with JEE and other middleware frameworks for nonintrusive application monitoring. It uses the Java agent mechanism to provide application mapping and performance data collection.

10.4.2.4 Skyline

Skyline (AnOmalY, 2022) is a near-real-time anomaly detection system designed to passively monitor hundreds of thousands of metrics without having to configure a model/threshold for each metric as Nagios does. Skyline was designed primarily for use in large high-resolution time series that requires continuous

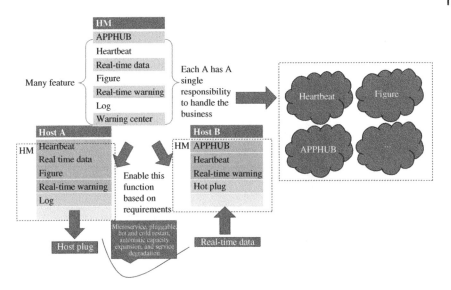

Figure 10.6 UAVStack HM structure.

monitoring. Once a metric stream is set up (from StatsD or Graphite or other sources), other metrics are automatically added to Skyline for analysis. The simple and extensible algorithm of Skyline can be used for automatic detection. Once an indicator anomaly is detected, the whole time series will be expanded to WebApp to check where the anomaly is and take action. The interior of Skyline consists of three components: Horizon, Analyzer, and Webapp. Horizon receives external datapoints, forward them to Redis, and removes obsolete datapoints from Redis (datapoint refers to data at a particular point in time, including timestamp and value). Analyzer takes the metrics data from Redis and uses an algorithm to determine if it is abnormal. Finally, Webapp charts metrics for the exception. The simple workflow of Skyline is shown in Figure 10.7.

- Horizon is the data collector for Skyline, which consists of three roles: Listener, Worker, and Roomba. A Listener receives external data. Each Listener is a process that starts two types of Listeners: TCP and UDP. They use different application layer protocols and use different data serialization methods. The Worker is responsible for processing Chunk in the public Queue. When Horizon starts up, it will create WORKER_PROCESSES Worker processes to continuously queue out Chunk from the Queue and serialize the datapoint in Chunk by MSgPack. It adds to the corresponding Redis queue by the metric to which it belongs. Roomba is responsible for cleaning the Datapoints outdated in each time series in Redis, leaving only the most recent data points to ensure that the Redis does not explode.

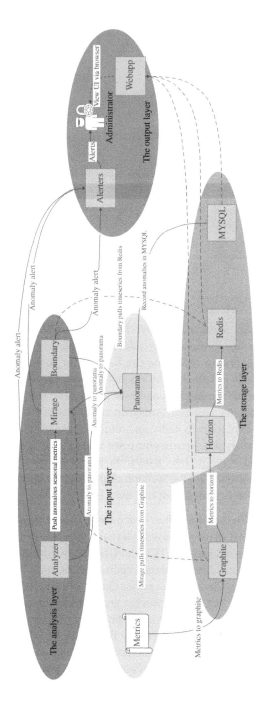

Figure 10.7 Skyline simplified workflow. Source: Based on https://earthgecko-skyline.readthedocs.io/en/latest/_images/skyline.simplified .workflow.annotated.gif.

- After processing by Horizon, several time series have been saved in Redis, and Analyzer is responsible for analyzing them and providing a series of algorithms to determine whether timeseries are anomalous. Analyzer is also a thread that works in much the same way as Roomba. Once started, ANALYZER_PROCESSES processes are created and all-time series under FULL_NAMESPACE are equally allocated. Each time series is fed into the Algorithms module to determine if it is abnormal and return an abnormal Datapoint and report the abnormal algorithm. Algorithm is the core of anomaly judgment. Skyline has nine built-in algorithms to determine whether a Datapoint sequence is abnormal or not. Users can configure the algorithm to be used according to the characteristics of their application (ALGORITHMS configuration item) or customize their own determination algorithm.
- Webapp provides a diagram of anomalous metrics based on the Flask framework, which is a relatively simple module that does not expand. The basic principle is to poll anomalies. json in the background, gets the name of the exception's metrics and the corresponding exception datapoint, and then requests the time series sequence (including FULL/name MINIspace) from the background according to the metrics name, and display it in a chart.

10.4.3 Summary

This section introduces AIOps' existing open-source systems and frontier algorithms. As the hardware and software systems supporting the digital world become larger and more complex, the requirements for intelligent operation and maintenance will become higher and higher. AIOps is an inevitable trend of the development of operation and maintenance technology. As industries grow, AIOps will eventually spread to companies that use Internet technology. All parties of "production, learning, research and application" are also actively following up, and eventually a complete AIOps ecosystem will be formed, with different professional divisions and cooperation to promote the faster landing of AIOps.

At the same time, the core of the algorithm is data. In order to provide a more comprehensive operation and maintenance system and make AI play a greater role in operation and maintenance, comprehensive and diversified data collection are essential. Extract the most useful information for operation and maintenance from the system to help operation and maintenance personnel understand the latest and most complete operation status of the data center and serve for AIOps scenarios. The algorithm analyzes data of different dimensions in different scenarios, and the application of the algorithm is more refined. Therefore, it is necessary to adjust or adapt the AIOps anomaly detection algorithm appropriately for specific refined scenarios. Therefore, the algorithm of AIOps develops in the direction of data diversification, refinement, and diversification of algorithm scenes. The ultimate goal of AIOps is to achieve fully automated and intelligent system operation and maintenance, in which the intelligent operation and maintenance system completely takes over the human work and independently achieves the optimization of availability, cost, and efficiency. At present, AIOps has not covered the whole field of operation and maintenance systems, and there is still a long way to go to be fully intelligent.

10.5 Machine Learning-Based Network Security Monitoring and Management Systems

Various open-source systems provide a series of tools to complete specific data collection, monitoring, alarm, and data processing functions, but these tools are concerned with their own data collection and monitoring. It is difficult to form an overall monitoring, operation and maintenance system, which leads to data fragmentation and lack of a unified view of resources. Therefore, it is difficult to carry out unified global calculation and statistical analysis.

Based on the machine learning methods of the previous chapters of this book and various open-source security operations and management software, this section proposes an overall architecture of machine learning-based network security monitoring and management systems, forming a whole closed loop of data acquisition, statistical analysis and security control, and realizing the unified management and scheduling of the network.

10.5.1 Architecture

A machine learning-based network security monitoring the overall architecture of the management system is shown in Figure 10.8. The overall architecture is formed by the following parts: physical facility layer, virtual resource layer, orchestration layer, policy layer, semantic description layer, and application layer. It is through the Center for Intelligent Analytics of Big Data to complete the overall state awareness and policy scheduling and through the programmable measurement and audit to complete the data audit function.

10.5.2 Physical Facility Layer

The physical facility layer refers to the infrastructure of all kinds of network equipment and security equipment, including routers, switches, security equipment, computing, storage equipment, and all kinds of measurement audit equipment. It constitutes the infrastructure of IT architecture and uses machine learning techniques to carry out network security monitoring and management of the

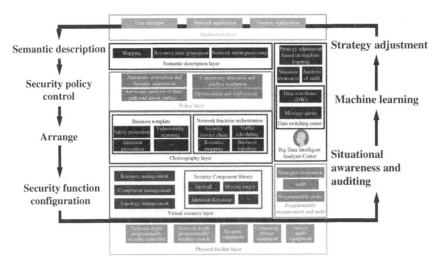

Figure 10.8 Machine learning-based network security monitoring and management systems.

network objects and data sources. The physical facility layer provides a rich source of measurement data, including device and link performance data (e.g. SNMP (SNMP, 2022), ICMP (ICMP, 2022)), underlying log type data (e.g. logs for various devices), advanced log type data (e.g. firewall logs, IDS, IPS system logs), and measurement design device data (e.g. depth pack detection data such as DPI).

10.5.3 Virtual Resource Layer

With the development of virtualization and containerization technologies, VMs and containers have become an important part of infrastructure. Virtual resource pools, as a key element in the fabric of converged infrastructure, are a collection of shared servers, storage, and networks that can be reconfigured faster to meet application requirements, enabling administrators to support changes in business requirements more easily and quickly than ever before. In a cloud-computing environment, resources are no longer decentralized hardware, but physical servers are consolidated to form one or more logical pools of virtual resources, including computing, storage, and network resources. Resource pools can delegate control over host (or cluster) resources, and the advantages are clear when using resource pools to divide all resources within a cluster. Users can create multiple resource pools as direct children of a host or a cluster and configure them. Users can then delegate control of the resource pool to other individuals or organizations. Users can use attack-spoofing technology, access control, intrusion detection, to name a few, to form a security component library.

10.5.4 Orchestrate Layer

As the variety and number of businesses and functions increase, the deployment environment is more complex, and different businesses and functions need to be orchestrated to simplify cross-environment, cross-enterprise business processes in integrated services, systems, and applications. Orchestration enables automated deployment of network services with the ability to quickly deploy, dynamically adjust, and reuse. Common network functions include security service chain, traffic scheduling, resource mapping, business topology, etc.

10.5.5 Policy Layer

The policy layer is responsible for combining the semantic description of network intent with the semantic description of resource states and gives the strategy for the current network by intelligent methods. Network policies describe the actions that a network performs to achieve a goal and the order in which they are executed. A network policy can be divided into multiple policies for ease of execution, or multiple policies can be combined into a single combination of policies to implement the modular execution of network policies. OSDF (Comer and Rastegarnia, 2018) proposed a template-based policy generation method. The system defines the network policy library in advance and stores different types of network policies in the policy library. When the user intends to input, the key information can be obtained by using the method of natural language processing and mapped to the corresponding network policy according to the policy library. Han et al. (2016) designed a set of interfaces in the SDN environment to convert the input intention into OpenFlow flow table rules and deliver them to the physical network. Before implementing the network policy, the policy should be verified in order to ensure the smooth operation of the network. In an enterprise environment, policies manage the various permissions to access data. These policies can be represented in different forms, such as natural language, xml-based formats such as XACML (XACML, 2022), or firewall code. Because of their complexity, distribution, and the size, these policies can contain exceptions or errors that can lead to security vulnerabilities. Inconsistency refers to rules that may be found in a set of rules or policies that lead to the opposite decision, such as denying and allowing access requests in certain circumstances (Shaikh et al., 2017). In addition, if a pending policy is found to conflict with the current network policy, the conflict needs to be eliminated. Currently, the main policy is to resolve conflicts based on priority and eliminate low priority by setting priorities.

10.5.6   Semantic Description Layer

The network needs to satisfy the intent of the application layer, but it does not give how to implement it. In practice, forwarding decisions and resource allocation are still based on network policies. Therefore, the intent needs to be understood. Nagios can be used as an implementation for monitoring resource status. Nagios, Zabbix, and Prometheus can be used to monitor resource status. The semantic description layer makes semantic understanding of the input provided by the application layer, and through the natural language processing method, the input provided by the application layer is extracted by keyword, lexical analysis, semantic mining, and so on. However, the current ability of natural language processing technologies is limited, and further development of natural language processing technologies is needed. In addition, we need to get the current network resource status and semantically describe the resource status to inform the policy layer of the current network resource status.

10.5.7   Application Layer

The application layer is responsible for obtaining the user's intention to the network, obtaining the input to the network through the user interface, network application and security application, and unifying the input into a standard form. The input obtained by the application layer does not need to be implemented. The most common way to obtain input is natural language, mostly using semantics (subject, predicate, guest language, modifier) to form the representation. For example, if a user wants to realize "I want to disconnect A from B," we can input it, and ⟨A, disconnect, B⟩ will be output. There should be an interface to implement it. Foster et al. (2011) used high-level abstractions to describe packet-forwarding rules. Anderson et al. (2014) provided simple primitives to describe the forwarding behaviors and network structures of the underlying switches. Both are designed based on DSL and can fully describe user intents.

10.5.8   Center for Intelligent Analytics of Big Data

After the policy is issued to the actual network, because the state of a network is constantly changing, the policy needs to be automatically optimized and adjusted according to the desired state and the current network state to ensure that the network always meets the intent requirements. Machine learning methods are used to classify and predict network status information and adjust for changes in the state of the network. Through situational awareness, security threats are identified, analyzed, and addressed from a global perspective to prepare for the next step in decision-making and action. For the centralized management of network state information, data exchange components such as Kafka (Kafka, 2022) RocketMQ (RocketMQ, 2022) can be used. Kafka is a distributed, publish/subscribe-based messaging system that provides message persistence in an $O(1)$ manner with time complexity, and high throughput, and supports offline and real-time data processing, as well as horizontal online scaling. RocketMQ is an open-source message middleware with pure Java, distributed and queue model, which has high performance, high reliability, high real-time, and distributed characteristics. Exception detection can be based on the Flink (Apache Flink, 2022; Carbone et al., 2015)/Spark (Spark, 2022; Zaharia et al., 2010) Machine Learning Library. FlinkML (FlinkML, 2022) is a library of machine learning tools within Flink. The goal of FlinkML is to provide scalable machine learning algorithms, good APIs, and tools to minimize the effort required to build end-to-end machine learning systems. MLlib (MLlib, 2022) is the machine learning library in Spark. Its goal is to make practical machine learning algorithms scalable and easy to use.

10.5.9   Programmable Measurement and Auditing

After the policy is issued to the actual network, the status information of the network needs to be monitored in real time to ensure that the forwarding behavior of the network conforms to the user's intention. In addition, the state of the network is constantly changing, and the network state at the beginning of execution and the network state in the process of operation may not be consistent. Therefore, at this time, we also need to monitor the status of the network information. A range of tools such as Suricata (Sur, 2022), Nmap (NMAP, 2022), and Snort3 (Snort, 2022) can be used to monitor and audit policies. In-band network telemetry provides a solution for real-time monitoring of network status. In-band network telemetry is a network-monitoring framework that can collect and report the status of network equipment and the current state of the network directly in the data plane, so as to realize real-time, fine-grained, and end-to-end network monitoring. By injecting a probe into the data plane, the data plane is judged to be forwarded according to the corresponding policy, and whether the user intent is correctly implemented (Zheng and Cao, 2013).

10.5.10   Overall Process

The intent can be obtained from the user, and the requirements can be collected from the application; they can be summarized into a unified format and given to the semantic description layer. The semantic description layer turns intent into a semantic description and provides it to the policy layer. The semantic description layer also provides a semantic description of the state of the resource. The policy layer automatically generates security policies by analyzing semantic descriptions, resolves consistency issues and conflicts, and optimizes and deploys global security policies. The orchestration layer orchestrates various business templates and network functions to simplify the process. Security features are configured at the virtual resource layer based on policy, including resource management, component management, topology management, and the management of components such as firewalls and intrusion detection in the security component library. Situational awareness and auditing can obtain the network status after the policy is implemented. Machine learning automates the processing of data in message queues, and the network can adjust the strategy based on the judgment given by machine learning.

10.5.11 Summary

This section introduced a network security monitoring and management system based on machine learning. Due to the different data formats provided by various open-source tools, it is difficult to form a unified overall architecture by focusing only on data monitoring, operation, and maintenance in its own domain, which is inconvenient for unified management. This tends to lead to the lack of unified view of resources, and it is difficult to carry out unified global calculation and statistical analysis.

This section aimed at the overall architecture of the network security monitoring and management system based on machine learning, combining data acquisition, statistical analysis and security control, and forming a complete convenient and controllable system. This architecture applies a lot of machine learning, including natural language processing for semantic descriptions of network resources and intentions, machine learning for automatic generation of policies, consistency detection and conflict resolution, and machine learning for situational awareness to perceive and predict network conditions. Unified management of operation and maintenance systems is necessary, and it is also a development trend to use machine learning to endue it with intelligence.

10.6 Conclusion

The chapter provided a comprehensive overview of the network management and operation tools and systems, from traditional approaches to the current intelligent ways. We compared and discussed the representative tools at different stages of the development of network management and operation. In addition, we also proposed a machine learning-based network security monitoring and management system, combining data acquisition, statistical analysis, and security control.

References

FlinkML is the machine learning (ML) library for flink. https://nightlies.apache.org/flink/flink-docs-release-1.5/dev/libs/ml/, 2022.

Honeypot, a computer security mechanism. https://en.wikipedia.org/wiki/Honeypot_(computing), 2022.

MLlib is apache spark's scalable machine learning library. https://spark.apache.org/mllib/, 2022.

Apache Rocketmq is a unified messaging engine, lightweight data processing platform. https://rocketmq.apache.org/, 2022.

What is a security operations center (SOC)? https://www.mcafee.com/enterprise/en-us/security-awareness/operations/what-is-soc.html, 2022.

Snort3. https://www.snort.org/snort3, 2022.

Suricata. https://suricata.io/, 2022.

Apache Flink Stateful Computations Over Data Streams. https://flink.apache.org/, 2022.

Internet Control Message Protocol. https://en.wikipedia.org/wiki/Internet_Control_Message_Protocol, 2022.

Apache Kafka. https://kafka.apache.org/, 2022.

Metis. https://github.com/Tencent/Metis/blob/master/README.en.md, 2022.

NMAP. https://nmap.org/, 2022.

Detecting anomalies with skyline. https://anomaly.io/detect-anomalies-skyline/index.html, 2022.

What is simple network management protocol (SNMP)? https://www.thousandeyes.com/learning/techtorials/snmp-simple-network-management-protocol, 2022.

What is apache spark? https://spark.apache.org/, 2022.

UAVStack. https://uavorg.github.io/main/#/, 2022.

Extensible access control markup language. https://en.wikipedia.org/wiki/XACML, 2022.

Nagios the industry standard in it infrastructure monitoring. https://www.nagios.org/, 2022.

Prometheus. https://prometheus.io/docs/introduction/overview/, 2022.

ZABBIX 6.0 LTS. https://www.zabbix.com/, 2022.

Carolyn Jane Anderson, Nate Foster, Arjun Guha, Jean-Baptiste Jeannin, Dexter Kozen, Cole Schlesinger, and David Walker. NetKAT: Semantic foundations for networks. In Suresh Jagannathan and Peter Sewell, editors, *The 41st Annual ACM SIGPLAN-SIGACT Symposium on Principles of Programming Languages, POPL '14*, San Diego, CA, USA, January 20–21, 2014, pages 113–126. ACM, 2014. doi: 10.1145/2535838.2535862.

Ismail Butun and Patrik sterberg. A review of distributed access control for blockchain systems towards securing the internet of things. *IEEE Access*, 9:5428–5441, 2021. doi: 10.1109/ACCESS.2020.3047902.

Paris Carbone, Asterios Katsifodimos, Stephan Ewen, Volker Markl, Seif Haridi, and Kostas Tzoumas. Apache Flink™: Stream and batch processing in a single engine. *IEEE Data Engineering Bulletin*, 38(4):28–38, 2015. URL http://sites.computer.org/debull/A15dec/p28.pdf.

Douglas Comer and Adib Rastegarnia. OSDF: An intent-based software defined network programming framework. In *43rd IEEE Conference on Local Computer Networks, LCN 2018*, Chicago, IL, USA, October 1–4, 2018, pages 527–535. IEEE, 2018. doi: 10.1109/LCN.2018.8638149.

Yingnong Dang, Qingwei Lin, and Peng Huang. AIOps: Real-world challenges and research innovations. In *2019 IEEE/ACM 41st International Conference on Software Engineering: Companion Proceedings (ICSE-Companion)*, pages 4–5, 2019. doi: 10.1109/ICSE-Companion.2019.00023.

OSCAR DCA. "Enterprise AIOPS implementation recommendations" white paper. https://pic.huodongjia.com/ganhuodocs/2018-04-16/1523873064.74.pdf, 2018.

Dorothy E. Denning. An intrusion-detection model. In *Proceedings of the 1986 IEEE Symposium on Security and Privacy*, Oakland, California, USA, April 7–9, 1986, pages 118–133. IEEE Computer Society, 1986. doi: 10.1109/SP.1986.10010.

Nate Foster, Rob Harrison, Michael J. Freedman, Christopher Monsanto, Jennifer Rexford, Alec Story, and David Walker. Frenetic: a network programming language. In Manuel M. T. Chakravarty, Zhenjiang Hu, and Olivier Danvy, editors, *Proceeding of the 16th ACM SIGPLAN International Conference on Functional Programming, ICFP 2011*, Tokyo, Japan, September 19–21, 2011, pages 279–291. ACM, 2011. doi: 10.1145/2034773.2034812.

Yoonseon Han, Jian Li, Doan Hoang, Jae-Hyoung Yoo, and James Won-Ki Hong. An intent-based network virtualization platform for SDN. In *12th International Conference on Network and Service Management, CNSM 2016*, Montreal, QC, Canada, October 31 - November 4, 2016, pages 353–358. IEEE, 2016. doi: 10.1109/CNSM.2016.7818446.

Alexander Poth, Mark Werner, and Xinyan Lei. How to deliver faster with CI/CD integrated testing services? In Xabier Larrucea, Izaskun Santamaria, Rory V. O'Connor, and Richard Messnarz, editors, *Systems, Software and Services Process Improvement - 25th European Conference, EuroSPI 2018*, Bilbao, Spain, September 5–7, 2018, Proceedings, volume 896 of *Communications in Computer and Information Science*, pages 401–409. Springer, 2018. doi: 10.1007/978-3-319-97925-0_33.

Riaz Ahmed Shaikh, Kamel Adi, and Luigi Logrippo. A data classification method for inconsistency and incompleteness detection in access control policy sets.

International Journal of Information Security, 16(1):91–113, 2017. ISSN 1615-5270. doi: 10.1007/s10207-016-0317-1.

John Viega, J. T. Bloch, Y. Kohno, and Gary McGraw. ITS4: A static vulnerability scanner for C and C++ code. In *16th Annual Computer Security Applications Conference (ACSAC 2000)*, 11–15 December 2000, New Orleans, Louisiana, USA, page 257. IEEE Computer Society, 2000. doi: 10.1109/ACSAC.2000.898880.

Kenji Yamanishi and Junichi Takeuchi. A unifying framework for detecting outliers and change points from non-stationary time series data. *Proceedings of the 8th ACM SIGKDD International Conference on Knowledge Discovery and Data Mining*, 2002.

Matei Zaharia, Mosharaf Chowdhury, Michael J. Franklin, Scott Shenker, and Ion Stoica. Spark: Cluster computing with working sets. In Erich M. Nahum and Dongyan Xu, editors, *2nd USENIX Workshop on Hot Topics in Cloud Computing, HotCloud'10*, Boston, MA, USA, June 22, 2010. USENIX Association, 2010. URL https://www.usenix.org/conference/hotcloud-10/spark-cluster-computing-working-sets.

Li Zhang and Vrizlynn L. L. Thing. Three decades of deception techniques in active cyber defense – retrospect and outlook, 2021.

Qiang Zheng and Guohong Cao. Minimizing probing cost and achieving identifiability in probe-based network link monitoring. *IEEE Transactions on Computers*, 62(3):510–523, 2013. doi: 10.1109/TC.2011.244.

11

Conclusions, and Research Challenges and Open Issues

11.1 Conclusions

With the fast development of 5G, Internet of Things (IoT), Industrial IoT (IIoT), Cloud/Edge Computing, and Industry 4.0, networking systems are experiencing a remarkable increase in the complexity, dynamicity, and the security concerns. Artificial intelligence (AI) and machine learning (ML) have been widely applied and succeeded in many areas in terms of improving performance and efficiency of decision-making. They are well placed to address the above concerns of networking systems. AI and ML for network and security management have received tremendous attention in recent years from both academia and industry. This book provided a deeper understanding of this topic from three different points of views.

First, in Chapter 2 we elaborated the architecture of ML-empowered network and security management. Under this architecture, we investigated the potential AI and ML techniques in academia, in terms of supervised learning, semi- and unsupervised learning, and reinforcement learning, that can enable the automation of network and security management tasks. In addition, we surveyed the existing industry products, standards, projects, and proof-of-concepts on network and security management, in order to allow readers to have a better view of industry progress on AI- and ML-enabled network and security management.

Second, we presented a series of typical AI- and ML-enabled solutions for specific network and security management tasks, including learning network intent for autonomous network management in Chapter 3, virtual network embedding via hierarchical reinforcement learning in Chapter 4, ML for network traffic analysis in Chapter 5, online encrypted traffic classification based on lightweight neural networks in Chapter 6, context-aware learning for robust anomaly detection in Chapter 7, anomaly classification with unknown, imbalanced and few labeled log data in Chapter 8, and zero-trust networks in Chapter 9.

AI and Machine Learning for Network and Security Management, First Edition.
Yulei Wu, Jingguo Ge, and Tong Li.

Finally, in Chapter 10, we showcased an intelligent network management and operation system and illustrated how the AI and ML techniques can be adopted in a system to enable intelligent network and security management.

11.2 Research Challenges and Open Issues

In this section, we will provide and discuss a list of research challenges and open issues on the automation of network and security management. We appreciate that this is not the list of exclusive challenges and issues, but we hope this can be useful as a start point for advancing the further research in this area.

11.2.1 Autonomous Networks

- How to unify the expression of intents inferred from different tasks is an important issue. Intents for some tasks are suitable for being expressed from the perspective of constraints, such as connectivity, and for other tasks they may be depicted in terms of performance, such as QoS. A unified way of expressing intents may be considered from the construction of a common primitive, which expresses all the upper-level intents.
- With the increasing number of intent symbols, how to efficiently search for the symbol structure from the huge symbol space will become a challenge. Enumeration of all structures is unrealistic. This problem may be alleviated by combining prior distribution and random search. The prior distribution is used to give priority for trying historical structures. Random search is used to sample structures instead of trying all of them.
- User intents are expressed in close to natural language, and how to automatically translate them into appropriate intention symbol structures is a challenge. As more and more intention symbol structures are learnt and accumulated from data, they are stored in the agents network knowledge base. When a user proposes a specific intention to perform a task, the agent should be able to automatically recognize the user's intention and call the corresponding symbol structure or use existing symbols to form a new task structure. This question may refer to natural language processing methods, such as the sequence-to-sequence method. The input is the user's intent language sequence, and the output is the intent symbol sequence to realize the translation from the user's intention language to a symbolic structure.

11.2.2 Reinforcement Learning Powered Solutions

Reinforcement learning (RL) has been widely used in automating network tasks. In this section, we will use virtual network embedding (VNE) as a typical example to illustrate potential challenges.

- The reward functions of RL are hard to define. In RL, an agent improves its strategies according to the returned rewards, and the function of reward is usually defined manually. Most of the existing works (Yan et al., 2020, Wang et al., 2019) define the reward function without rigorously mathematical validation, and it cannot guarantee the eventual training of an optimal strategy. To address this problem, we should pay more attention to the mathematical analysis instead of verifying the effectiveness of the reward function directly by simulation results. In other words, the measurement of reward functions should both consider simulation performance and mathematical analysis.
- It is hard to set up a real network to verify the effectiveness of the proposed algorithm for carrying out a network task. Almost all the works validate the algorithm within a simulation environment (Yao et al., 2018a,b). It is too resource-consuming to set up a real network, and the Internet service provider (ISP) is reluctant to use the proposed algorithms in the entire production network. This problem is decided by the reality and the objective conditions and a convincing framework that combines the reality and simulation environment is urgently needed. Besides, the proposed algorithms need to consider more about the implementation details to enhance their deployment performance.
- RL-based algorithms such as VNE algorithms have not been verified in an elaborate way. For example, RL-based algorithms are usually verified within a middle-size ISP in a simulation case (Yan et al., 2020, Wang et al., 2019, Yao et al., 2018a,b). Due to the complexity of the VNE problem, there is no large-size ISP simulation environment for verification. There are a few works (Yan et al., 2020, Amaldi et al., 2016) that take the algorithm complexity into consideration. However, their algorithms are not validated within a large-size ISP simulation environment. More complexity analysis should be included in the VNE works, which is important in the real environment and is one of the key points that can determine whether the deployment is successful or not.

11.2.3 Traffic Classification

- It is not easy to collect a reliable dataset for traffic classification, which has a great impact on the accuracy of classification algorithms. First, traditional methods label the data manually, which has low efficiency and cannot guarantee accuracy. Second, some works (e.g. (Liu et al., 2018)) have proposed automatic methods, but their effectiveness cannot be verified. A convincing dataset is an urgent need, and its effectiveness should also be verified in an elaborate manner. Different algorithms can then be compared in a more proper way and their strengths and weaknesses can be identified easily.

- Existing traffic classification methods lack consideration for reality. In AI-based models, the classification labels are fixed, which is not suitable in a real-world setting, since there are always unknown traffic categories. On the one hand, the unknown traffic should be recognized as early as possible. On the other hand, the unknown traffic should be classified and labeled correctly. Zhang et al. (2020) proposed a model for classifying unknown traffic, but it failed to determine the label for real traffic. More specifically, the model first recognized the unknown traffic and then clustered them with the k-means method. However, the number of categories and the specific category are unknown. Therefore, a more specific model for unknown traffic classification should be exploited elaborately, which can classify the unknown traffic into right categories.
- Fine-grained traffic classification has not been solved properly. For example, there are application-level classification methods, but the traffic classification within the application (e.g. different functions in the application) has not been developed. Usually, traffic classification is carried out based on (1) protocols (e.g. HTTP, SSL, SMTP, DNS, or QUIC); (2) traffic types (e.g. video, chat, or browsing); (3) applications (e.g. Amazon, Apple, Microsoft, or Google); and (4) websites. A more refined classification is needed, which can further improve QoS.

11.2.4 Anomaly Detection

Anomaly detection can be carried out using various types of data, including temporal data, spatial data, spatiotemporal data, and graph data. Log data, as a typical example of spatiotemporal data, have been widely used in anomaly detection of networking systems. In the following, we mainly provide some challenges about leveraging log data in anomaly detection.

- Log parsing is responsible for extracting parameters from logs and transforming each log message into a log event. It can automate the phase of log analysis. However, most of the existing log anomaly detection methods discard extracted parameters. If these parameters can be used sensibly, log anomaly detection could be performed more accurately.
- Existing studies on log anomaly detection focus on training a model to make it perform well on multiple log datasets. However, in a real production environment, operators prefer to perform better on a specific log dataset. In order to make this, we can combine different methods to conduct log anomaly detection

instead of using a single method. For example, we can combine the thresholds setting, regular expression matching, machine learning, and deep learning methods to conduct log anomaly detection.

- Log vectorization is an important process in log anomaly detection. Usually, we use the off-the-shelf, word-embedding matrix or train a word-embedding matrix at the same time of the model-training phase. However, in a real-production environment, loading a word-embedding file takes considerable time and memory space. Training a word-embedding matrix at the same time of the model-training phase will increase the training time overall and may lead to over-fitting. We can consider using compression techniques to reduce memory consumption and use distributed technologies to improve loading speed and solve the problem of memory limitation of a single node.

11.2.5 Zero-Trust Networks

- To make the most comprehensive decision when performing authorization and authentication, a large number of services, traffic, and device logs need to be collected in a zero-trust network. Therefore, it is important to design a reasonable data collection mechanism. However, the current data plan still has many problems. For example, when collecting network traffic, many schemes cannot guarantee the packet loss rate when collecting high-speed traffic. In addition, when zero-trust networks need to obtain information from other organizations in a federated setting, how to ensure data privacy also needs further consideration. After the data are collected, how to manage the data efficiently, securely, and deredundantly are also crucial.
- Authentication and authorization are the two cores of zero-trust networks. However, traditional authentication and authorization schemes, which only performed at the user login stage, are not suitable for zero-trust networks, because users' status and environment may change at any time, and the originally secure environment may become insecure. Therefore, it is necessary to design a continuous authentication and authorization mechanism. At the same time, in order to minimize the computational overhead and delay during authentication and authorization, the continuous authentication algorithm should be as lightweight and easy to deploy as possible.
- After collecting information and capturing the access requests, the Policy Engine in the zero-trust network has to make decisions on whether the subject has permission to access the object. ML-based Policy Engine has to be carefully designed. For example, in order to overcome the uncertain noise and jitter in the network, the robustness of the model should be improved on the premise of ensuring safety. In addition, to maintain the availability of the system, the number and reasons of error blocking should also be carefully analyzed.

References

Edoardo Amaldi, Stefano Coniglio, Arie M. C. A. Koster, and Martin Tieves. On the computational complexity of the virtual network embedding problem. *Electronic Notes in Discrete Mathematics*, 52:213–220, 2016. ISSN 1571-0653. doi: 10.1016/ j.endm.2016.03.028. URL https://www.sciencedirect.com/science/article/pii/ S1571065316300336. INOC 2015 7th International Network Optimization Conference.

Chang Liu, Zigang Cao, Gang Xiong, Gaopeng Gou, Siu-Ming Yiu, and Longtao He. MaMPF: Encrypted traffic classification based on multi-attribute Markov probability fingerprints. In *2018 IEEE/ACM 26th International Symposium on Quality of Service (IWQoS)*, pages 1–10, 2018. doi: 10.1109/IWQoS.2018.8624124.

Cong Wang, Fanghui Zheng, Sancheng Peng, Zejie Tian, Yujia Guo, and Ying Yuan. A coordinated two-stages virtual network embedding algorithm based on reinforcement learning. In *2019 7th International Conference on Advanced Cloud and Big Data (CBD)*, pages 43–48, 2019. doi: 10.1109/CBD.2019.00018.

Zhongxia Yan, Jingguo Ge, Yulei Wu, Liangxiong Li, and Tong Li. Automatic virtual network embedding: A deep reinforcement learning approach with graph convolutional networks. *IEEE Journal on Selected Areas in Communications*, 38(6):1040–1057, 2020. doi: 10.1109/JSAC.2020.2986662.

Haipeng Yao, Xu Chen, Maozhen Li, Peiying Zhang, and Luyao Wang. A novel reinforcement learning algorithm for virtual network embedding. *Neurocomputing*, 284:1–9, 2018a.

Haipeng Yao, Bo Zhang, Peiying Zhang, Sheng Wu, Chunxiao Jiang, and Song Guo. RDAM: A reinforcement learning based dynamic attribute matrix representation for virtual network embedding. *IEEE Transactions on Emerging Topics in Computing*, 9(2):901–914, 2018b.

Jielun Zhang, Fuhao Li, Feng Ye, and Hongyu Wu. Autonomous unknown-application filtering and labeling for DL-based traffic classifier update. In *IEEE INFOCOM 2020 - IEEE Conference on Computer Communications*, pages 397–405, 2020. doi: 10.1109/INFOCOM41043.2020.9155292.

Index

Note: Page numbers in *italics* denote figures and page numbers in **bold** denote tables.

AI and Machine Learning for Network and Security Management, First Edition.
Yulei Wu, Jingguo Ge, and Tong Li.
© 2023 The Institute of Electrical and Electronics Engineers, Inc. Published 2023 by John Wiley & Sons, Inc.

IEEE Press Series On
Networks and Services Management

The goal of this series is to publish high quality technical reference books and textbooks on network and services management for communications and information technology professional societies, private sector and government organizations as well as research centers and universities around the world. This Series focuses on Fault, Configuration, Accounting, Performance, and Security (FCAPS) management in areas including, but not limited to, telecommunications network and services, technologies and implementations, IP networks and services, and wireless networks and services.

Series Editors:

Dr. Veli Sahin
Dr.Mehmet Ulema

Printed and bound by CPI Group (UK) Ltd, Croydon, CR0 4YY

18/10/2023

08152841-0001